QUESTIONNAIRE DESIGN

MARKET RESEARCH IN PRACTICE SERIES

Published in association with The Market Research Society
Consultant Editors: David Barr and Robin J Birn

Kogan Page has joined forces with The Market Research Society (MRS) to publish this unique series of books designed to cover the latest developments in market research thinking and practice.

The series provides up-to-date knowledge on the techniques of market research and customer insight and best practice in implementing them. It also shows the contribution market research and customer information management techniques can make to helping organisations of all kinds in shaping their strategy, structure, customer focus and value creation.

The series consists of several essential guides that focus on the core skills developed in the MRS training and qualifications programmes (www.mrs.org.uk). It provides practical advice and case studies on how to plan, use, act on and follow-up research, and on how to combine it with other sources of information to develop deep insights into customers.

Fully international in scope of content, its readership is also from all over the world. The series is designed not only for specialist market researchers, but also for all those involved in developing and using deeper insights into their customers — marketers in all disciplines, including planning, communications, brand management, and interactive marketers.

Other titles in the series:

Business to Business Market Research, Ruth McNeil
Consumer Insight, Merlin Stone
The Effective Use of Market Research, Robin J Birn
Market Intelligence: How and why organizations use market research, Martin Callingham
Market Research in Practice: A guide to the basics, Paul Hague, Nick Hague & Carol-Ann Morgan
Researching Customer Satisfaction and Loyalty, Paul Szwarc

Kogan Page Ltd
120 Pentonville Road
London N1 9JN
Tel: 020 7278 0433
www.kogan-page.co.uk

MRS. MARKET RESEARCH IN PRACTICE

QUESTIONNAIRE DESIGN

HOW TO PLAN, STRUCTURE AND WRITE SURVEY MATERIAL FOR EFFECTIVE MARKET RESEARCH

IAN BRACE

KOGAN PAGE

London & Philadelphia

Publisher's note

Every possible effort has been made to ensure that the information contained in this book is accurate at the time of going to press, and the publishers and authors cannot accept responsibility for any errors or omissions, however caused. No responsibility for loss or damage occasioned to any person acting, or refraining from action, as a result of the material in this publication can be accepted by the editor, the publisher or any of the authors.

First published in Great Britain and the United States in 2004 by Kogan Page Limited
Reprinted 2005, 2006, 2007

120 Pentonville Road
London N1 9JN
United Kingdom
www.kogan-page.co.uk

525 South 4th Street, #241
Philadelphia PA 19147
USA

© Ian Brace, 2004

ISBN-10   0 7494 4181 X
ISBN-13   978 0 7494 4181 4

British Library Cataloguing-in-Publication Data

A CIP record for this book is available from the British Library.

Library of Congress Cataloging-in-Publication Data

Brace, Ian, 1949–
Questionnaire Design: how to plan, structure and write survey material for effective market research/ Ian Brace.
   p. cm.
  ISBN 0-7494-4181-X
1. Market surveys--Methodology. 2. Questionnaires--Methodology. I. Title.
HF5415.3.B6?3 2004
658.8'3--dc22

                                    2004010045

Typeset by Datamatics Technologies Ltd, Mumbai, India
Printed and bound in Great Britain by Bell and Bain Ltd, Glasgow

Contents

The Market Research Society   *vii*
The editorial board   *ix*
Preface   *xi*

Introduction   **1**

1. **Objectives in writing a questionnaire**   **7**
   Introduction 7; The questionnaire in the survey process 7;
   Stakeholders in the questionnaire 9; The objectives of the
   study 10; Recruitment questionnaires 13; Collecting
   unbiased and accurate data 13

2. **The data collection media**   **23**
   Introduction 23; Interviewer-administered interviews 24;
   Self-completion surveys 36

3. **Planning the questionnaire**   **43**
   Introduction 43; Defining the information required 44;
   Sequencing the sections 44; Exclusion question 45;
   Screening questions 47; Main questionnaire 49

4. **Types of question and data**   **54**
   Introduction 54; Question types 54; Open and closed
   questions 55; Spontaneous questions 57; Prompted
   questions 60; Open-ended questions 61; Pre-coded
   questions 65; Data types 70

5. **Rating scales and attitude measurement**   **78**
   Attitude measurement 78; Itemized rating scales 79;
   Attitudinal rating scales 86; Rating scales in customer
   satisfaction research 96; The dimensions 99; Comparative
   scaling techniques 102; Measuring brand image 107

Contents

6. Writing the questionnaire   **113**
Introduction 113; Use of language 113; Avoiding ambiguity
in the question 118; Determining the pre-codes 119;
Using prompts 124; Order bias and prompts 127;
Question order 133; Standardizing questions 137;
Tracking studies 138; Omnibus studies 139

7. Laying out the questionnaire   **141**
Introduction 141; Interviewer-administered paper
questionnaires 141; Self-completion paper
questionnaire 151; Electronic questionnaires 157

8. Piloting the questionnaire   **163**
Introduction 163; Why pilot questionnaires? 164; Types
of pilot surveys 165

9. Ethical issues   **172**
Introduction 172; Responsibilities to respondents 174;
Responsibilities to clients 180

10. Social desirability bias   **181**
Response bias 181; Social desirability bias 181; Dealing
with SDB 185; Determining whether SDB exists 193

11. International surveys   **196**
Introduction 196; Client presence 197; Common or
tailored approaches 197; Translating the questionnaire 203;
Demographic data 206; Cultural response differences 206;
Laying out the questionnaire 207

Appendix 1: Example questionnaire   *209*
Appendix 2: The Market Research Society Code of Conduct   *253*
References   *277*
Further reading   *281*
Index   *283*

The Market Research Society

With over 8,000 members in more than 50 countries, The Market Research Society (MRS) is the world's largest international membership organization for professional researchers and others engaged in (or interested in) market, social and opinion research.

It has a diverse membership of individual researchers within agencies, independent consultancies, client-side organizations, and the academic community – at all levels of seniority and in all job functions.

All MRS members agree to comply with the MRS Code of Conduct (see Appendix), which is supported by the Codeline advisory service and a range of specialist guidelines on best practice.

MRS offers various qualifications and membership grades, as well as training and professional development resources to support these. It is the official awarding body in the UK for vocational qualifications in market research.

MRS is a major supplier of publications and information services, conferences and seminars, and many other meeting and networking opportunities for researchers.

MRS is 'the voice of the profession' in its media relations and public affairs activities on behalf of professional research practitioners, and aims to achieve the most favourable climate of opinion and legislative environment for research.

The Market Research Society (Limited by Guarantee) Company
Number 518685
  Company Information: Registered office and business address:
  15 Northburgh Street, London EC1V OJR
  Telephone: 020 7490 4911
  Fax: 020 7490 0608
  e-mail: info@marketresearch.org.uk
  Web site: www.mrs.org.uk

The editorial board

SERIES EDITORS

David Barr has been Director General of the Market Research Society since July 1997. He previously spent over 25 years in business information services and publishing. He has held management positions with Xerox Publishing Group, the British Tourist Authority and Reed International plc. His experience of market research is therefore all on the client side, having commissioned many projects for NPD and M&A purposes. A graduate of Glasgow and Sheffield Universities, David Barr is a Member of the Chartered Management Institute and a Fellow of The Royal Society of Arts.

Robin J Birn has been a marketing and market research practitioner for over 25 years. In 1985 Robin set up Strategy, Research and Action Ltd, which is now the largest international market research company for the map, atlas and travel guide sector, and the book industry. He is a Fellow of the Market Research Society and is also the editor of *The International Handbook of Market Research Techniques*.

ADVISORY MEMBERS

Martin Callingham was formerly Group Market Research Director at Whitbread, where he ran the Market Research department for 20 years and was a non-executive director of the company's German restaurant chain for more than 10 years. Martin has also played his part in the market research world. Apart from being on many committees of the

MRS, of which he is a Fellow, he was Chairman of the Association of Users of Research Agencies (AURA), has been a council member of ESOMAR, and has presented widely, winning the David Winton Award in 2001 at the MRS Conference.

Nigel Culkin is a Fellow of the Market Research Society and member of its Professional Advisory Board. He has been a full member since 1982. He has been in academia since 1991 and is currently Deputy Director, Commercial Development at the University of Hertfordshire, where he is responsible for activities that develop a culture of entrepreneurism and innovation among staff and students. He is Chair of the University's Film Industry Research Group (FiRG), supervisor to a number of research students and regular contributor to the media on the creative industries.

Professor Merlin Stone is Business Research Leader with IBM's Business Consulting Services, where he works on business research, consulting and marketing with IBM's clients, partners and universities. He runs the IBM Marketing Transformation Group, a network of clients, marketing agencies, consultancies and business partners, focusing on changing marketing. He is a director of QCi Ltd., an Ogilvy One company. Merlin is IBM Professor of Relationship Marketing at Bristol Business School. He has written many articles and 25 books on marketing and customer service, including *Up Close and Personal: CRM @ Work, Customer Relationship Marketing, Successful Customer Relationship Marketing, CRM in Financial Services* and *The Customer Management Scorecard*, all published by Kogan Page, and *The Definitive Guide to Direct and Interactive Marketing*, published by Financial Times-Pitman. He is a Founder Fellow of the Institute of Direct Marketing and a Fellow of the Chartered Institute of Marketing.

Paul Szwarc began his career as a market researcher at the Co-operative Wholesale Society (CWS) Ltd in Manchester in 1975. Since then he has worked at Burke Market Research (Canada), American Express Europe, IPSOS RSL, International Masters Publishers Ltd and PSI Global prior to joining the Network Research board as a director in October 2000. Over the past few years Paul has specialized on the consumer financial sector, directing multi-country projects on customer loyalty and retention, new product/service development, and employee satisfaction in the UK, European and North American markets. Paul is a full member of the Market Research Society. He has presented papers at a number of MRS and ESOMAR seminars and training courses.

Preface

When I was asked if I would be interested in writing this book, I was not at all sure that there would be enough to say to fill it. When I talked to other people about the subject, their reaction, particularly amongst non-researchers, was usually that it was going to be a short book. It did not take long, though, for me to realize that the opposite was going to be the case.

After 30 years of writing market research questionnaires, I had forgotten how much I now took for granted: the issues of question wording, bias, question order, layout and translations are all things that market researchers deal with on a day-to-day basis. They learn the skills through training, and hone them through practice.

It is increasingly the case nowadays that the questions have already been written. Most of the big research companies use standard formats or techniques for much of their business; some big manufacturing companies have standard approaches to specific types of research study; or studies have been carried out before. For many market researchers there is less opportunity now than there once was to hone these skills through continual use. All the more need, therefore, for a work to which they could refer.

Mainly, though, this book is aimed at students and new entrants to the market research industry. It is intended to provide them with an overview of the role of the questionnaire in the survey process, together with information on all of the options, alternatives, dilemmas and dangers that they are faced with when they set out to write a questionnaire that they hope will collect accurate data about people, their behaviour and their attitudes.

There is rarely a correct way to ask any question. Almost everything can be asked in a number of different ways. What I have tried to do in this book is to avoid being prescriptive and to provide students or practitioners with guidance on how to think about the questions and the questionnaire. They can then decide for themselves what is the best approach for their situation.

Inevitably, the book reflects my own experience and the types of research project on which I have worked. However, as that experience has covered most types of research and most markets, I hope that readers will not find it too narrow.

Of course there are many people I must thank for their help. In particular I must thank Professor Clive Nancarrow, Phil Graham, Sue Nosworthy, Dr Steve Needel and Stuart Thomlinson for their input and for providing material, and Nigel Spackman for his support. I also owe many thanks to Pat Molloy and Geoffrey Roughton at Pulse Train for agreeing to provide a copy of their Visual QSL software on the CD ROM, which will enable readers to write their own questionnaires. I must also thank David Barr at the Market Research Society for suggesting that I write this book in the first place. Finally I must thank my wife, Pat, for living with this book for so long.

Introduction

It is clear to anyone undertaking data collection through a questionnaire survey that the questionnaire is an important element in its success. However, just how important writing a good questionnaire is can often be underestimated. After all, anybody can write a set of questions, can't they? But if those questions are the wrong questions, poorly phrased, or in the wrong order, the answers obtained may be worse than meaningless: they may be misleading.

In all surveys, there are two generally recognized types of error: sampling error and non-sampling errors. Sampling error arises from the random variation in the selection of respondents. The extent of it can be calculated and its effects can be taken into account. Sampling error can be reduced, most commonly by increasing the size of the sample, which usually means additional cost. To halve the sampling error requires the sample size to be quadrupled, so achieving a reduction in sampling error can be expensive.

Non-sampling errors arise from mistakes made in areas such as the coding and data entry processes of the survey, and through errors committed by interviewers, but also through mistakes made when the questionnaire is written. Not only can these mistakes be fatal to the success of the survey – if a key question or response code is omitted, or respondents are led to give particular answers – but they are not always obvious. Even when obvious, the impact is not always quantifiable, nor capable of being measured or corrected for. However, reducing questionnaire error, in contrast to sampling error, need not add significantly to the cost of a survey, provided that the questionnaire writer understands how to write a questionnaire; one

1

that will obtain the most accurate data to address the objectives of the study.

Good questionnaire writing is a no- or low-cost option in any survey, which has major rewards in delivering the best, or most accurate, answers.

WHAT IS A QUESTIONNAIRE?

Questionnaires are written in many different ways, to be used in many different situations and with many different data-gathering media. The purpose of this book is to provide some general rules and principles that can and should be applied to writing any type of questionnaire. The book is written principally with students and practitioners of market research in mind, but the principles it contains should also be of use to social researchers, political opinion and advocacy pollsters and anyone else who needs to write a questionnaire to collect information by means of a structured interview.

A structured interview is one in which each subject or respondent is asked a series of questions according to a prepared and fixed interviewing schedule – the questionnaire. Thus this book will not apply to qualitative research interviews, where the interview is carried out to a prepared topic guide, because the interview schedule, although prepared, is not fixed. It will, however, apply to the recruitment interview, usually used in qualitative research to identify eligible subjects to participate in later depth interviews or group discussions or focus groups.

The term 'semi-structured interview' will be avoided as it can mean different things to different people. For some it implies a questionnaire consisting almost entirely of open-ended questions with probing instructions. This provides a framework for a degree of consistency between interviews conducted by a number of different interviewers, whilst providing them with scope for greater exploration than is normally possible. For other people the term simply means a questionnaire that contains both open-ended and closed questions.

Structured interviews are carried out using a range of different data collection media. Interviewers can be used to ask questions face to face with the respondent or subject; interviews can be carried out by telephone; questionnaires can be left with subjects to complete themselves;

questionnaires can be mailed to subjects; or questionnaires can be accessed by subjects through the Internet. It is likely that, in the not-too-distant future, questionnaires will be accessed by respondents through their television sets. Each of these media has its own opportunities and problems, but the general principles of questionnaire construction and writing apply to all of them.

OBTAINING THE BEST ANSWERS

This book could be called 'Obtaining the best answers' because that is what we are trying to achieve in market research surveys – the 'best' or most accurate answers. We are not, or should not be, trying to obtain particular answers to support our position or our client's position. The role of the researcher is to be as objective as possible in order to provide the ultimate decision makers – whether that is ourselves, our client or our client's client – with the best, most accurate picture that we can paint. That is equally true both for researchers in agencies and for researchers working in client companies. Setting out to tell our clients or sponsors simply what they want to hear is rarely best in the long term, and is questionable ethically.

However, we must recognize that the data we collect through interviews are rarely completely accurate. And why should they be? We are using volunteer respondents who have agreed to give up their time, frequently for no reward. We ask them to recall events that to them are often trivial, such as the breakfast cereals that they bought, or the choice of flavours of yoghurt offered in the supermarket. We frequently ask them to analyse and report their emotions and feelings about issues that they have never consciously considered, such as their feelings about different brands of paint. Even if they can recognize their feelings and emotions, can they articulate them? Why should they make any effort to do so? The interview may be taking place on a doorstep, or by telephone, when the respondent's first consideration is where the children are, or whether the pie in the oven is likely to burn. They may be irritated because they have been interrupted whilst watching a favourite television programme. Or the interview may be taking place in a shopping mall, where the respondents are anxious to complete their shopping and go home.

As researchers, we have to recognize that we cannot expect to be given perfectly accurate information by our respondents. We must construct and use the questionnaire to help respondents give the researcher the best information that they can. How to achieve that is what this book sets out to cover.

WHY DO WE NEED A QUESTIONNAIRE?

In all cases the role of the questionnaire is to provide a standardized interview across all subjects. This is so that all respondents are asked the questions that are appropriate to them, and so that, when those questions are asked, they are always asked in exactly the same way.

Asking the questions in the same way to different people is key to most survey research. Imagine what would happen if the same question were asked differently of different respondents. It would be impossible for the survey researcher to interpret the answers. It may be argued that in some instances the same questions should be asked differently of different people, that wording should be tailored to each respondent's vocabulary or knowledge of the topic. Without this tailoring process, respondents will not be able to communicate to the researcher all of the information that is either relevant or that they wish to convey. There is certainly a case for asking a question differently where there are a small number of discrete and identifiable groups covered by the survey. But with large-scale surveys where there is anything more than a few dozen respondents, it is impossible to handle and interpret data without a standardized question format.

WHAT DOES IT DO?

The questionnaire is the medium of communication between the researcher and the subject, albeit sometimes administered on the researcher's behalf by an interviewer. In the questionnaire, the researcher articulates the questions to which he or she wants to know the answers and, through the questionnaire, the subjects' answers are conveyed back to the researcher. The questionnaire can thus be described as the medium of conversation between two people, albeit that they are remote from each other and never communicate directly.

STANDARDIZED SURVEYS

Many market research companies now use standardized and often branded approaches for some of the more common research requirements – advertising tracking, advertising pre-testing, brand positioning, customer satisfaction – which use standard questionnaires or questionnaire formats. This reduces the need for the researcher to determine and decide on the questions to be asked. However, using standard techniques does not remove the need for the researcher to be aware of the principles of questionnaire design. Standardized surveys are often written with a particular research universe or product sector in mind and need to be adapted for other populations and product sectors. A technique designed for researching fast-moving consumer goods may need considerable alteration for the retail or financial sector.

Many standardized approaches allow some flexibility, often in the way of additional questions that can be added to the end of the standardized interview. The questionnaire writer therefore needs to know what questions can be asked, how to ask them and how to assess their value, given that they follow the standard questions.

All researchers therefore need to know how to write a questionnaire.

A REMOTE CONVERSATION

The questionnaire has already been described as a medium of remote conversation between researcher and respondent. This is of course a major difference between quantitative survey research and qualitative research, and quantitative researchers must be aware of their remoteness from their subjects and allow for it in all that they do. In particular, researchers must not allow their remoteness from respondents to lead them to forget that each respondent is a person. There can be a tendency for researchers to see respondents purely as sources of information. They then write long, complex and boring questionnaires that fail to treat the respondents with the respect that is due.

One of the consequences of the remoteness between researcher and respondents is the difficulty that structured questionnaires have in eliciting creative responses. The lack of interaction between researcher and respondents, and the consequent inability to tailor questions to the specific respondent, means that the questionnaire survey should generally be seen as a reactive medium. It is good at obtaining answers to the questions it asks (although we shall see many ways in which it can fail to do even this). It does not provide answers to questions that are not asked, and it is not a good way of tapping into the creativity of consumers. If that is what is required, qualitative research techniques offer far better solutions.

There are many pitfalls that the questionnaire writer has to avoid. Throughout the book, some of the most common errors are illustrated in the 'Seen in print' boxes. These are examples taken from a range of different sources that demonstrate how easy it can be to depart from best practice or even basic principles and collect data that are meaningless or incapable of interpretation. Although called 'Seen in print', the examples come from Web-based and telephone interviews as well as from paper questionnaires. Minor changes have been made in many cases in order to spare the blushes of those responsible, but all are taken from live surveys.

The CD ROM that accompanies the book contains questionnaires in different formats for the example project included in the Appendix. This includes electronic formats and a link to a Web site to access the Web-based version. It also contains a version of Pulse Train's Visual QSL electronic questionnaire-writing software, which will enable readers to construct their own questionnaires.

1 Objectives in writing a questionnaire

INTRODUCTION

This chapter considers *what* the researcher is trying to achieve with the questionnaire. Later chapters will then look at *how* this can be achieved.

The role of the questionnaire is to elicit the information that is required to enable the researcher to answer the objectives of the survey. To do this the questionnaire must not only collect the data required, but collect the data in the most accurate way possible.

Collecting accurate data means getting the most accurate responses, so a key objective in writing the questionnaire is to help the respondents to provide them. The questionnaire's role does not stop there, though. There are other stakeholders whose interests must also be met.

THE QUESTIONNAIRE IN THE SURVEY PROCESS

The questionnaire represents one part of the survey process. It is, however, a very vital part of the process. A poorly written questionnaire will not provide the data that are required or, worse, will provide data that are incorrect.

The first task with any survey is to define the objectives that the study is to answer. These will relate to the issue at hand and may be very specific, such as to determine which of two alternative product formulations is preferred, or rather broader, such as to segment the market into different user groups. Where the objectives are specific, the questionnaire writer's task is usually rather more straightforward than where the survey is exploratory in nature. A specific objective usually implies that there is a specific question to be answered and it is the questionnaire writer's job to find the most appropriate way of answering that question.

Where research is exploratory, then the questionnaire writer's task is less predetermined, and a major part of the task is determining what data need to be collected and how they are best collected. With this type of project it is common to carry out preliminary qualitative research to determine what the issues are within the market, and how subjects in the market view them and talk about them. This will help the questionnaire writer to determine which questions to ask and the type of language to use in order to carry out the 'conversation' with respondents in a way that they will understand and will help them to provide the information that is sought.

A questionnaire writer who is not familiar with the vocabulary of a market can very quickly come unstuck. This does not just relate to complex business-to-business markets, but can arise almost anywhere. A questionnaire on the subject of bras to be asked of a sample of women was designed by a man, and referred throughout to 'front-opening' and 'back-opening' bras. Very soon after the piloting of the questionnaires had begun, the researcher received a visit from his fearsome head of field, who pointed out in no uncertain terms that, 'while men may "open" bras, women most definitely "fasten" them'.

Before any questions can be asked, though, the sample must be defined, and the sampling method and the data collection medium must be determined. These are all crucial stages in designing a survey that is appropriate to answering the objectives, and although outside the scope of this book, all will have an influence on the way in which the questionnaire is written.

After the interviews have been carried out and the data collected, they will need to be analysed. How the data are to be collated and analysed will have an influence on how the questionnaire is written and laid out, as well as determining some of the questions that will need to be asked for analysis purposes. A screening questionnaire for a focus group of eight people will not have to make the same allowances for data input to an analysis program that a survey of 1,000 people must make, nor ensure that all likely cross-analyses are anticipated and the appropriate questions asked.

Questionnaire writing thus does not exist in a vacuum, but is an integral part of the survey process. How the questionnaire is written thus affects the remaining survey processes, and what is to happen in those processes affects how the questionnaire is written.

STAKEHOLDERS IN THE QUESTIONNAIRE

Clearly there are a number of different stakeholders in the questionnaire, on each of whom the way in which it is written and laid out will have an effect. There can be up to five different groups of people who have an interest in the questionnaire, and each one has a different requirement of it:

- The clients, or people commissioning the survey, require the questionnaire to collect the information that will enable them to answer their business objectives.
- The interviewers, where used, want a questionnaire that is straightforward to administer, has questions that are easily understood by respondents, and has somewhere where they can easily record those responses.
- Respondents want a questionnaire that poses them questions that they can answer without too much effort, and that maintains their interest, without taking up too much of their time.
- The data processors want a questionnaire layout that allows for uncomplicated data entry, where necessary, and for the straightforward production of data tables or other required analyses.
- The researcher or questionnaire writer has to strive to meet all of these people's needs, and to do so whilst working within the parameters of a budget that has usually been agreed with the client, which in turn means working within an agreed interview length and survey structure.

It is not always possible to meet all of these needs at the same time.

One of the roles of the researcher is to juggle the demands of the different stakeholders. The two stakeholders who must be given the highest priority are the client – whose information needs must be met – and the respondent – whose cooperation we rely on first to agree to be interviewed and then to answer our questions truthfully, which can sometimes require significant mental effort. Respondents are generally volunteers who are giving their time, frequently for no reward, and, apart from the impact on the quality of the data, we have no right to bore them or antagonize them, which can only rebound on their willingness to take part in future surveys. Against their needs, though, we sometimes have to balance those of the interviewer and data processor, in the knowledge that, if we make the questionnaire too complex or difficult for them, we are increasing the risk of errors occurring.

The questionnaire writer's job can be summarized, then, as being to write a questionnaire that collects the data required to answer the objectives of the study as objectively as possible and without irritating or annoying respondents, whilst minimizing the likelihood of error occurring at any stage in the data collection and analysis process.

THE OBJECTIVES OF THE STUDY

Relating research objectives to business objectives

The brief that the researcher receives may sometimes include the business objectives for the study and the research objectives required to achieve them. For example:

Business objective: to enter the mobile telecoms market with a pricing package that is attractive to at least 60 per cent of the current contract market.

Research objectives:

- to determine the distribution of the amount that mobile telecoms users who have a contract pay per month;
- to determine how that amount is made up from standing charges, call charges and special offers and discounts;
- to determine level of satisfaction with current supplier;
- to determine the level of price advantage that would be required for them to consider switching supplier.

However, it is not uncommon for researchers to be given only the business objectives or only the research objectives.

If researchers are provided only with the business objectives, then the implication is that they should determine what the research objectives should be in order to meet the business objectives. These should be agreed with the client or business manager, to ensure that no misunderstandings have occurred regarding the business objectives and that no areas of information have been omitted.

Sometimes researchers are supplied only with the research objectives. It is perfectly possible for the questionnaire to be written from these alone. However, the more background that questionnaire writers have as to how the data are to be used, the more they are able to ensure that all relevant questions are included, that every question serves a purpose, and that response codes used are appropriate to the business objective. In the above example, the business manager may have had a belief that the target market for the new service should be people aged less than 30 years, but nevertheless wished to examine the whole market. This may not have been apparent from the research objectives and could have resulted in the question recording age on the questionnaire having the category 25- to 34-year-olds, and omitting the age break at 30. It is therefore incumbent on the questionnaire writer to obtain as much information as possible about the business objectives in order to maximize the value of the study.

Sometimes client researchers will ask their internal clients to provide a list of the questions to which they want answers, perhaps under the heading of 'information needs'. These are not necessarily questions that can be asked of respondents – they may often contain 'company jargon' – but they can provide a clearer understanding of the underlying issues driving the research and the business objectives.

Relating the questionnaire to the research objectives

The first task therefore is to determine what the questions are that need to be asked. These will be a function both of the research objectives and of the survey design to be used. Thus it may be clear from the information needs of the study that certain questions must be asked, eg whether or not a car is owned, the number and ages of children in the family, whether or not the respondent ever buys pasta sauce. The research technique to be used may also require that certain types of question are asked, eg a paired comparison product test will almost certainly require questions to compare the respondent's preference between the products, or an advertising awareness study will require questions about advertising recall.

Proprietary or specific techniques will often determine not only what types of questions must be asked but will be quite specific about the format of these questions. Some advertising tracking techniques will not only require that questions be asked about advertising awareness but will also determine the almost exact wording of the question and where in the interview it should be asked. Another example would be where a trade-off or conjoint technique is to be used, when the format of the relevant questions may be predetermined.

The objective is not simply to take the study objectives and to write a question against each one. That is generally far too simplistic and can yield facile and misleading information. A series of processes is needed to arrive at the questionnaire from the study objectives. It is one of the skills of the researcher to turn the objectives of the study into a set of information requirements, and from there to create questions to provide that information and then to turn those into a questionnaire.

Study objectives: to determine which of two possible recipes for pasta sauce, A and B, is preferred.

At a simplistic level this objective could be answered by asking a sample of the relevant market to taste each of the two recipes and to say which they preferred. However, the first thing to do is to determine what information is required, and that will entail asking questions of the brief. Is it enough to know that x per cent prefer Recipe A and y per cent prefer Recipe B? Do we need to know whether the people who prefer Recipe A differ from those who prefer Recipe B in any way, such as demographic characteristics, weight of usage of pasta sauce, and which brands or recipes they currently use? Can either or both of the recipes be amended following the research to improve their appeal, which would mean that questions about what was liked and disliked about each one should be included? Is it possible to create a new recipe combining some of the characteristics from each of A and B?

Only after the brief has been interrogated in this way can we determine either the final survey design or the information required to address the objective in full.

RECRUITMENT QUESTIONNAIRES

Recruitment questionnaires are used in qualitative research and for recruitment of respondents for some types of quantitative research (eg clinics held in central locations). The purpose of this type of questionnaire is to identify eligible respondents in order to invite them to attend the main research session, for example a focus group or car clinic. Consequently, the data collected should be limited to that required to determine whether or not respondents meet the criteria that would define them as a member of the target group for the research. Identification of someone as being part of the target group does not necessarily mean that the person will be invited to the main research session, as there may be quota controls on certain sub-groups within the target group (age, gender, product usage, etc), which may have already been filled.

The recruitment questionnaire does not, therefore, have to address all of the objectives of the research study but should be limited to the minimum number of questions required to establish eligibility.

COLLECTING UNBIASED AND ACCURATE DATA

Clearly, the data collected should be as accurate as possible. However, complete accuracy is almost impossible to obtain in surveys where respondents are asked to report their behaviour or their attitudes.

Many problems arise because of problems within the questionnaire itself. These can include:

- ambiguity in the question;
- order effects between questions;
- order effects within a question;
- inadequate response codes;
- wrong questions asked because of poor routeing.

Some of the problems outside of the direct control of the researcher in trying to collect accurate and unbiased data include:

- questions asked inaccurately by the interviewer;
- failure of the respondent to understand the question;

- failure of the interviewer to record the reply accurately or completely;
- failure of the questionnaire to record the reply accurately or completely;
- inattention to the interview because of respondent boredom and fatigue;
- mistakes made by the interviewer because of boredom and fatigue;
- desire by the respondent to answer a different question to the one asked;
- inaccuracy of memory regarding behaviour;
- inaccuracy of memory regarding time periods (telescoping);
- asking respondents to describe attitudes on subjects for which they hold no conscious attitude;
- respondents lying as an act of defiance;
- respondents wishing to impress the interviewer;
- respondents not willing to admit their attitudes or behaviour either consciously or subconsciously;
- respondents trying to influence the outcome of the study and giving answers that they believe will lead to a particular conclusion.

Some of the main biases are analysed by Kalton and Schuman (1982).

Ways in which the questionnaire and questions can be written and structured to minimize the effects of these phenomena will be covered in later chapters on questionnaire construction and question writing. In this chapter we will consider the problems that each of these causes, with the exception of the last three, which are part of a subject known as 'social desirability bias'. This, and the ways in which it can be countered, is a sufficiently important subject to warrant its own chapter, Chapter 10.

Questions asked inaccurately by the interviewer

It is not uncommon to hear an interviewer paraphrase a question in order to make it sound more conversational. Those who have written a questionnaire and then used it to interview a number of people are likely to have found themselves doing it, as they realize that a question that looks accurate on paper often sounds stilted when spoken. Where the interviewer is the same person as the questionnaire writer it may be permissible to amend the wording as the interview proceeds. The author knows the intent of the question and will take care not to alter the sense or meaning of it. Then the author is most likely asking the questions as part of a pilot exercise designed to determine the best wording.

However, when someone else paraphrases it, it is likely that some aspect of the question will be changed, and the response will be different to the one that would have been obtained from the original question. Good interviewer training will instil into the interviewer that the wording on the questionnaire is to be kept to. If, after that training, the interviewer feels the need to alter the wording, then it is a sign of a poorly written question. The role of the interviewer is to hold a conversation with the respondent on behalf of the researcher. The question writer must ensure that this is what happens.

Interviewers can ask questions wrongly because they do not understand them themselves, or because they are too long, and particularly if they involve many sub-clauses. Well-trained interviewers will always make themselves familiar with the questionnaire and the questions before starting the first interview, but if questions are too long and complex, mistakes will happen.

With some business-to-business interviews, the interviewer may not understand the terminology used. A thorough briefing of the interviewers should be carried out and it may be advisable to provide a glossary of terms that respondents may use when giving open-ended verbatim comments. These can be made available on-screen or on paper. They may also be of benefit to coders and editors at the analysis stage of the survey.

Failure of the respondent to understand the question

If the interviewer fails to understand a question, then it is reasonable to expect that a respondent will too. Again, long and complex questions will be the most likely to cause problems, or questions that use words that are not part of the respondent's everyday vocabulary.

Respondents may fail to understand a question because it is not in their competence to answer it. Thus it would be a mistake to ask people what they think is a fair price for certain high-specification audio equipment if they do not own any, have no intention of owning any and do not understand the implications of the high-specification features. Some respondents may recognize that they do not have the knowledge to answer the question and say so, in which case they will be recorded as 'Don't know'. Others, though, will believe that they do understand the implications, and provide an answer, but one based on a failure to understand the question.

Ambiguity in a question can mean that the respondent cannot understand what is being asked or understands a different question from the one intended.

Failure of the interviewer to record the reply accurately or completely

Interviewers record responses inaccurately in many ways. Simply mis-hearing the response can occur. This is particularly likely to happen where, on a paper questionnaire, there is a long and complex routeing instruction following a question. The interviewer's attention may well be divided between listening to the respondent's answer and deter-mining which question should be asked next. The interviewer may be trying to maintain the flow of the interview, and not have it interrupt-ed by a lengthy wait whilst the subsequent question is found, but this is bound to increase the risk of mishearing the answer. This, of course, is not an issue with computer-based questionnaires, where routeing to the next question is automatic.

With open-ended (verbatim) questions, interviewers may not record everything that is said. There is a temptation to paraphrase and précis the response again in order to keep the interview flowing and so as not to make the respondent wait whilst the full verbatim is recorded.

It is common to provide a list of pre-codes as possible answers to an open question. Interviewers scan the list and code the answer that most closely matches the response given. This is open to error on two counts. First, none of the answers may match exactly what the respon-dent has said. The interviewer (or respondent, if self-completion) then has the choice of taking the one that is closest to the given response or there is frequently an option to write in verbatim responses that have not been anticipated. There is a strong temptation to make the given response match one of the pre-coded answers, thus inaccurately record-ing the true response. To minimize the chances of this happening, the pre-coded list may contain similar, but crucially different, answers. The danger then is that when the interviewer (or respondent) scans the list he or she sees only the answer that is close to but different from the given response and codes that as being 'near enough'. In many ways, this is a worse outcome, as it misleads the researcher.

Failure of the questionnaire to record the reply accurately or completely

The main failure of questionnaires in this respect is in not providing a comprehensive list of possible answers as pre-codes for interviewers and respondents to record the response accurately. The response to the question 'Do you like eating pizza?' sounds as if it should be a simple 'yes' or 'no', but respondents may wish to qualify the answer depending on whether it is home-made or shop-bought, the toppings or the occasion. If they are unable to do so, an answer of 'Don't know' may be recorded. Whatever is recorded is not the complete response.

It is common to see a question such as 'How often do you visit the cinema?' given the possible answers:

> More than once a week.
> Once a week.
> Once a month.
> Once every three months.
> Less often than once every three months.

Such an answer list cannot accurately record the behaviour of someone who went to the cinema twice in the last week and not at all in the three months before that. Either the respondent or the interviewer has to decide what is the least inaccurate response.

This type of questionnaire failure, leading to inaccurately recorded data, has, however, become accepted for many types of survey, principally because the alternative of allowing for all possible responses would be too complicated to process and analyse.

Inattention to the interview because of respondent boredom and fatigue

Mistakes of response made by respondents because of failure to understand the question or to give sufficient thought to their response are exacerbated when respondents become tired of or bored by the interview process.

When that happens, respondents will adopt strategies designed to get them to the end of the interview as quickly as possible and with as little thought or effort as possible. Thus with repeated questions, such as rating scales, they will often go into a pattern of response that bears little or no relationship to their actual answers. With self-completion rating scales this strategy will often be something like marking all the boxes that are second from the right-hand side of the page. This strategy is easily spotted by the analyst and dealt with, but where a random strategy is adopted it may be impossible to spot.

With behavioural questions less thought is give to the responses as fatigue sets in. Sometimes any answer will be given just to be able to proceed to the next question. Towards the end of an interview answers are sometimes given that contradict those given earlier, because of boredom and fatigue.

The point at which boredom and fatigue will set in can be difficult to judge beforehand. It will depend on the level of interest of the respondent in the subject matter and the skill of the questionnaire writer in providing a varied and interesting experience.

No matter what the subject, interest is retained longer if the interview experience is itself interesting. Few people think that they could talk for an hour and a half about tomato ketchup. However, a skilled qualitative researcher can keep the interest of a group discussion or focus group on any subject for that length of time and have the participants thank them afterwards for an interesting time. It is more difficult to achieve that in a structured questionnaire survey, but that should be the aim of all questionnaire writers.

Few structured interviews, however, can retain the interest of any respondent for as long as 90 minutes (with the possible exception of cars or a hobby subject), and a realistic expectation for most topics is that fatigue will set in at after about 30 minutes for most respondents on most subjects.

Mistakes made by the interviewer because of boredom and fatigue

A long and tedious interview affects not only the respondent but also the interviewer. Like everybody else, interviewers make mistakes. Whether the interview is on the telephone or face to face, responses can be misheard, or a wrong code recorded. And these errors become more frequent if the interviewer is tired of or bored with the interview. An interview that is tedious for the respondent is also tedious for the interviewer. This can be made worse for the interviewer by the embarrassment felt in being responsible for boring the respondent. There can then be a temptation for the interviewer to help ease the respondent's boredom by reading the questions more quickly, leading to an increase in the number of errors of misunderstanding as well as recording errors on the part of the interviewer.

This, however, is not a problem confined to techniques using interviewers. With self-completion surveys, where there is no interviewer, a long and tedious questionnaire simply results in respondents failing to finish the interview. This means that the response rate falls and the sample of completed interviews is less representative of the population than it could have been.

Desire by the respondent to answer a different question to the one asked

Sometimes respondents will 'interpret' the question in a way that fits their circumstances. When asked how often they go to the cinema, respondents who see films at a club may choose to include those occasions in their response because that is the closest they come to going to a cinema. If the interviewer is made aware of this, then a note can be made and a decision taken later by the analyst as to whether to include this or not. However, often the interviewer will not be told, and, with most computer-aided systems, including Web-based surveys, there is no mechanism provided for respondents to alert the researcher to their interpretation of the question.

Inaccuracy of memory regarding behaviour

Memory is notoriously unreliable regarding past behaviour. It is invariably more accurate for respondents to record their behaviour as it happens, using a diary or similar technique. However, the cost or feasibility of that type of approach often rules it out, and the behavioural data that are collected in most studies are behaviour as reported by memory.

The accuracy of recall will depend on many factors, including the recency, size and significance to the individual of the behaviour in question. Most people will be able to name the bank they bank with, but will be less reliable about which brand of tinned sardines they last bought.

Frequently what is reported is an impression of behaviour, the respondents' beliefs about what they do, rather than an accurate recording of what they have done. Tourangeau, Rips and Rasinski (2000) list the following reasons for memory failure by respondents to surveys:

There are several major sources of memory failure:

* Respondents may not have taken in the critical information in the first place;
* They may be unwilling to go through the work of retrieving it;
* Even if they do try, they may be unable to retrieve the event itself, but only generic information about events of that type;
* They may retrieve only partial information about the event and, as a result, fail to report it; or
* They may recall erroneous information about the event, including incorrect inferences incorporated into the representation of the event.

Researchers are generally aware that recall information can be unreliable. However, what is sometimes overlooked is the bias introduced into the responses by the third of the sources of memory failure listed above. When respondents generalize about types of events they will tend to report not only what they believe that they do, but also what they believe that they do most of the time. Even if what they say is accurate, minority behaviour will tend to be unreported.

Inaccuracy of memory regarding time periods (telescoping)

Particularly notorious is the accuracy of memory related to time. Respondents will tend to report that an event occurred more recently than it actually did. Researchers and psychologists have long been aware of this phenomenon. The first important theory of telescoping was proposed by Sudman and Bradburn (1973). They wrote: 'There are two kinds of memory error that sometimes operate in opposite directions. The first is forgetting an episode entirely... The second kind of error is compression (telescoping) where the event is remembered as occurring more recently than it did.'

Thus, asked to recall events that occurred in the last three months, respondents will tend to include events that occurred in what feels like the last three months but is usually a longer period. Additional events are therefore 'imported' into that period and mistakenly reported (forward telescoping). In contrast, other events are forgotten or thought to have occurred longer ago than they really did (backward telescoping) and are therefore not reported. The extent to which telescoping occurs will depend on the importance of the event to the respondent and the time period asked about.

Asking respondents to describe attitudes on subjects for which they hold no conscious attitude

Researchers often ask respondents to reveal their attitudes about a range of subjects that the respondents have never before given conscious thought to. Many respondents may feel that they have an attitude towards issues such as street crime and how to deal with it, but few will have consciously thought about the issues surrounding the role of pizza in their lives. Questionnaires frequently present respondents with a bank of attitude statements on subjects that, while of importance to the manufacturer, are very low down on the respondent's list of burning issues. Studies have shown that the data reported are more stable over time where respondents are not given time to think about their attitudes but are asked to respond quickly to each statement (Tourangeau, Rips and Rasinski, 2000). Attitudinal questions will often include an instruction to respondents to give their first reaction and not to spend time considering each statement.

Respondents lying as an act of defiance

Some people see market research as a tool of 'big business', and many people hold negative attitudes towards multinational corporations. They are held responsible by these people for many of the world's problems from the globalization of products and services to political instability. Confronted with a market research interview, these people may see an opportunity to disrupt and distort the information held by big business, even if only in a small way. This may be seen as 'doing their bit' in the 'war against international capitalism'.

Consequently, these people will appear to cooperate, but will deliberately lie about their behaviour and attitudes in the expectation that somehow they will be helping to disrupt the commissioning organization's business. Sometimes they can be spotted at the analysis stage because of inconsistencies in their responses, which have been made up as they go along, but this may not always be the case.

Such people are probably few in number, and the tendency is to ignore them in the belief that they will cancel each other out, with one pizza-eater denying that he or she eats pizza counterbalanced by a non-pizza-eater claiming to be an avid consumer. Opt-in media such as Web-based panels are particularly prone to this type of activity, as they are relatively easy to target.

The questionnaire writer has much to consider. The overriding objective is to achieve the most accurate data that will satisfy the research objectives and the business objectives, by avoiding all of these reasons for inaccuracy, at the same time as meeting the needs of all the various stakeholders in the questionnaire.

2 The data collection media

INTRODUCTION

The researcher has an array of different ways in which to collect the data, and it is an array that continues to grow. They can, however, be broadly divided into two categories: interviewer-administered; and self-completion.

It is not unusual, though, for interviewer-administered interviews to contain self-completion sections, and a third category could be added, that of interviewer-supervised self-completion. These are interviews where the respondents are left to complete the interview themselves, but with an interviewer in attendance to answer any queries. The interviewer may well have acted as recruiter for a self-completion interview in a central location.

Each of the types of data collection media provides its own opportunities in terms of questionnaire construction, but equally each has its own drawbacks.

INTERVIEWER-ADMINISTERED INTERVIEWS

The key benefits of having an interviewer administer the questionnaire are:

- Queries about the meaning of a question can be dealt with.
- A misunderstood question may be corrected.
- Respondents can be encouraged to provide deeper responses to open questions.

Sometimes a question can be unintentionally ambiguous. Although this should have been spotted and corrected before the questionnaire was finalized, it is possible for such questions to slip through. If respondents cannot answer because of the ambiguity, then they are able to ask the interviewer for clarification. Interviewers, though, must be careful not to lead respondents to a particular answer when giving their clarification, and should report back to the researcher that clarification was required.

Interviewers can sometimes spot that respondents have misunderstood the question by the response that they give, which may be inconsistent with previous answers, or simply inconsistent with what the interviewer already knows (or suspects) about the respondents and their situation. Such an inconsistency can be challenged, the question repeated and the response corrected if necessary.

An interviewer administering the questionnaire thus gives an opportunity for mistakes of the questionnaire writer to be corrected, but it also gives the questionnaire writer an opportunity to probe for information on open questions. At the simplest level, a series of non-directive probes (eg 'What else?') can be used to extract as much information as possible from the respondent. If a bland and unhelpful answer is anticipated, the interviewer can be specifically asked to obtain further clarification. For example, the question 'Why did you buy the item from that shop in particular?' is likely to get the answer 'Because it was convenient.' An interviewer can be given an instruction not to accept an answer that only mentions convenience, and the questionnaire will supply the probe 'What do you mean by convenient?'

Interviewer-administered questionnaires can be used in either face-to-face interviews or in telephone interviews. Each of these has its advantages and disadvantages in questionnaire writing. The choice of which is to be used will have been strongly influenced by the overall survey design, but the appropriateness of the medium to the questions to be asked will also play a part.

Face-to-face

In the UK, face-to-face interviewing has been the dominant mode of data collection for many years. Although this dominance has been reduced by telephone interviewing and more recently by Internet-based interviewing, the majority of market research interviewing in the UK and much of Europe is still face-to-face interviewer-administered. In the USA, face-to-face interviewing has never accounted for the same high proportion of interviews.

Many of the advantages of telephone interviewing are associated with access to respondents, survey control and speed. These do not relate to questionnaire design but can be deciding factors in the survey design.

Advantages of face-to-face interviewing

One clear advantage of face-to-face interviewing is the ability to show prompt cards easily to respondents. These cards can be used in questions where prompted awareness or recognition of names is required, where respondents are being asked to select their answer from a scale, or where it is desirable to prompt with a list of possible responses.

Table 2.1 *Advantages and disadvantages to questionnaire writer of medium*

Face-to-face interviewing		Telephone interviewing	
Advantages	**Disadvantages**	**Advantages**	**Disadvantages**
Ability to show response cards.	Self-presentation bias.	Relative anonymity can reduce bias.	Use of prompts can be difficult.
Ability to show stimulus material.	Selection bias.		Difficult to show stimulus material.
More complex questions can be asked.	Third-party bias.		

The ability to show things also means that products and ideas can be shown to respondents for their reactions. This is obviously important for evaluating any product or advertising, or where reaction is required to new ideas or concepts for products or advertising. Frequently, surveys evaluating products and concepts will be carried out in a central location. This facilitates:

* transportation of the product – particularly if it is something bulky like a washing machine;
* demonstration of the product – making sure it is cooked or served correctly;
* security of a concept or a new product that might be of significant interest to a competitor.

Where the product or concept is portable, or where the product is left with the respondent to be tried, then in-home face-to-face interviewing is often preferred.

Face-to-face CAPI

CAPI (computer-assisted personal interviewing) is the use of a portable computer that provides the questions and pre-codes on the screen. The computers can be either tablet computers with a touch screen for responses to be recorded by touching a 'pen' on to the screen, or laptop personal computers where answers are recorded by clicking the cursor on the appropriate box. Laptops may have multimedia capabilities. In central locations, desktop personal computers may be used. Personal digital assistants (PDAs) can be used in some circumstances where the number of questions is relatively small. (PDAs have also been used successfully as a self-completion medium.) Pocket PCs connected through a local WiFi network are now also used in appropriate circumstances.

Whichever type of computer is used, it can either provide the interviewer with a questionnaire and means of recording responses, or allow the respondent to participate in the interview through self-completion of part or all of the questionnaire. Either way, it brings a number of advantages for the questionnaire writer. Principal amongst these is the ability to include complex routeing between questions, which could cause problems for interviewers if given as a written instruction. Thus, the question that is asked of the respondent can be determined by a combination of answers from a number of previous questions. Such complex routeing would have resulted in a significant level of error if the interviewer had had to determine which question was to be asked.

Similarly, with CAPI, calculations can be programmed into the questionnaire, which it would not have been possible to ask the interviewer to carry out without risking a high level of error and a serious interruption to the flow of the interview. Thus an estimate of a household's annual consumption of a grocery product can be calculated. This would be impossible for respondents to estimate accurately. However, they may be able to make more accurate estimates of short-term consumption for each member of the family, from which total household consumption can be calculated. In business-to-business interviewing, volumes of consumption or output can be summed either as a total or within predetermined categories, for the interviewer to read back to the respondent to check the accuracy. This information can be used both as inputs to future questions and for question routeing.

The questionnaire writer has to worry less about the layout of the questionnaire with CAPI than with paper questionnaires. Eliminating many interviewer instructions as well as providing the means of recording pre-coded or numerical data makes this part of the questionnaire writer's task easier.

With pre-coded prompted questions, CAPI can randomize or rotate the order in which the response list is presented to the respondent on-screen. It is often preferable to use prompt lists on cards that can be handed to and easily read by the respondent. However, where the respondent is asked to read response lists from the screen, then randomization and rotation of response lists can present a significant advantage (see Chapter 6).

The combination of the abilities to calculate and to randomize response lists has led to the development of some complex techniques such as adaptive conjoint analysis. With this technique, the responses to questions asked at the beginning of the sequence are used to construct scenarios shown at later questions where the respondent is asked to provide preferences between them. Even the number of scenarios asked about is determined by the respondent's pattern of answers. Whilst this is theoretically possible with paper questionnaires (and a lot of show cards), the adaptive conjoint questionnaire is made easy to administer with the use of a computerized questionnaire.

Multimedia CAPI provides the questionnaire writer with more opportunities to present colour images, moving images and sound. Thus television or cinema advertisements can be played as stimuli either for recognition or for evaluation. When evaluating television or cinema advertisements on CAPI, care must be taken to ensure that all parties involved in implementing the findings are happy with the quality of the reproduction of the ad on the computer screen.

CAPI also presents self-completion options such as having icons or representations of brands that can be moved on the screen and placed in appropriate response boxes by the respondent.

Packs can be displayed, and supermarket shelves simulated. This creates opportunities to simulate a presentation, as it would appear in a store, with different numbers of facings for different products, as an attempt to reproduce better the actual in-store choice situation.

Respondents can be asked to simulate their choice process. Or they can be asked to find a particular product with the time taken to find it automatically recorded. Using touch screens can make this easier for respondents.

Three-dimensional pack simulations can be shown and rotated by respondents, whilst they are asked questions about the simulations.

Electronic questionnaires thus provide the possibility of showing improved stimuli; of offering new ways of measuring consumer response; and of making the process more interesting and involving for the respondent.

One technique that allows respondents to become really involved with the interview is the 4D Shopper from Advanced Simulations LLC of Atlanta, Ga. This is demonstrated in Figure 2.1, which shows a series of screen shots from a program that allows respondents to simulate a shopping trip on the computer screen. The respondent can enter the store, approach the aisles, scan the shelves, pick up items, turn them to read the labels for nutritional or other information, and decide whether or not to purchase. The predominant colouring of the store can be changed to simulate each respondent's regular supermarket.

Disadvantages of face-to-face interviewing

The main disadvantage of face-to-face interviewing is generally the cost of obtaining a sufficiently representative sample of the survey population. However, that is an issue of survey design and does not relate directly to the interview process.

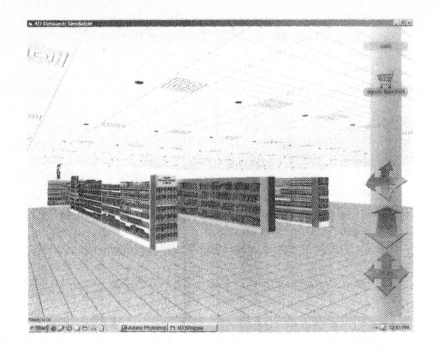

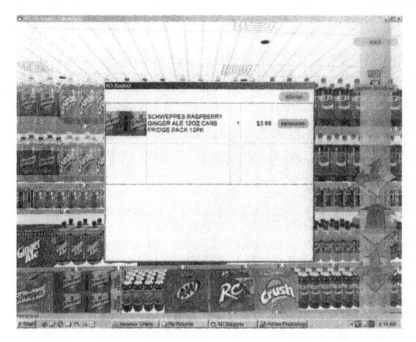

Figure 2.1   *Simulated shopping trip*

What can influence the accuracy of the data is the interaction between interviewer and respondent. Carefully chosen and well-trained interviewers are essential if the quality of the data is to be maximized. The biases that can be introduced by the presence of the interviewer, and the inaccuracies that can be caused if the interviewers fail to ask questions and record responses as they should have already been talked about in Chapter 1. How to minimize these is part of the skill of the questionnaire writer.

Telephone-administered questionnaires

Advantages of telephone interviewing

Most of the advantages enjoyed by telephone interviewing are to the benefit of the survey design rather than to the questionnaire design. Thus there are efficiencies in cost and speed, particularly where the sample is geographically dispersed, or where, as often happens in business-to-business surveys, the respondents are prepared to talk on the telephone but not to have someone visit them.

One advantage for data accuracy is that the telephone as a medium gives more anonymity to the respondents in respect of their relationship to the interviewer. This can help to diminish some of the bias that can occur as a result of respondents trying to impress or face-save in front of interviewers (see Chapter 10). It is also the experience of many researchers that respondents are more prepared to discuss sensitive subjects such as health on the telephone than face to face with an interviewer. Fuller responses are achieved to open questions, and they are more likely to be honest because the interviewer is not physically present with the respondent. Telephone interviewing thus becomes the medium of choice for interviews where there is a need for an interviewer-administered interview, coupled with a sensitive subject matter.

Computer-assisted telephone interviewing (CATI) brings many of the same advantages to this medium as CAPI does to face-to-face interviewing. These include an ability to include complex routeing and calculations within the interview, and the automatic randomization or rotation of question order and of prompt lists within questions.

Disadvantages of telephone interviewing

From the point of view of the questionnaire writer, telephone interviewing has a number of disadvantages.

First, there is limited ability to show material such as prompt lists or stimuli. The inability to show prompt lists is not as much of a problem as might be imagined. Where the list is short it can be read out by the interviewer and remembered by the respondents.

When it is straightforward for the respondents to understand, they can hold the question and answer in their head until the time comes for them to respond. It is important that the interviewer reaches the end of the options before the respondent answers, so that the complete list of possible responses is read out.

For longer lists of response options, or repeated lists such as scales, respondents can be asked to write them down.

The inability to show material such as concepts or advertising is a drawback to telephone interviewing. Radio ads or the soundtrack from television ads can be played over the telephone as a prompt for recognition. Care must be taken to distinguish responses that arise because of the quality of the recording as heard by the respondent, which can be variable, from those relating to content. Other ways must be sought, though, for visual material.

It is possible to mail material to respondents for them to look at during the interview. This creates a lengthy and more expensive process. The respondents have to be recruited and agreement obtained in an initial interview; the material then has to be sent; the main interview can then be carried out once the material has arrived.

It may be desirable for respondents not to see the material before a certain point in the interview. In that case, the initial contact would complete the interview up until that point, when respondents would be asked permission for the researcher to send them material and to call them again to complete the interview. This procedure runs the risk of a high proportion of respondents refusing the researcher permission to send the material, particularly if the interview has not been particularly interesting up to that point. There will also be a proportion of respondents who will have received the material but whom it will be impossible to recontact for a variety of reasons. The number of initial interviews must therefore exceed the desired number of completed interviews by a margin that the researcher must estimate beforehand. This oversampling inevitably adds to the cost of the project.

With some populations, it is possible to speed up this process. In business-to-business studies, it is now common to e-mail material to respondents. This means that the gap between the first and second contacts or parts of the interview can be reduced to minutes. By reducing that period, fewer respondents are lost between the two stages. Alternatively, the material can be faxed, but the quality of reproduction is generally significantly less, and monochrome.

A possible method of showing material, particularly in business-to-business surveys, is to ask the respondent to log on to a Web site where the material is displayed. The respondent can log on whilst the interviewer continues to talk on the telephone, so there is no loss of continuity in the interview. This is more difficult for consumer surveys because of the large number of households that have one line for both telephone and Internet connection, and cannot use both at the same time. The increase in the use of broadband, though, may make this a viable option for consumer surveys in the near future.

Interviews started on the telephone can be continued on the Internet, by asking the respondent to log on to a Web site that contains the remainder of the questionnaire. There is an inevitable loss of numbers, however, because control passes to the respondents, some of whom will never log on to the Web site and so will not complete the interview.

SELF-COMPLETION SURVEYS

Self-completion methods, whether paper based or electronic, can benefit from the complete absence of an interviewer from the process. This removes a major source of potential bias in the responses, and makes it easier for respondents to be honest about sensitive subjects.

However, self-completion studies can also suffer from there being no interviewer to identify when a respondent has misunderstood, or to ask for clarification where there are inconsistencies, or to probe for fuller answers.

From the aspect of the survey design, self-completion questionnaires are often considerably cheaper per interview to administer than interviewer-administered ones, although this is not always the case. Against that must be balanced the difficulties of achieving a representative sample when there is such a high degree of self-selection as is typical with self-completion studies, and particularly when there is a low response rate.

Paper questionnaires

Paper self-completion questionnaires are typically sent by mail to people who qualify or are thought to qualify as eligible for the study. They may be members of a panel who have agreed to take part in surveys, or they may be taken from a database such as customers of a company or members of an organization.

Advantages of paper questionnaires

With a paper self-completion questionnaire, respondents have time to consider their answers. They can leave the questionnaire whilst they think about an issue, or whilst they go away to check something or look up some information. With little time pressure on them, they can write lengthy and full answers to open questions if they wish to do so.

Descriptive material can be included for evaluation. Written descriptions and pictures of new concepts, products or ideas can be included, and again the respondents have the time to read and digest these before giving their responses. For photographs and drawings, as well as written material, a level of production quality can be achieved that is appropriate to the study.

Disadvantages of paper questionnaires

With a paper self-completion questionnaire, it is impossible to stop respondents from reading through all of the questions before responding. Frequently the question sequence is carefully chosen by the questionnaire writer in order to reveal certain pieces of information at a specific point in the interview. That is impossible with this type of questionnaire.

Certain measures cannot therefore be taken. It is not possible to ask a spontaneous brand awareness question if the questionnaire includes brand names in any of the other questions. Respondents may have read through the questionnaire and will have been prompted by mentions of a brand before completing the spontaneous awareness question.

Having time to consider answers, whilst often an advantage, is not always what the questionnaire writer wants. With attitudinal and image questions, it is often the first reaction that is sought, rather than a considered response. An instruction in the question for respondents to give their first reaction cannot be enforced, nor encouraged in the way that an interviewer can, either face to face or by telephone.

Where prompt material has been sent to the respondents for their reaction, it is difficult to retrieve all of it. This can present a security concern if the material is commercially sensitive.

Web-based self-completion

There are several different ways of carrying out surveys using the Internet. The questionnaire can either be delivered by e-mail or accessed via a Web page. The main approaches are summarized by Bradley (1999) as follows:

- *Open Web* – a Web site open to anyone who visits it.
- *Closed Web* – respondents are invited to visit a Web site to complete a questionnaire.
- *Hidden Web* – the questionnaire appears to a visitor only when triggered by some mechanism (eg date, visitor number, interest in a specific page). This includes pop-up surveys.
- *E-mail URL embedded* – a respondent is invited by e-mail to the

survey site, and the e-mail contains a URL or Web address on which respondents click.

- *Simple e-mail* – an e-mail with questions contained in it.
- *E-mail attachment* – the questionnaire is sent as an attachment to an e-mail.

The last two of these, the simple e-mail and e-mail attachment, are rarely used in commercial research for a variety of practical reasons. Attachments require respondents to download the questionnaire, complete it and then return it. This requires a lot of cooperation and has been shown to lead to low response rates. Questionnaires embedded within e-mails can have their layout distorted, depending on the e-mail software with which it is opened. This can lead to the questionnaire being incomprehensible to the recipient. Both of these routes also suffer from the inability to include complex routeing.

Most practitioners now use questionnaires hosted on a Web site to which respondents are invited or routed in some way. This book will therefore concentrate on the Web-based questionnaire.

As noted above, the invitation to the Web site or questionnaire can be delivered in a number of ways:

- It can be delivered by e-mail to people on a panel or to a mailing list of customers or people who might qualify for the survey.
- Pop-ups can be used to direct respondents to the questionnaire whilst they are visiting another site. (These are particularly useful where the objectives of the survey relate to the site being visited, such as evaluating the site.)
- Invitations can be posted as banner ads on other sites (eg ISP home pages) or respondents can be directed to the site following a recruitment interview by telephone or face to face.

Advantages of Web-based self-completion

There are many different ways of capturing a sample online. There are also many issues regarding how representative such samples are of a population that contains people other than those with Internet access. These issues are outside the scope of this book and are well covered elsewhere.

Web-based questionnaires have the same strength as paper self-completion questionnaires in that, in theory at least, respondents can complete the questionnaire in their own time, going away from it if they are interrupted, and returning to it later. In practice, there is little evidence that respondents leave a questionnaire whilst they think about it and return later.

In terms of data collection, the major differences between online surveys and other forms of data collection are the same as between postal self-completion and interviewer-administered surveys. Any advantages are those that come from being technology driven (Ilieva, Baron and Healey, 2002).

Some of the differences between online and other forms of data collection are given by Taylor (2000) as:

- It is a visual medium, allowing images, messages and longer lists of response options. (One survey of motorists has a list of more than 90 different car makes and models for respondents to code their vehicle against. This level of detail would not be possible in any other medium.)
- It captures the unedited voice of the consumer, so that open-ended responses can be richer, longer and more revealing.
- It may be more effective in addressing sensitive issues (medical issues, in particular, may be more easily discussed).
- Scales may elicit different response patterns – it has been the experience both of Taylor and of other researchers that the extremes of scales are used less often.
- More 'Don't knows' may be generated, which is likely to be a function of the 'Don't know' code appearing as a response option.

In addition to online surveys being more effective with sensitive issues, evidence from Kellner (2004) and Basi (1999) supports the view that because there is no interviewer there is less social desirability bias and the respondents answer more honestly (see Chapter 10). This means that data on 'threatening' questions, where respondents feel a need to appear to be socially acceptable, are likely to represent better how the survey population really feels, although this is not yet proven (Sparrow and Curtice, 2004). It also helps to achieve high response rates to questions regarding household income, for example.

The distribution of usage of the points on rating scales has been shown to be different, with less use of the extreme points than is found with face-to-face or telephone interviewing. However, Cobanoglu,

Warde and Moreo (2001) have shown that mean scores for data collected via a Web-based questionnaire are the same as for other self-completion methods, postal and fax surveys. This supports the view that using a Web-based questionnaire should be seen as an alternative method of administering a self-completion survey.

Most studies of how people respond to Web-based questionnaires have found that they are completed more quickly than their equivalent telephone or face-to-face administered versions. Being quicker can help to make it a more pleasurable experience for respondents.

The presentation of the questionnaire can also help to make its completion pleasurable. With a little flair and imagination, Web questionnaires can be designed to have visual appeal, an equivalent level of which is often too costly to achieve with paper questionnaires. In addition to the page design, techniques such as showing icons to represent each brand can be used for respondents to move around the screen and drop into the appropriate response box. By involving the respondents more, the interview is more likely to keep their attention and continue to provide good-quality data through to the end of the questionnaire.

Demonstration of material can also be achieved with a Web-based survey in many of the same ways as with CAPI surveys. Television advertisements can be shown, although the quality with which they are seen will depend on the specification of the equipment that the respondent is using to view it. High-quality representation of still images can be achieved, so that pack designs can be shown either for new or for existing products. There is software available that allows the respondent to rotate the pack representation in three dimensions and even to change elements of it such as colour or text. This kind of technique allows much more interaction in the interview, again involving the respondents and maintaining their interest.

One of the disadvantages of paper self-completion questionnaires is that the respondents can look ahead. With Web-based questionnaires the questions are presented in the sequence that the researcher wants them to be. Generally, Web-based questionnaires will allow respondents to go back over questions already answered in order either to check or to change previous answers. However, it is unlikely that respondents will go completely through the interview and then go back to the beginning and change all of their answers.

As with other electronic questionnaires, CATI and CAPI, the Web-based questionnaire can change the order of questions between

Table 2.2 *Comparison of interviewer-administered and self-completion questionnaires*

	Interviewer-administered		Self-completion	
	Paper	**Electronic**	**Paper**	**Electronic (Web-based)**
Advantages	– flexible – inexpensive to set up	– allows complex routeing – can rotate questions and responses – builds links between questions – uses advanced stimuli (face to face) – no data entry – fast analysis	– flexible – wide-reaching	– allows complex routeing – can rotate questions and responses – builds links between questions – uses advanced stimuli – no data entry – fast analysis
Disadvantages	– requires data entry – limited routeing	– can be slow to set up – investment in CAPI or CATI – questionnaire software skills needed	– requires high-quality production – respondent can read through – no spontaneous measures – limited rotations	

respondents; rotate or randomize response lists; customize response lists against previous answers; cope with complex routeing; and carry out calculations within the interview.

Disadvantages of Web-based self-completion

As with all self-completion media, a major disadvantage is not having an interviewer on hand to clarify questions or to repair misunderstandings.

It might be thought that an issue with Web-based questionnaires would be the difficulty of recording open-ended verbatim responses. Most respondents are not accomplished typists, and it might be expected that questions that require responses to be typed in verbatim would be poorly completed, and be at best completed perfunctorily and in abbreviated fashion. However, experience has shown that, whilst this is undoubtedly an issue with some respondents, the overall level of detail to which this type of question is completed is high. The ability of respondents to take their time and think about their answer appears to more than cancel out any typing difficulties, and responses are generally as complete as for interviewer-administered questionnaires.

Web-based surveys have other disadvantages compared to face-to-face surveys, such as the inability to touch or smell stimuli, but these tend to be issues of survey design rather than questionnaire design.

3 Planning the questionnaire

INTRODUCTION

A questionnaire that is going to provide accurate, good-quality information needs to be thought about and planned, before a single question is written. The sequence of the different topics that may be covered by the questionnaire, the sequence of individual questions and the sequence in which prompted responses are given can all dramatically affect the accuracy and reliability of the collected data. It is also essential to plan the questionnaire carefully so that all respondents are asked the questions that they should be asked and are not asked questions that are irrelevant to them.

From the research objectives and, if possible, the business objectives as well, it should be clear what data need to be collected, in outline if not in detail. Once the researcher knows the definition of the research universe, the data collection medium and the survey design, the questions themselves can be drafted. The steps in planning are:

1. Define the principal information that is required.
2. Determine what else is required for analysis purposes.
3. Map the flow of the subject areas or sub-sections within the questionnaire.

The questionnaire writer should ask the questions that are relevant to the objectives and not be tempted to ask questions of areas that might be interesting but are not relevant. To do so is to waste resources in terms of the time of everyone involved, including the respondents, and to spend money unnecessarily.

DEFINING THE INFORMATION REQUIRED

It should be clear from the research objectives and the business objectives what information areas the questionnaire needs to cover. This is the principal information such as product and brand awareness and usage, behavioural patterns, attitudes, satisfaction with service, response to concept or test product, etc. The level of detail to which it is required should also be apparent from the research and business objectives.

Other information required

It may not always be obvious from the research objectives what additional information is required for analysis purposes. This may include demographic or classification data, but could be far broader than that. In an attitudinal study, for example, it could include brand and product usage and brand loyalty so that attitudes can be cross-analysed by products used and weight of usage. It is important that how the data are to be analysed is thought about at the planning stage. If the appropriate data are not collected, the analysis cannot be carried out.

SEQUENCING THE SECTIONS

The questionnaire can be properly planned once the principal and analysis information requirements have been decided. It is most commonly divided into three sections:

- exclusion or security question;
- screening questions;
- main questionnaire.

EXCLUSION QUESTION

A common, although not universal, practice is to exclude respondents from research surveys who work in market research, marketing or the client's industry. This will normally be the first question, so that they can be identified and excluded as quickly as possible and neither the respondent's nor the interviewer's time is wasted.

Exclusion by industry or profession is carried out partly to protect the confidentiality of the content of the survey, which could find its way to the desk of a competitor through any one of these routes. It is also carried out to avoid the over-representation of unusual behaviour and attitudes. Someone who works in marketing or market research is likely to have different patterns of behaviour, particularly in relation to new products, and to respond differently to attitudinal questions to the public at large. People in these industries do of course make up a finite proportion of the markets and should ideally be included in their correct proportion for the data to represent fully the market in question. However, their proportion in any market is likely to be very small, and any over-representation could distort the study findings.

People who work in the industry that is the subject of the survey pose not only a threat to the security of the study, but may well have behavioural characteristics that are very different from the rest of the population. Their different behaviour could be due to staff discounts on the products in question or to a high degree of familiarity with the product. If they are buying the product at a staff shop or at a staff discount, then these people are genuinely outside of the market and should be excluded both for this reason and for the security of the survey.

Some companies take the issue of security further and exclude journalists from some or all of their surveys. There is a risk that if journalists are shown a new concept or new product, they might be tempted to write a story about it, and there is a risk that what was a closely guarded new idea could quickly become the subject of a press article. The researcher should weigh up the risk of this and decide whether or not to exclude any profession based on the risk that it poses to the project. A behavioural study of the consumption of bread is unlikely either to reveal any new concepts to respondents or to stimulate the writing of an article. However, a study evaluating a new design for a car is likely to arouse a great deal of interest. The motoring press is always keen to find out about new ideas, and security needs to be kept tight if the idea is not to be publicly revealed before the client wants it to be.

This question is usually asked as a prompted question, at which respondents are shown a list of industries and professions. It is advisable to include in that list jobs and professions in addition to those you wish to exclude. This reduces the possibility of a respondent trying to manipulate the outcome. Sometimes respondents will do this unintentionally. Most people's natural inclination is to try to be helpful and answer questions positively. This may particularly occur early in an interview before fatigue sets in and whilst they are curious about the survey. Some people will 'stretch' the eligibility of someone in their household and say that they work in one of the industries or professions, believing that they are being helpful. If the only industries and professions offered are the exclusions, then respondents may be eliminated from the study unnecessarily.

Some respondents will deliberately try to manipulate the outcome, by saying that someone in their family works in one of the professions or industries because they realize that this is a screening criterion. They may wish not to be interviewed and, correctly, think that by saying that someone in their household works in one of the professions or industries they will be excluded. Or they may want to be interviewed and, mistakenly, think that qualification depends on someone in their household qualifying at this question.

Including a number of professions or industries in which many people work can reduce the effect of all of these biases, by allowing more people to answer positively without unnecessarily excluding themselves.

TYPICAL EXCLUSION QUESTION

SHOW CARD A.

Do you or anybody in your household work in any of the industries or professions on this card?

ACCOUNTANCY
ADVERTISING*
COMPUTERS OR INFORMATION TECHNOLOGY
MARKETING/MARKET RESEARCH*
ALCOHOLIC DRINK PRODUCTION OR RETAILING*
BANKING OR INSURANCE
GROCERY RETAILING
NONE OF THESE

* RESPONDENT TO BE EXCLUDED FROM INTERVIEW. (Asterisks are not shown on the card.)

SCREENING QUESTIONS

Following the exclusion question, the next part of the questionnaire will be to screen the respondents for eligibility for the survey, depending on whether or not they belong to the research population. Few studies do not have a requirement for a screening section. In many surveys the researcher only wants to interview people with certain characteristics, either behavioural or attitudinal. We do not wish to find out at the end of the interview that the respondent does not meet the criteria to be included in the sample definition.

Even where the sample is defined as being all adults, there will often be quota requirements on age or social grouping that have to be determined before proceeding with the interview.

It is not unusual with face-to-face interviewing for criteria such as these not to be asked at the beginning but estimated by the interviewer, who confirms them only at the end of the interview. For gender this usually runs little risk, but for age and social grouping there is a clear risk that the estimation is incorrect. The interviewer discovers this error usually at the end of the interview when completing the classification details. The respondent may then fall into a different quota group than expected, or in a quota group that is already full, or outside of any required quota grouping.

If the respondent falls outside of any required quota group, the interviewer has to decide whether to discard the interview and possibly not be paid for it, or to send it in as part of the assignment and hope that it will be accepted because another interviewer has made a similar but compensating error. Unscrupulous interviewers may be tempted to falsify the data to make it appear that the respondent was in quota. Experienced interviewers make sure that they do not put themselves in this situation by checking with respondents at the beginning of the interview if there is any doubt and by estimating age and social grouping only at the beginning of the assignment, when all quota groups are still open. It can be difficult to ask questions such as these, which can be sensitive for some people, at the beginning of the interview, but ensuring that the respondent is in quota before the main interview begins can avoid wasted time and the temptation to falsify data later.

With all data collection other than face-to-face interviewing these questions must be asked at the beginning to ensure eligibility.

It is not uncommon for eligibility criteria to include both behavioural and attitudinal questions, or to include complex behavioural criteria. The screening questions can then take several minutes to administer and seem like an interview in their own right to respondents. Lengthy screening also takes up interviewer time, and if paper questionnaires are being used, leads to errors in the assessment of eligibility. The complexity of the eligibility criteria should be a consideration in the survey design, and kept as simple and as straightforward to administer as possible.

As with the exclusion question, the interest of the researcher should be disguised in order to avoid 'helpful' respondents answering positively to everything, and to avoid the possibility of respondents trying to guess which answers they should give in order to be included or excluded as they wish. Respondents may also feel pressure to say that they have bought something when they have not, for fear of appearing mean or ungenerous, or lacking social status.

It is not good practice to ask, for example, 'Have you bought a wide-screen television in the last six months?', as respondents' reasons for answering 'yes' or 'no' may have little to do with whether they actually have or not. A less biased version of the question is given in Figure 3.1.

SCREENING QUESTIONS

SHOW LIST. (On card, screen or paper, or read out, depending on interview medium.)

Which, if any, of the items on this card (list which I am going to read out) have you bought in the last six months, either for yourself or for anybody else?

TELEPHONE
TELEVISION
DIGITAL RADIO
DVD PLAYER
MICROWAVE OVEN
NONE OF THESE

IF BOUGHT TELEVISION IN PAST SIX MONTHS, SHOW LIST.

Which of these describes the television that you bought?
PLASMA SCREEN

FLAT SCREEN
WIDE SCREEN
SURROUND SOUND
DOLBY SOUND

RESPONDENT IS ELIGIBLE FOR INTERVIEW IF BOUGHT WIDE-SCREEN
TELEVISION IN PAST SIX MONTHS.

Figure 3.1

MAIN QUESTIONNAIRE

The main questionnaire can now be planned.

Once into the main questionnaire, the writer must consider the order in which the various topics are presented to the respondents. As a rule, it is better to work from the most general topics through to the most specific. Thus, the interview might start with questions about the respondent's behaviour in the market in general, before proceeding through to specific questions about the client's product and then to reaction to a new proposition for the client's product. There are two reasons for this.

First, if the questions regarding the specific product or brand of interest were asked first, then the respondents would be aware of the question writer's interest and this would bias their answers to the more general market questions that come later. Raising the respondents' consciousness of the product or brand in question will tend to lead to it being over-represented as a response in any questions that follow. This may include questions about consumption of products or brands in the market generally and lead to overestimation of consumption of the brand of interest.

Secondly, starting with general questions allows the respondents to think about their behaviour in the market before getting into the detail. Respondents are rarely as interested in the market as is the researcher or the client. They may find it difficult to respond immediately to questions about the detail of a particular brand or product. Starting with questions that are more general helps the respondents to ease into the subject, recalling their overall behaviour and how they feel about brands and products before reaching the detailed questions.

There are many exceptions to this general rule when there is a good research reason for not starting with the more general questions, but the questionnaire writer should always be prepared to justify the decision.

It is important to map the questionnaire so that it flows logically from one subject area to the next. Avoid returning to a topic area previously asked about. This makes the questionnaire appear not to have been thought through, can confuse respondents who think that they have dealt with this already, and can frequently require interviewers to refer back in the questionnaire for information already given, which may lead to errors.

A flow diagram can assist in ensuring that all topics are covered and that respondents are asked the sections that are relevant to them. In the example flow chart (Figure 3.2), the objective is to determine what journey types buses are used for; to determine why the bus or other public transport is preferred to using a car; and to obtain a rating of different types of public transport. People who do not use any form of public transport are not to be asked this last section. This diagram does not tell us precisely what questions need to be asked. What it determines is how the question areas that the different categories of respondents (bus users, non-bus users who use other public transport, and people who use no public transport) need to be asked will flow.

The flow chart also demonstrates that there will be some routeing issues. Whether or not the respondent has use of a car appears three times in different paths. Complex routeing will be required if the questionnaire writer decides that this question should appear only once, in order to facilitate analysis. Alternatively, the same question can appear three times, once in the path of each respondent category. The latter approach is less likely to result in interviewer error if using paper questionnaires, or in routeing errors within electronic questionnaires.

Behaviour before attitude

It is generally advisable to start any section of the interview with behavioural questions before going on to ask attitudes and images. This is in part to allow the respondents to assess their behavioural position and then to explain their behaviour through their attitudes. Behavioural questions, are usually easier to answer because they relate to fact and require only recall. If respondents find it difficult to answer behavioural questions, then this is usually because the questionnaire writer has been too ambitious in the level of detail expected, and the reliability of the information that is being reported will be in doubt.

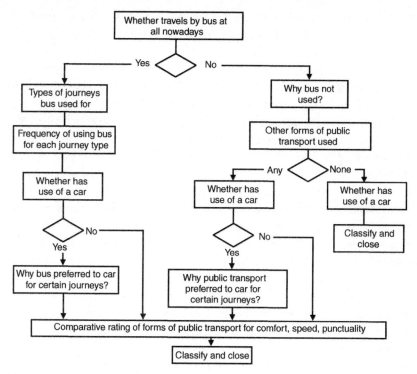

Figure 3.2 *Flow chart to plan questionnaire*

If attitudes are asked first there is a danger that respondents will take a position that is not thought through and that is contradicted by their behaviour. They may well then misreport their behaviour in order to justify their attitudes.

Spontaneous before prompted

It may appear obvious, but great care must be taken not to prompt respondents with possible answers before asking questions designed to obtain their spontaneous response. Thus you cannot ask 'Which brands of instant coffee can you think of?' if you have already asked 'Which of the brands of instant coffee on this list do you buy?' An example like this appears obvious, but there are many occasions where it is not so obvious that this is happening.

Sometimes it can be virtually impossible to obtain a 'clean' measure of spontaneous brand awareness, particularly where purchase or consumption of a brand is one of the screening criteria for eligibility. This will normally mean that respondents will have been exposed to a list of brands in the screening questions. Thereafter it is impossible to obtain a measure of spontaneous awareness.

This is a particular issue with certain types of surveys such as advertising testing. Here respondents may be recruited based on their brand consumption in order to evaluate a new advertisement. Part of that evaluation may be to show the test advertisement among other ads. For television ads this would be as part of a clutter reel; for press ads they would be contained within a mock-up of a newspaper or magazine. The test ad will, however, stand out from the rest if the respondents have been sensitized to the brand or the category through the screening questions. To ameliorate this, a series of mock screening questions are sometimes asked, which relate to the products and categories shown in the other ads. Whilst this is unlikely to reduce the sensitization of the respondents to the test ad's category, it does raise the level of sensitization so that it is the same for all the ads, thereby cancelling out the differential effect. This type of strategy often needs to be adopted where it is essential that prompting occurs earlier than is desirable.

Prompting also extends to attitudes. A questionnaire may include a series of attitude statements to which respondents are asked to respond. If attitudes on the same subject are to be assessed spontaneously, that must be asked before the attitude statements have been shown or respondents will continue to play back the attitudes with which they have been prompted.

Sensitive sections

If the interview is to include questions of a sensitive nature, then they should not be asked right at the beginning of the interview. Where the questionnaire is interviewer administered, this allows a relationship to be built between interviewer and respondent, so that the respondent is more willing to disclose sensitive information. The trust that has hopefully been built between them reassures the respondent that the information will not be abused.

With Web-based questionnaires, these questions should also be positioned towards the end of the interview. Although there is no interviewer, there is still a relationship built between the respondent and 'the survey'. Having been prepared to divulge less sensitive information in earlier questions, it may be less difficult for respondents then to disclose data that are more sensitive. Such questions at the beginning of the interview are likely to be seen as more intrusive and provoke a greater level of non-response or termination of interview.

A further reason for asking sensitive questions later in the interview is that if the interview is terminated at this point by the respondent, most of the data have already been collected and may be usable. In extreme cases where it is expected that the level of termination due to intrusiveness of the questions will be high, being able to salvage as much information as possible will be part of the questionnaire writer's strategy, and all key questions for analysis will have been asked before the intrusive questions. However, if questions are so intrusive as to cause a significant level of offence, then the questionnaire writer should consider the ethical position carefully before including them. (See Chapter 9 for what may constitute a sensitive topic.)

Classification questions

Partly because they can be seen as intrusive, classification questions are normally asked at the end of the interview. They are also positioned here because they are usually disconnected with the subject matter of the interview. Asking them earlier in the interview would disrupt the flow of the 'conversation'. Information such as gender, age, income, social grouping, final level of education, television viewing, number of children in household, etc rarely relate directly to the subject of the study. However, they are proven discriminators in many behavioural and attitudinal fields and so are invaluable for cross-analysis purposes.

The researcher should resist the temptation to ask for more classification data than are needed simply because it might be useful for cross-analysis. This is often personal information and respondents do not always understand why it is needed. The questionnaire writer should think carefully about what is and what is not required.

4 Types of question and data

INTRODUCTION

Questions can be asked and data recorded in many ways. Different types of questions are appropriate for different purposes and different types of data can be used and analysed differently. It is important for the questionnaire writer to understand the range of question types available because the choice of question type will determine the information that is elicited. It is also important to understand the different types of data that will be generated, because that will determine the types of analysis that can be carried out. The questionnaire writer should thus be thinking about how the data are to be analysed at the time that the questions are being formulated so that the information collected can be analysed in the way that is required.

QUESTION TYPES

Any question in an interview can be classified in a number of different ways:

- open or closed, depending whether or not the answer can come only from a finite number of possible responses;
- spontaneous or prompted, depending on whether respondents are asked to reply in their own words or given a number of options from which to choose a response;
- open-ended or pre-coded, depending on whether the answer is recorded verbatim or against one or more of a number of predetermined answers.

We are using here the definition of an open-ended question that is commonly used in market research, which is that the responses are recorded verbatim, and distinguishing it from an open question, which seeks a response that may or may not be recorded verbatim. Whether a question is open-ended or pre-coded is determined by how responses are recorded rather than the question itself. However, the topic is included in this chapter rather than Chapter 6 ('Writing the questionnaire') because open questions and open-ended (verbatim) recording of responses frequently go together, and are frequently confused.

Open questions are usually asked spontaneously, and any prompted question is likely to be closed. Prompted questions will usually be pre-coded, but open questions can be recorded either as open-ended (verbatim) or pre-coded responses.

OPEN AND CLOSED QUESTIONS

An open question is one where the range of possible answers is not suggested in the question and which respondents are expected to answer in their own words. An open question may expect a short answer, as in 'Which brand of breakfast cereal did you eat today?', where the anticipated answer would simply be a brand name, or it may expect respondents to talk as long as possible using their own words in order to give fully their answer, as in 'Why do you eat that brand of breakfast cereal more than any other?' Open questions always seek a spontaneous, that is unprompted, response. In conversation, one person trying to start another person talking about a topic would use an open question.

The responses may be recorded verbatim as an open-ended question ('Why do you eat...?') or, with interviewer-administered surveys, a list of the most commonly given responses may be provided that can be coded ('Which brand did you eat...?').

Closed questions, on the other hand, tend, in conversation, to bring it to a stop. This is because there is a predictable and usually small set of answers to a closed question that the respondent can give. Any question that simply requires the answer 'yes' or 'no' is a closed question, and not helpful to opening out a conversation. An evening spent with a new acquaintance with both of you asking only closed questions would be very dull indeed.

In a research interview, closed questions also include any question where the respondent is asked to choose from a number of alternative answers. Thus any prompted question is a closed question.

Examples of closed questions are:

- 'Have you drunk any beer in the last 24 hours?'
- 'Are you aged under 25?'
- 'Which of these brands of tinned meat do you buy most often?'
- 'Which of the phrases on this card best indicates how likely you are to buy this product?'

The examples above are all closed questions, the first two because they can only be answered 'yes' or 'no', and the last two because there is a frame of possible responses from which the respondent is asked to choose.

Closed, and therefore pre-coded, questions are popular with researchers and interviewers alike because there is a set of answers known beforehand that can be listed on the questionnaire. With a paper questionnaire the interviewer only has to circle the appropriate code and that code can easily be entered into the data file by those responsible for data entry. With an electronic questionnaire, either the interviewer or the respondent only has to check the appropriate box and the data are automatically recorded and stored, ready for analysis. This type of question is usually easy to administer and cheap to process.

A questionnaire that measures behaviour is likely to consist mostly of closed questions ('Which of these brands...?', 'When did you last...?', 'How many did you buy?'), whereas one exploring attitudes is likely to have a higher proportion of open questions. From the point of view of maintaining the involvement of the respondent, the interview should consist of a mixture of both types of question.

SPONTANEOUS QUESTIONS

A spontaneous question is any question for which the respondent is not given a repertoire of possible answers from which to choose. All open-ended questions are by their nature spontaneous, but not all spontaneous questions need be open-ended.

Spontaneous questions will be used when the questionnaire writer does not know what the range of responses is likely to be, or wants to collect the response in the respondent's own words. These will then be open-ended questions with the response recorded verbatim for later coding.

The decision whether or not to make a spontaneous question open-ended depends on whether it is important to record the response verbatim and whether the full range, or at least the majority, of likely responses is known.

One of the difficulties with spontaneous questions is that the amount of effort that respondents are prepared to make with spontaneous questions varies depending on how interested they are in the subject and on the medium of the interview.

Common uses of spontaneous questions

Spontaneous open questions are frequently used in market research to measure awareness and attitudes, for example:

* brand awareness;
* awareness of brands seen advertised;
* recall of brands or products used or bought;
* advertising content recall;
* attitudes towards a product, or activity or situation;
* likes and dislikes of a product or concept.

The first three in this list would normally be pre-coded on an interviewer-administered questionnaire, where the interviewers can easily code the response without prompting the respondents.

With spontaneous questions we are trying to determine what is at the forefront of people's minds, which they can easily access. We interpret this as saliency in the case of brands, or as importance in the case of attitudes. Spontaneous questions are not a good measure of the brands people have heard of, nor of behaviour, nor of all the full range of attitudes or emotions. Prompted questions usually elicit more complete and accurate responses in terms of behaviour.

Spontaneous brand awareness

Spontaneous brand awareness is a measure of which brands are the most salient in the respondents' minds. It would be the result of the following or similar questioning: 'Which brands of breakfast cereal have you heard of?' 'Please tell me all the brands of washing powder that you can think of.' The objective here is to obtain every brand that the respondent can think of, and so probes asking for 'What else?' or 'Any more?' will be used extensively in interviewer-administered interviews. The list of possible brands will usually be given as pre-codes on the questionnaire for the interviewer to record responses.

Frequently the first brand mentioned will be recorded separately, to give a measure of 'top of mind awareness'. With CAPI and CATI questionnaires, the order in which brands are mentioned can be recorded automatically.

With self-completion questionnaires (including Web-based), spontaneous questions must be recorded as open-ended responses to avoid prompting the respondents. With paper self-completion questionnaires, it is not possible to obtain spontaneous awareness if any brands are mentioned anywhere in the questionnaire. Respondents will read through the questionnaire and will be prompted by any brand names that appear.

Sometimes we wish to know precisely how respondents give a brand name. Then, in any data collection medium, the responses will be recorded verbatim. The researcher can then determine whether it is the brand, sub-brand or variant that is mentioned, or what combination of these. This is particularly used in advertising research where it can be important to know precisely what level of branding is being communicated.

Spontaneous brand awareness can be used to demonstrate how the effort that respondents are prepared to make varies according to where the interview takes place. It has been demonstrated on numerous occasions that the average number of brands that are given spontaneously in face-to-face street interviews is significantly lower than with face-to-face in-home interviews. Not only is the average number lower in the street, but the distribution of the brands mentioned is also different. In the street, where less effort is made, the dominant brands in a market will tend to be mentioned. Their spontaneous brand awareness figures may be similar to those obtained from in-home interviews. The smaller and newer brands get lower prompted awareness levels from street inter- views, or in any type of interview where the respondent is prepared to make less effort.

Spontaneous advertising awareness

When evaluating the effect of an advertising campaign, spontaneous advertising awareness is usually a key measure. Exactly how this is measured, though, differs between researchers.

One way is to ask spontaneous brand awareness first, followed by a spontaneous awareness of brands seen advertised, followed by content recall of the advertising claimed to have been seen. All questions require spontaneous responses; the first two are likely to be pre-coded with a list of brands, and the third question will be open-ended:

'Which brands of breakfast cereal have you heard of?'
'Which brands of breakfast cereal have you seen or heard adver- tising for recently?'
'What did the advertising say, or what was it about?'
Repeat the last question for all brands for which advertising has been seen.

An alternative approach is not to ask brand awareness first, but to ask the respondent to recall spontaneously any advertising for any brand in the category:

'Please describe to me any advertising that you have seen recently for a breakfast cereal. What did it say? What was it about?'
'What brand was that for?'
Repeat until the respondent can recall no more advertising.
'Please tell me any other brands of breakfast cereal that you have seen advertising for.'

Proponents of this approach argue that, by leading with the brand recall in the first approach, the best-known brands score well as respondents assume that they have seen advertising for them, whether or not they have actually been advertising. By leading with advertising content recall, without mentioning any brands, the second approach attains a truer measure of memorability of the advertising.

Spontaneous attitudinal questions

Spontaneous questions regarding attitudes can be either open-ended or pre-coded. Typical spontaneous attitudinal questions are:

- 'What, if anything, do you like about...?'
- 'What, if anything, do you dislike about...?'
- 'How do you feel about...?'
- 'Please describe to me your feelings about...?'

The responses to these questions would most likely be recorded verbatim as open-ended answers. This enables the capture of the full range of answers in the code frame, which may include some that were not anticipated. This also allows the researcher to see the precise language used by respondents to describe their feelings and attitudes.

Preliminary qualitative research may have been carried out so that the full range of attitudes held on the issue in question has been determined. The study may be a repeat of a previous one in which the attitudes were defined. In these cases summaries of the main attitudes may be pre-coded on interviewer-administered questionnaires, in order to save the time and expense of coding the responses at the analysis stage. With any kind of self-completion questionnaire pre-coding is not a possibility if the attitudes are to be expressed spontaneously.

PROMPTED QUESTIONS

Spontaneous responses rarely tell the researcher the complete picture regarding what the respondent knows or feels, but only what is front-of-mind. However, most people find it difficult to articulate everything that they know or feel about a subject, or they forget that they know something, or they have given one answer and aren't prepared to make any further effort to think of additional answers. Prompting with a set of options tells the researcher what people know or recognize, rather than what is front-of-mind, if we are measuring awareness or recognition.

Alternatively, prompting helps people to recall actions and behaviour, and to express their answers in the framework desired by the researcher.

For prompted awareness questions that follow a spontaneous question on the same issue it may sometimes be helpful to include the phrase '... including any that you have already mentioned'. Whether or not this phrase is included, the analysis should always re-record any answers mentioned spontaneously on to the prompted recognition answer for each respondent.

With self-completion paper questionnaires it is not possible to ask both spontaneous and prompted questions on the same subject. Because respondents can read through the complete interview before answering questions, any lists or sets of answers that appear in the questionnaire can act as a prompt to any question.

OPEN-ENDED QUESTIONS

An *open-ended* question is an open question where the response is recorded verbatim. An open-ended question is nearly always also an open question. (It would be wasteful to record yes–no answers verbatim.) Open-ended questions are also known as 'unstructured' or 'free-response' questions.

Open-ended questions are used for a number of reasons:

- The researcher cannot predict what the responses might be, or it is dangerous to do so. Questions about what is liked or disliked about a product or service should always be open-ended, as it would be presumptuous to assume what people might like or dislike by having a list of pre-codes.
- We wish to know the precise phraseology that people use to respond to the question. We may be able to predict the general sense of the response but wish to know the terminology that people use.
- We may wish to quote some verbatim responses in the report or presentation to illustrate something such as the strength of feeling that respondents feel. In response to the question 'Why will you not use that company again?', a respondent may write in: 'They were — awful. They mucked me about for months, didn't respond to my letters and when they did they could never get anything right. I shall never use them again.' Had pre-codes been given on the questionnaire this might simply have been recorded as 'Poor

61

service'. The verbatim response provides much richer information to the end user of the research.

* Through analysis of the verbatim responses, clients can determine if the customer is talking about a business process, a policy issue, a people issue (especially in service delivery surveys), etc. This enables them to determine the extent of any challenges they will face when reporting the findings of the survey to their management.

Common uses for open-ended questions include:

* likes and dislikes of a product, concept, advertisement, etc;
* spontaneous descriptions of product images;
* spontaneous descriptions of the content of advertisements;
* reasons for choice of product/store/service provider;
* why certain actions were taken or not taken;
* what improvements or changes respondents would like to see.

These are all directive questions, aimed at eliciting a specific type of response to a defined issue. In addition, non-directive questions can be asked, such as what, if anything, comes to mind when the respondent is shown a visual prompt, and whether there is anything else that the respondent wants to say on the subject. Questions that ask 'What?' or 'Why?' or 'How?', or for likes and dislikes, will commonly be open-ended.

Open-ended questions are easy to ask but suffer from several drawbacks:

* In interviewer-administered surveys they are subject to error in the way and the detail with which the interviewer records the answer.
* Respondents frequently find it difficult both to recognize and to articulate how they feel. This is particularly true of negative feelings, so that asking open-ended questions about what people dislike about something tends to generate a high level of 'Nothing' or 'Don't know' responses.
* Without the clues given by an answer list, respondents sometimes misunderstand the question or answer the question that they want to answer rather than the one on the questionnaire.
* Analysing the responses can be a difficult, time-consuming and relatively expensive process.

In addition, some commentators (Peterson, 2000) see verbosity of respondents as a problem with open-ended questions. It is argued that if one respondent says only one thing that he or she likes about a product, but another says six things, then the latter respondent will be given six times the weight of the former in the analysis. To even this up, only the first response of the more verbose respondent is counted. In practice, interviewers are trained to extract as much detail as possible from respondents at open-ended questions. The objective is to identify the full range of responses given by all respondents and to determine the proportion of the sample that agrees with each of them.

To analyse the responses, a procedure known as 'coding' is used. Manual coding requires a sample of the answers to be examined and the answers grouped under commonly occurring themes, usually known as a 'code frame'. If the coder is someone other than the researcher, then that list of themes needs to be discussed with the researcher to see whether it meets the researcher's needs. The coder may have grouped answers relating to low price and to value for money together as a single theme, but the researcher may see them as distinct issues and want them separated. The researcher may be looking for specific responses to occur that have not arisen in the sample of answers listed. It may be important for the researcher to know that few people mention this, but in order to be sure that this is the case, the theme must be included on the code frame. When the list of themes has been agreed, each theme is allocated a code, and all questionnaires are then inspected and coded according to the themes within each respondent's answer.

Manual coding is a slow and labour-intensive activity, particularly when there is a large sample size and the questionnaire contains many open-ended questions. Most research agencies will include a limit to the number of open-ended questions in their quote for a project, because it is such a significant variable in the costing.

There are a number of computerized coding systems available, which are increasingly used by larger research companies. These rely either on an initial word-recognition search procedure to identify the themes, or on manual compilation of a code frame. They generally still require significant manual input to sort and edit the themes and to sort and code the responses on-screen. With CATI, CAPI and Web-based surveys, the interviewer or respondent will have typed the responses in. Where the interview is paper based, though, all of the responses have to be typed in before the computerized coding can be carried out. This nullifies some of the cost savings made.

Probing

With most open questions it is important to extract from respondents as much information as they can provide. The first reason they give for having bought that brand may be the same for all brands and will not discriminate. Although it is the first that comes to mind, it may not be the one in which the researcher is most interested. First responses given to open questions are often very bland, and non-directional probing is required to try to fill out the answer.

Probing is very different from prompting, and the two must not be confused. In prompting, respondents are given a number of possible answers from which to choose, or are given clues to the answers through visual or picture prompts. Probing makes no suggestions regarding answers to the respondent. A typical probe with instructions is:

'What else did you like about the product?' PAUSE. THEN PROBE: 'What else?' CONTINUE UNTIL NO FURTHER ANSWERS.

The object here is to keep respondents talking in reply to the initial question in their own words until there is no more that they can or wish to say. They are not led in any direction.

Do not use phrases such as 'Is there anything else?' as a probe. That form of probe allows or even encourages the respondents to say 'No, nothing else.' If the probe is 'What else?', this makes a presumption that there is more that the respondent wants to say and puts the onus on the respondent to indicate that he or she has no more to say. This helps the researcher to obtain the fullest answer rather than helping the respondent to say as little as possible.

It is occasionally possible to anticipate unhelpful answers and ask for these specific responses to be elaborated. A common example is when respondents give 'convenience' as an answer to why they use a particular shop or travel by a particular type of transport. This is a common answer given to this type of question, but is frustratingly unhelpful. Where it is anticipated that this will occur, an instruction may be given to interviewers to probe for more information regarding in what way it was convenient, and what 'convenience' means to the respondent.

PRE-CODED QUESTIONS

Pre-coded open questions

Frequently with interviewer-administered surveys, a list of pre-codes is provided with open questions for the interviewer's use. This may simply be a brand list on which to code the response to a question such as 'Which brand of breakfast cereal did you eat today?' or it may be used in order to categorize more complex responses (see Figure 4.1).

Q. Why did you buy that particular brand of mayonnaise?
DO NOT PROMPT

IT'S THE ONE I ALWAYS BUY	1
THE ONLY ONE AVAILABLE	2
THE CHEAPEST	3
ON SPECIAL OFFER	4
THE FLAVOUR I WANTED	5
THE PACK SIZE I WANTED	6
OTHER ANSWER (WRITE IN)	7

Figure 4.1 *Pre-codes used to categorize responses to open questions*

This requires the questionnaire writer to second-guess what the range of responses is going to be. It is usually done to save time and cost in coding open-ended verbatim responses. This approach might also be used to try to provide some consistency of response by forcing the open responses into a limited number of options. It is important that there is always a space provided for the respondent or interviewer to write in answers that are not covered by the pre-codes. It is unlikely that the questionnaire writer will have thought of every possible response that will be given, and it is not unusual for quite large proportions of the responses to be written in as 'other answers'. However, there is still a danger that respondents or interviewers will try to force responses into one of the codes given rather than write in a response that is close to, but does not quite fit, one of the pre-codes.

The richness and illustrative power of the verbatim answer is lost by providing pre-codes, as are any subtle distinctions between responses, but the processing time and cost will be reduced. Consistency with other surveys may also be increased.

The code list may be based on qualitative research that has suggested the range of answers that could be expected or on the results of previous studies. If questionnaire writers adopt this approach, because they want to categorize the responses in a particular way, then they should consider treating it as a closed multiple choice question with a prompt list from which respondents can choose the answer that comes closest to their response.

Pre-coded closed questions

Closed questions will tend to be pre-coded. Either a prompt list of possible answers is used or there is a known and finite number of responses that can be given. These are provided on a code list for the interviewer or the respondent to select. There is little point in not providing such a list and requiring the answers to be written in, with the consequent cost and time of having to code the responses.

Dichotomous questions

The simplest of closed questions are dichotomous questions, which have only two possible answers:

'Have you drunk any beer in the last 24 hours?'
Yes
No

It is possible that respondents could refuse to answer or say that they 'Don't know'.

Dichotomous questions such as this are easy to write and easy to ask. Complex pieces of information can often be broken down into a series of dichotomous questions that respondents can be led through, with a greater expectation of accuracy than would be achieved with a single question.

'Have you bought a bicycle in the last 12 months as a present for a child in your family that cost over £200?'

Is more easily asked, and understood as:

'Have you bought a bicycle in the last 12 months?'
  IF YES:
  'Was it for your own use or for someone else's?'
  IF SOMEONE ELSE'S:
  'Was that other person a child?'
  IF A CHILD:
  'Is that child a member of your family?'
  IF MEMBER OF THE FAMILY:
  'Did it cost £200 or more, or less than £200?'

As can be seen, additional information is also picked up along the way. When the questioning is through a single question, we can only determine the penetration of the defined group. By breaking the questions down we can also determine the penetration of bicycle purchasers and whether for self or as a gift. This is information that may be capable of being checked against other sources to establish the accuracy of the sample, or it may be new information, not previously available.

However, care must be taken that the question really is dichotomous. Consider the question 'Will you buy a new bicycle in the next six months?' This may appear to be dichotomous, capable of being answered 'yes' or 'no'. But if they were the only answers offered it would result in a high proportion of 'Don't know' answers because future behaviour is unpredictable. Some respondents will be certain that they will not buy a bicycle in the next six months; others will be certain that they will. Others, though, will not be sure. They may think that there is a possibility that they will, but have not been given this option as an answer.

The real question here is about current expectations or intentions. It could therefore be asked as: 'At the moment, do you intend (or expect) to buy a new bicycle in the next six months?' This could now be treated as a dichotomous question, but is still probably better asked as a scale, from 'Definitely will buy' to 'Definitely will not', encompassing less certain positions along the way. This would allow respondents to express better their true uncertainty regarding their future behaviour (see Chapter 5).

Multiple choice

Closed questions with more than one possible answer are known as multiple choice (or multi-chotomous) questions. Such a question might be: 'Which brand or brands of beer have you drunk in the last seven days?' Clearly, there is a finite number of answers; the range of possible answers is predictable; and the question does not require respondents to say anything 'in their own words'. With an interviewer-administered questionnaire, the brands can be listed without the respondent being prompted. Thus, a spontaneous answer can be easily recorded and coded for analysis. With self-completion questionnaires, the respondent must be asked to write in the brand name.

The list of possible answers provided should be exclusive and as exhaustive as possible.

'Don't know' responses

Questionnaire writers are often unsure as to whether they should include a 'Don't know' response to pre-coded questions. With interviewer-administered questionnaires, it is argued, the inclusion of 'Don't know' legitimizes it as a response and gives the interviewer permission to accept it and not to probe for a fuller answer. If it is not on the questionnaire, the interviewer will be more likely to probe for a response that is on the pre-code list before having to write in that the respondent is unable or unwilling to answer the question.

'Don't know' can be a legitimate response to many questions where the respondent genuinely does not know the answer, and there should be no difficulty in identifying questions where a 'Don't know' code must be included:

- 'Which mobile phone service does your partner subscribe to?'
- 'When was your house last repainted?'
- 'From which store was the jar of coffee bought?'

With other questions, though, it is not always so clear. These tend to be questions either of opinion, where a likelihood of action is sought, or of recent behaviour, which the respondent could be expected to remember:

- 'Where in the house would you be most likely to use this air freshener?'
- 'What method of transport did you use to get here today?'
- 'Which brand of tomato soup did you buy most recently?'

A good reason for having a 'Don't know' code on interviewer-administered paper questionnaires is that without it the response may be left blank. The researcher cannot then be sure that the question was asked. Knowing that the respondent could not or would not answer the question gives a positive assurance to the researcher that the interview was administered correctly.

This can also provide important information about the knowledge of respondents and their ability to answer this question. Isolated responses of this type might indicate that those respondents were not recruited correctly to the desired criteria. Widespread responses of this type might indicate that the information asked is beyond the scope of this research universe (eg asking post room managers in businesses about the size of the company's stationery bill) or that the question is poorly worded and not understood by many of the respondents. This is generally information worth knowing and should encourage the inclusion of 'Don't know' codes on the questionnaire.

Bias can be introduced if a brand name is pressed for if there is no 'Don't know' code. This is because it is more likely that the brand leader (or best-known brand if that is different) will be the one that comes to mind first, or will be the one that respondents guess that they are most likely to have bought recently. Less-well-known brands may get under-represented, so a bias has been introduced through the lack of a 'Don't know' code.

With CAPI and CATI questionnaires it is usual to provide a 'Don't know' code for most questions, as, without being able to record that, it may not be possible to move on to the next question.

With self-completion questionnaires, the provision of a 'Don't know' code has to be considered question by question. Such a code on every question may indeed encourage respondents not to think sufficiently about their response, and if there is any uncertainty, to answer 'Don't know'. It is prudent, therefore, to limit the use of 'Don't know' categories to those questions where the researcher believes it to be a genuine response. With Web-based self-completion questionnaires there are other issues regarding not encouraging respondents to give 'Don't know' as an answer, while enabling them to continue to the next question. These issues are considered as a matter of questionnaire layout in Chapter 7.

DATA TYPES

Responses are measured using four types of data:

* nominal;
* ordinal;
* interval;
* ratio.

These are frequently described as 'measurement scales', though most researchers would not necessarily recognize all of them as scales. It is important for the questionnaire writer to recognize which type of data is being collected for each question, as this will determine the type of analysis that can be carried out.

Nominal data

Nominal data are data that are classified into discrete categories by name, eg male, female; New York, Chicago, Los Angeles; purchaser of pizza, non-purchaser of pizza. Depending on the type of data collection system used, a number will often be assigned to each category. However, that number is purely arbitrary and implies no value that can be given to the response category. The numbers are given for identification purposes only. Thus if a sampling point is described as 'Urban' and is given a code of 1, and 'Rural' is assigned a code 2, there is no relative value implied between the two categories (see Figure 4.2). Respondents are classified into one category or another. The categories should be exhaustive (ie everybody should fit somewhere) and mutually exclusive (ie there is no overlap between them).

There is no numerical relationship between the categories. The responses are usually presented in an order that is the most convenient for the respondent, which may be alphabetically, or by size, or by geography. In Figure 4.2 the fact that Safeway is given a code 3 and Sainsbury's a 4 is arbitrary and has no meaning other than as a way of recording the response.

Nothing can be done with the data except to count the number of responses against each code. It is meaningless to calculate an average across the responses or to carry out any other calculation based on the value of the code.

Q. Which of these supermarkets in your opinion sells the best-quality fresh vegetables?

Asda	1
Morrison	2
Safeway	3
Sainsbury	4
Somerfield	5
Tesco	6

Figure 4.2 *Assigning code numbers for identification purposes*

Ordinal data

Ordinal data are usually found in questionnaires as ranking scales, otherwise known as 'comparative scales'. Respondents are asked to put nominal categories in order according to a criterion contained in the question. This is often order of preference, as in:

Please put the following flavours of yoghurt in the order in which you prefer them, starting with 1 for your first choice through to 5 for your least preferred:

Blackcurrant	3
Black cherry	1
Peach	4
Raspberry	5
Strawberry	2

Other ranking questions might include ranking by order of:

▓ a product characteristic – sweetness, consistency, strength;
▓ frequency of use – most used, next most used, etc;
▓ recency of use – last used, next to last used, etc;
▓ perceived price – most expensive to least expensive;
▓ ease of comprehension – easiest to understand to most difficult.

Ranking puts the nominal data into the appropriate order, but tells the researcher nothing about the distance between the points. In the example above, strawberry yoghurt might be liked almost as well as black cherry, with both of them liked considerably more than blackcurrant. The researcher cannot deduce this from the data. Nor can the researcher determine whether the last choice, raspberry, is actively disliked and would never be chosen by this respondent, or whether it is firmly in the repertoire of flavours. It may even be the case that the respondent actually likes none of these five flavours and the ranking is based on which flavours are least disliked.

Ranking can be used to force differences between brands, products or services, which would not be apparent with rating scales. On a five-point rating scale of sweetness, from not at all sweet to very sweet, the five flavours of yoghurt may all be rated fairly or very sweet, giving the researcher insufficient discrimination in the resulting data. By using ranking, that discrimination is forced out.

The task of ranking can become too difficult for respondents where there are a large number of items.

Suppose that we want to ask respondents to give their order of preference for, say, 15 flavours of yogurt. With electronic self-completion interviews, either Web-based or CAPI, this is relatively straightforward provided the number of flavours presented is not too large, as respondents can be asked to drag and drop the flavour descriptions into their rank order of preference.

With interviewer-administered and paper questionnaires the task is rather more onerous. Ranking 15 flavours of yoghurt would be a tedious exercise. Even if they could do it, for many people it would be unrealistic, as they may have a number that they like and a number that they dislike, but have some in between that they have no feelings about. The length of the task and its unrealistic nature would be likely to lead to fatigue, with a consequent lack of care given to the responses. There may be a knock-on effect to the rest of the interview, damaging the quality of the responses thereafter. This problem can be approached in a number of ways.

Respondents can be asked to rank their preferred flavours up to a predetermined number and their least preferred, or those that they don't like at all, if this is more appropriate. Or, as in Figure 4.3, they may be asked to rank their preferred three and then to nominate their least preferred three, but with no order recorded for the least preferred.

In a face-to-face interview, each flavour can be presented on a card. Respondents are asked to put their five preferred flavours (or the five sweetest flavours, or whatever is appropriate to the question) in one

Q. SHOW CARD.

On this card are 15 different flavours of yoghurt.

a) Which one do you prefer most?

b) Which is your second preference?

c) Which next?

d) And which three do you like least?

	Preferred	Second preference	Third preference	Three liked least
Apricot	1	2	3	4
Banana	1	2	3	4
Black cherry	1	2	3	4
Blackcurrant	1	2	3	4
Gooseberry	1	2	3	4
Grapefruit	1	2	3	4
Mandarin	1	2	3	4
Passion fruit	1	2	3	4
Peach	1	2	3	4
Pear	1	2	3	4
Pineapple	1	2	3	4
Raspberry	1	2	3	4
Rhubarb	1	2	3	4
Strawberry	1	2	3	4
Tangerine	1	2	3	4

Figure 4.3 *Ranking preferences*

pile, and the five least preferred (or least sweet) in a second pile. They are then asked to rank-order the cards in each pile, from preferred to least preferred, or sweetest to least sweet. There is rarely difficulty ranking the top five, as the respondent is likely to have a reasonably clear view about them. However, the bottom five can often present difficulties to respondents in discriminating between them as they are all rejected, and equally so. The number of items in the bottom group should be carefully thought about and different options piloted wherever possible, in order to find what is a sensible number to ask about. This type of exercise then gives a notional rank order equal to the midpoint for all of the items not ranked in the top or bottom five. This is not unrealistic, as respondents will often know what they like and what they dislike, and have a group of items in between about which they have no strong views.

Interval scales

Interval scales provide for a rating of each item on a scale that has a numerically equal distance between each point, and an arbitrary, and therefore meaningless, zero point. Such scales are used in order to determine the relative strength of relationships between items. The five flavours of yoghurt could be individually rated on a scale from 1 to 10 for how much each is liked. There is an equal interval between each point, but a score of 8 does not necessarily mean that the item is preferred twice as much as another item scored 4. Nor does a score of 2 given to a flavour imply that it is thought to be twice as good as one with a score of 1. The advantage of the interval scale over the ordinal scale is that the researcher can tell whether an item is liked or disliked (or thought to be sweet or not, etc) by its rating. It will, however, not always be possible to assign a rank order for the items from this information.

Figure 4.4 gives the results for two respondents asked to rate the five yoghurt flavours on a 10-point interval scale. The first respondent has given a different score to each flavour, so that not only can we rank-order that person's preferences, but we can now tell that the person likes black cherry and strawberry rather better than he or she likes blackcurrant, whilst peach and raspberry are not liked. The second respondent, however, likes all five flavours and it is difficult to deduce a meaningful rank order of preference from the interval scale responses.

In practice, the researcher is rarely dealing with data at an individual level but with aggregated data over the whole sample. Interval scales allow mean scores and standard deviations to be calculated across the sample for each item. Using mean scores can often appear to overcome this, as over a large sample it is rare for the mean score for two items to be identical. The analyst, though, must be careful that any two mean

Please give each flavour a mark between 1 and 10 based on how much you like it.

	Respondent 1		Respondent 2	
	Rating 1 to 10	Deduced ranking	Rating 1 to 10	Deduced ranking
Blackcurrant	5	3	9	1=
Black cherry	9	1	8	3=
Peach	2	4	9	1=
Raspberry	1	5	8	3=
Strawberry	8	2	8	3=

Figure 4.4 *Rating on an interval scale*

scores are significantly different with a desired level of confidence before concluding that across the sample one item is rated differently to another.

Many of the scales used in measuring attitude, brand perceptions, customer satisfaction, etc are interval scales. These include the semantic differential scale, Likert scale and others covered in Chapter 5.

Ratio scales

Ratio scales are a particular type of interval scale. The distance between each point on a ratio scale is constant, but the zero point has a real meaning, such that the ratio between any two scores also has a meaning. Age is a ratio scale, with a 50-year-old person being twice as old as a 25-year-old. Income is another.

This type of scale is also used to ask questions such as:

※ 'Out of the last 10 cans of baked beans that you bought, how many were Heinz?'
※ 'What proportion of your household income do you spend on your rent or mortgage?'
※ 'How long ago did you buy your car?'

Of the last 10 cans of baked beans that you bought, how many were Heinz?

None	❏
1	❏
2	❏
3	❏
4	❏
5	❏
6	❏
7	❏
8	❏
9	❏
10	❏

What proportion of your household income do you spend on your rent or mortgage?

0% to 5%	❏
6% to 10%	❏
11% to 15%	❏
16% to 20%	❏
21% to 25%	❏
26% to 30%	❏
31% to 40%	❏
41% to 50%	❏
51% to 60%	❏
61% to 80%	❏
81% or more	❏

How long ago did you buy your car?

Within the last month	❏
Between one month and three months ago	❏
Longer than three months and up to six months ago	❏
Longer than six months and up to one year ago	❏
Longer than one year and up to two years ago	❏
Longer than two years and up to three years ago	❏
Longer than three years and up to five years ago	❏
Longer than five years and up to ten years ago	❏
Longer ago than ten years	❏

Figure 4.5 *Recording on a ratio scale*

In some instances we might choose to record the responses directly and sometimes within categories. For these three questions the recording of the responses may be as in Figure 4.5.

Note that the response categories are not necessarily of equal length. These have been chosen to suit the purposes of the researcher or to reflect the expected distribution of the data. The proportion of income spent on rent or mortgage could have been recorded as a direct percentage and categorized at the analysis stage. The reason for putting this into bands is that most respondents will not know the answer to the exact percentage point, and if they are asked for it, this could lead to a higher level of non-response at this question. The length of time since respondents bought their car could be recorded as days, months or years. No one would bother to work out the number of days, however, and only the most recent buyers would easily be able to give the time in months. The researcher here is particularly interested in differences between people who have bought their car relatively recently, so it is important to be able to distinguish between very recent purchasers (within the last three months) and less recent purchasers.

The fact that the recording of the data is categorized does not affect the underlying property that there is a relationship between the responses, and the researcher can identify a respondent who buys twice as many cans of Heinz beans, or spends twice as much on rent or mortgage, or bought a car twice as long ago as another. The accuracy of this calculation is restricted only by the size of the categories used to collect the data.

With allocation of appropriate scores to each point, or average values to each range, we can now calculate mean values and standard deviations for the sample, and carry out statistical tests.

5 Rating scales and attitude measurement

ATTITUDE MEASUREMENT

The measurement of attitude poses more problems than does the measurement of behaviour. Respondents are able to respond relatively easily to behavioural questions, limited only by their memory of events, the amount of effort they are prepared to give to answering the questions and the degree to which they are prepared to be truthful. It is easier for respondents to say how they travelled here today, which brand of pasta sauce they last bought or which phone company they are with than it is for them to describe their attitude towards the government's transport policy, to say how they feel about the use of convenience foods or to describe their perception of the telephone company's brand image.

Respondents need to be helped to express attitudes and describe images, particularly to describe them in a format that we can analyse. The most commonly used approach to measuring attitude is the itemized rating scale.

ITEMIZED RATING SCALES

Itemized rating scales are used to help the researcher obtain a measure of attitudes. The researcher first develops a number of dimensions – attitude statements, product or service attributes, image dimensions, etc. Respondents are then asked to position how they feel about each one using a defined rating scale.

A rating scale is an interval scale (see Chapter 4) on which respondents are asked to give their answer using a range of evenly spaced points, which are provided as prompts.

Rating scales are widely used by questionnaire writers. They provide a straightforward way of asking attitudinal information that is easy and versatile to analyse, and that provides comparability across time. However, there are many different types of rating scales, and there is skill in choosing which is most appropriate for a given task.

All of the itemized rating scales given in Figure 5.1 are from actual surveys. The wording on each scale is tailored to be appropriate to the question, and all have five points representing a gradation from positive to negative. The first two are balanced around a neutral mid-point with equal numbers of positive and negative statements for the respondent to choose from.

Being interval data, scores can be allocated to each of the responses to assist in the analysis of responses. The allocated scores are most likely to be from 1 to 5, from the least to the most positive, or from −2 to +2, from the most negative to the most positive with the neutral point as zero.

In all of these examples the scales presented to respondents run from the most positive to the most negative or, if rotated, from the most negative to the most positive for half of the respondents. It is usual to present the responses in this way for clarity and to assist the respondent to find the most appropriate answer.

However, there are occasions when there is a reason for an alternative order that overrides this. Consider Figure 5.2. This is from an Australian Web-based survey, and the questionnaire writer has placed the mid-scale neutral statement at the end of the list offered because of the subject matter. This is because there is a tendency for respondents to deny being influenced by advertising, or even to acknowledge to themselves that they are influenced. The neutral statement has been placed last in the list in the expectation that, by offering the four statements that acknowledge advertising influence together as a block, the visual impact will be such

SHOW CARD.

How likely are you to use the train for this journey in the near future?

Very likely	1
Quite likely	2
Neither likely nor unlikely	3
Quite unlikely	4
Very unlikely	5
Don't know (not on card)	6

SHOW CARD.

Using the scale on this card please indicate how effective are the management and staff in seeming well organized and systematic in carrying out their work.

Highly effective	1
Effective	2
Neither effective nor ineffective	3
Not very effective	4
Not at all effective	5

SHOW CARD.

Thinking about travelling in and around the city, which of the statements on this card best describes how you feel about using the bus?

The only method I would use	1
One of the methods I would be happy to use	2
It's not my preferred way to travel but I would consider it	3
I would only use it if there was nothing else available	4
I would never use it	5

Figure 5.1 *Some examples of itemized rating scales*

that respondents will themselves be more prepared to consider that they may be influenced. The questionnaire writer has tried to bias the responses, but is doing so in order to offset another known bias. When scoring the responses, the researcher must remember that the mid-point score must be given to the last statement in the list.

Based on everything you saw or heard in this ad, how likely will you be to purchase this product in the future?

Please select one.

Much more likely to buy it 1

Somewhat more likely to buy it 2

Somewhat less likely to buy it 3

Much less likely to buy it 4

The ad had no effect on my likelihood to buy it 5

Figure 5.2 *An alternative order for responses*

Balanced scales

It is usual to balance scales by including equal numbers of positive and negative attitudes. If there are more positive than negative attitudes offered, then the total number of positive responses tends to be higher than would have otherwise been the case. An advantage is given to the attitude that has the greater number of dimensions for the respondent to select from.

Consider the balanced scale when asking respondents to describe the taste of a product:

Very good
Good
Average
Poor
Very poor

With two positive and two negative statements the respondents are not led in either direction. However, if the scale was:

Excellent
Very good
Good
Average
Poor

then the three positive dimensions would tend to be chosen more often. In most circumstances, it is important to balance the scale in order to avoid this bias.

However, there are occasions when an unbalanced scale can be justified. Where it is known that the response will be overwhelmingly in one direction, then more categories may be given in that direction to achieve better discrimination.

An example is frequently found when measuring the importance of service in customer satisfaction research. When asked to state how important various aspects of customer service are, few customers say that any are unimportant. After all, the customers will be looking for the best service that they can get. And the dimensions about which we ask are the ones that we believe are important anyway. The objective is mainly to distinguish between the most important aspects of service and the less important ones. An unbalanced scale might therefore be used, offering just one unimportant option, but several degrees of importance:

Extremely important
Very important
Important
Neither important nor unimportant
Not important

Here the questionnaire writer is trying to obtain a degree of discrimination between the levels of importance. The mid-point is 'important', and the scale implicitly assumes that this will be where the largest number of responses will be placed.

Even using scales such as these, it can be difficult for respondents to acknowledge which aspects of service are the most important in their decision making. Indirect methods, such as establishing the correlation between performance and behaviour, or using a form of conjoint (trade-off) analysis, are generally preferable.

Unbalanced scales should only be used for a good reason and for a specific purpose, and by experienced researchers who know what the impact is likely to be (see Figure 5.3).

Number of points on the scale

The illustrations in Figures 5.1 and 5.2 show five-point scales, which are probably the most commonly used. A five-point scale gives sufficient discrimination for most purposes and is easily understood by respondents. The size of the scale can be expanded to seven points if

Seen in print

Q. SHOW CARD.

Which of these phrases best describes your overall opinion of the chances of winning a prize in this game?

VERY POOR	1
POOR	2
NEITHER FAIR NOR POOR	3
FAIR	4
GOOD	5
VERY GOOD	6
EXCELLENT	7
DON'T KNOW	8

With just two negative and four positive statements, the emphasis is clearly positive in this case. The researcher clearly knew that greater discrimination would be required between the positive scale positions.

Figure 5.3 *An unbalanced scale*

greater discrimination is to be attempted. Then the scale points can be written as:

Extremely likely
Very likely
Quite likely
Neither likely nor unlikely
Quite unlikely
Very unlikely
Extremely unlikely

or:

Excellent
Very good
Good
Neither good nor poor
Poor
Very poor
Extremely poor

The decision as to the number of points on the scale has to be taken with regard to the distinction that is possible between the points, the ability of respondents to discriminate between those points, and the degree of discrimination that is sought. The interview medium must also be considered. With telephone interviewing, scales with more than five points are difficult for respondents to remember. With self-completion questionnaires, the additional page space required for more points may be a factor.

'Don't knows'

In Figure 5.1, each of the scales is balanced around a neutral mid-point 'Neither agree nor disagree'. This is included to allow a response for people who have no strong view either way. This is frequently the case when the subject is groceries or other everyday objects. However, this point is also frequently used by respondents who wish to give a 'Don't know' response, but are not offered 'Don't know' as a response category and do not wish to, or are unable to, leave the response blank. The reluctance of respondents to leave a scale blank where they genuinely cannot give an answer has always been an issue with self-completion interviews, or where these scales form a self-completion section to an otherwise interviewer-administered interview. However, electronic interviews frequently do not allow respondents to pass to the next question if any line is left blank. Thus for CAPI, CATI and particularly Web-based interviews, distinguishing between genuine mid-point responses and 'Don't knows' can become a serious issue.

'Don't know' codes or boxes are frequently not provided, as the questionnaire writer does not wish to encourage this as a response but to encourage the respondent to provide a response that, in all likelihood, reflects an attitude unrecognized at a conscious level by the respondent. Also, non-response to one scale among a battery of scales can raise issues of how to treat the data when using certain data analysis techniques. The reluctance to accept 'Don't know' as a response is understandable. The questionnaire writer must consider whether it is preferable to be able to distinguish or not between genuine mid-point responses and people who did not want to, or could not, answer.

Odd or even number of points

Some practitioners prefer to use a scale with an even number of points. They eliminate the neutral mid-point in an attempt to force those who would otherwise choose it to give an inclination one way or the other. The response points for a six-point agree–disagree scale could be:

Extremely likely
Very likely
Quite likely
Quite unlikely
Very unlikely
Extremely unlikely

or:

Excellent
Very good
Good
Poor
Very poor
Extremely poor

In studies where it would be expected that most people would have a view, for example studies about crime, it can be argued that most people hold a view even if they do not recognize that they do. It is therefore legitimate, it is argued, to force a response in one direction or the other. When the subject is breakfast cereals, though, it must be recognized that many people may really have no opinion one way or the other.

It is possible to accept a neutral response if that is offered spontaneously by the respondent in an interviewer-administered survey. Studies have shown, though, that including a neutral scale position significantly increases the number of neutral responses compared to accepting them spontaneously (Kalton, Roberts and Holt, 1980; Presser and Schuman, 1980). This indicates that eliminating the middle neutral point does increase the commitment of respondents to be either positive or negative. However, the questionnaire writer must decide whether or not including a mid-point is appropriate for the particular question and subject matter. Often, another factor, such as precedence or comparability with other data, will be the deciding factor.

ATTITUDINAL RATING SCALES

A number of forms of rating scale have been developed specifically to address responses to a series of attitudinal dimensions. The three most commonly used are:

* Likert scale;
* semantic differential scale;
* Stapel scale.

Likert scale

The Likert scale (frequently known as an 'agree–disagree' scale) was first published by psychologist Rensis Likert in 1932. The technique presents respondents with a series of attitude dimensions (a battery), for each of which they are asked whether, and how strongly, they agree or disagree, using one of a number of positions on a five-point scale (see Figure 5.4).

With face-to-face interviewer-administered scale batteries, the responses may be shown on a card whilst the interviewer reads out each of the statements in turn. With telephone interviewing, the respondent may sometimes be asked to remember what the response categories are, but preferably would be asked to write them down.

The technique is easy to administer in self-completion questionnaires, either paper or electronic, and may often be given to respondents as a self-completion section in an interviewer-administered survey.

Responses using the Likert scale can be given scores for each statement, usually from 1 to 5, negative to positive, or −2 to +2. As these are interval data, means and standard deviations can be calculated for each statement.

The full application of the Likert scale is then to sum the scores for each respondent to provide an overall attitudinal score for each individual. Likert's intention was that the statements would represent different aspects of the same attitude. The overall score, though, is rarely calculated in commercial research (Albaum, 1997), where the statements usually cover a range of attitudes. The responses to individual statements are of more interest in determining the specific aspects of attitude that drive behaviour and choice in a market, or summations are made over small groups of items. The data will tend to be used in factor analysis, in order to identify groups of attitudinal

Below are a number of statements regarding attitudes to shopping. Please read each one and indicate whether you agree or disagree with it by ticking one box for each statement.

	Disagree strongly	Disagree	Neither agree nor disagree	Agree	Agree strongly
Being a smart shopper is worth the extra time it takes.	❏	❏	❏	❏	❏
Which brands I buy makes little difference to me.	❏	❏	❏	❏	❏
I take advantage of special offers.	❏	❏	❏	❏	❏
I like to try new brands.	❏	❏	❏	❏	❏
I like to shop around and look at displays.	❏	❏	❏	❏	❏

Figure 5.4 *Use of the Likert scale*

statements that have similar response patterns and that could there-fore represent underlying attitudinal dimensions. Factor analysis can be used to create a factor score for each respondent on each of the underlying attitudinal dimensions, thereby reducing the data to a small number of individual scores. These data are then often used in various forms of cluster or segmentation analyses, in order to segment the data into groups of respondents with similar attitudes.

There are four interrelated issues that questionnaire writers must be aware of when using Likert scales:

▦ order effect;
▦ acquiescence;

■ central tendency;
■ pattern answering.

The *order effect* arises from the order in which the response codes are presented. It has been shown (Artingstall, 1978) that there is a bias to the left on a self-completion scale. (Order effects are returned to in Chapter 6.)

Acquiescence is the tendency for respondents to agree rather than disagree with statements (Kalton and Schuman, 1982), also known as 'yea saying'.

In Figure 5.4, the negative end of the scale is placed to the left, to be read first. With the 'Agree' response to the left, the order effect and acquiescence would compound each other. With the 'Disagree' response to the left, there is a possibility of the biases going some way to cancelling each other.

Central tendency is the reluctance of respondents to use extreme positions. It has been shown (Albaum, 1997) that a two-stage question elicits a higher proportion of extreme responses. This work used the question:

> For each of the statements listed below indicate first the extent of your agreement and second how strongly you feel about your agreement.
>
> 'A product's price will usually reflect its level to quality.'
> agree_____ neither agree nor disagree_____ disagree_____
>
> How strongly do you feel abut your response?
> very strong_____ not very strong_____

With a large number of dimensions to be evaluated, this approach may be too time-consuming for most studies, but the questionnaire writer should be aware of this approach and of the different response patterns that it is likely to give. This approach is particularly appropriate for telephone interviewing, where the complete scale cannot be shown.

Pattern answering occurs when a respondent falls into a routine of ticking boxes in a pattern, which might be straight down the page or diagonally across it. It is often a symptom of fatigue or boredom. The best way to avoid it is to keep the interview interesting for the respondent. To minimize pattern answering, both positive and negative statements should be included. The respondent then has to read them or listen to them carefully in order to understand the polarity and to give consistent answers. Conflicting answers from the same respondent will identify where pattern answering has occurred.

Semantic differential scale

The semantic differential scale is a bipolar rating scale. It differs from the Likert scale in that opposite statements of the dimension are placed at the two ends of the scale and respondents are asked to indicate which they most agree with by placing a mark along the scale. This has the advantage that there is then no need for the scale points to be semantically identified. Any bias towards agreeing with a statement is avoided, as both ends of the scale have to be considered.

The original development of this scale by Osgood (Osgood, Suci and Tannenbaum, 1957) recommended the use of seven points on the response scale, and this number continues to be the favourite of researchers (McDaniel and Gates, 1993), although both five-point scales and three-point scales are used for particular purposes (Oppenheim, 1992).

With semantic differential scales the statements should be kept as short and precise as possible because of the need for the respondent to read and understand fully both ends of the scale. Attitudes can be difficult to express concisely, and it is sometimes difficult to find an opposite to ensure that the scale represents a linear progression from one end to the other. For these reasons semantic differential scales are usually better suited to descriptive dimensions.

As with all self-completion techniques it is wise to provide an example of how to complete the grid (see Figure 5.5).

Care must be taken to ensure that the two statements provided determine the dimension that the researcher requires. The opposite of 'modern' might be 'old-fashioned' or it might be 'traditional'. The opposite of 'sweet' might be 'savoury' or 'sour' or 'bitter'. This forces the questionnaire writer to consider exactly what the dimension is that is to be measured. This gives the semantic differential scale an advantage over the Likert scale where disagreeing with 'The brand is modern' could mean that the brand is seen as either old-fashioned or traditional, and the researcher does not know which.

Below are pairs of statements. Each one may or may not apply to the advertisement that you have just seen. Please read each pair and indicate which of the statements you agree applies to the ad by ticking one box for each pair of statements.

For example, if you agree strongly that the advertisement was 'mundane', you would tick the box closest to that statement, but if you only agreed slightly, then you should tick a box further away from the statement.

Example

| Fascinating | ❏ | ❏ | ❏ | ❏ | ❏ | ☑ | ❏ | Mundane |

Please complete the remaining items according to how you feel about the ad:

Boring	❏	❏	❏	❏	❏	❏	❏	Interesting
Important	❏	❏	❏	❏	❏	❏	❏	Unimportant
Relevant	❏	❏	❏	❏	❏	❏	❏	Irrelevant
Exciting	❏	❏	❏	❏	❏	❏	❏	Unexciting
Unappealing	❏	❏	❏	❏	❏	❏	❏	Appealing
Involving	❏	❏	❏	❏	❏	❏	❏	Uninvolving
Means nothing	❏	❏	❏	❏	❏	❏	❏	Means a lot to me

Scale items taken from Zaichkowsky (1999).

Figure 5.5 *Use of a semantic differential scale*

Some dimensions may have no opposite other than a negative statement of the attribute. The true opposite of 'fattening' applied to a food product would be 'slimming', but it is likely that the neutral 'not fattening' would make more sense in assessing perceptions of the product.

Figure 5.6 comes from an advertising study. Note that the questionnaire writer has reversed the polarity of the statements alternately. The statements have been shown to the respondent on a card. So although this is not a self-completion questionnaire, there is still a danger of pattern answering, which needs to be minimized.

Also note the difficulty that the questionnaire writer has in achieving exact opposites in the first pair of statements. The ad may be worth

Seen in print

SHOW CARD.

Here are two opposite ways in which someone could describe this ad. For example, 'worth remembering' at this end of the scale (POINT) or 'easy to forget' (POINT) at the other end of the scale. I'd like you to tell me which number on this scale best describes what you personally feel about this ad. You can use any number from 1 to 5.

CIRCLE NUMBER.

And how would you rate the ad in the second scale? POINT TO AND READ OUT DESCRIPTORS.

REPEAT FOR REMAINING SCALES.

Worth remembering	1	2	3	4	5	Easy to forget
Difficult to relate to	1	2	3	4	5	Involving or easy to relate to
Lively, exciting or fun	1	2	3	4	5	Dull
Ordinary or boring	1	2	3	4	5	Clever or imaginative
Helps make the brand different from others	1	2	3	4	5	Does not really make the brand appear any different from the others
Makes me *less* interested in the brand	1	2	3	4	5	Makes me *more* interested in the brand

Figure 5.6 *Example of a semantic differential scale*

remembering because it contains useful information, but that does not necessarily mean that it is not also easily forgettable. The questionnaire writer could have included both of the pairs 'Worth remembering – Not worth remembering' and 'Easy to forget – Difficult to forget', but has chosen to force a decision between two statements that are not strictly opposites in order not to have to extend the number of pairs asked about.

As with the Likert scale, dimensions of similar meaning should be given with reversed polarity in order to minimize pattern answering and to check internal consistency of responses.

Please indicate how accurately you feel each of the following words and phrases describes the GingerBread Store. Select a positive number for the phrases you think describe the store accurately. The more accurately you think it describes it, the larger the number you should choose. Select a minus number for the phrases you think do not describe it accurately. The less accurately you think the phrase describes the store, the larger the negative number you should choose. You can select any number from +5 for words and phrases you think are very accurate to −5 for words and phrases you think are very inaccurate.

The GingerBread Store

+5	+5	+5
+4	+4	+4
+3	+3	+3
+2	+2	+2
+1	+1	+1
is well laid out	has helpful staff	is attractive
−1	−1	−1
−2	−2	−2
−3	−3	−3
−4	−4	−4
−5	−5	−5

Figure 5.7 *Use of the Stapel scale*

Stapel scale

With the Stapel scale, named after Jan Stapel, the dimension or descriptor is placed at the centre of a scale that ranges from −5 to +5. Respondents are asked to indicate whether they agree positively or negatively with the statement, and how strongly, by selecting one of the points on the scale (see Figure 5.7).

The advantage of this type of scale over semantic differential scales is that it is not necessary to find an accur91ate opposite to each dimension to ensure bipolarity. The data can, however, be analysed in the same way as semantic differentials, and the scale, with 10 points, has the potential to provide greater discrimination than a five-point scale. By having no centre point, these scales also avoid the issue of whether or not there should be an odd or even number of points on the scale.

Stapel scales are, however, not widely used as they are thought to be confusing for respondents. They must be self-administered if the researcher is to be confident that the respondent has properly understood the task. This has limited their use in telephone interviewing and with much face-to-face interviewing. However, with imaginative layout, they could work well with online Web-based interviewing.

Graphic scales

A graphic rating scale is a continuous bipolar scale with fixed points at either end, which can be simply represented as a line (see Figure 5.8).

Please indicate by marking on the line how you rate the GingerBread Store for each pair of statements below:		
Well laid out	_____	Poorly laid out
Has helpful staff	_____	Has unhelpful staff
Attractive window display	_____	Unattractive window display

Figure 5.8 *Graphic rating scale*

The distance from the end points of the respondent's marks is measured to provide the score for each attitudinal dimension. Essentially this is a continuously rated semantic differential scale, which provides a greater degree of precision and avoids the issues of numbers of points on the scale. It is a simple way of measuring attitudes and image perceptions, but is impractical to use with paper questionnaires. Measuring the position marked on hundreds of paper questionnaires, with possibly dozens of scales on each one is not viable for most commercial projects. This technique cannot be used with telephone interviewing.

With CAPI interviewing, though, and to a greater degree with online Web-based interviewing, the continuous graphic scale is a realistic option. Respondents can drag a cursor along the line to the exact position that they want it, and that position is then automatically recorded.

When the technique is being used to measure attitudes to brands or products, as in Figure 5.9, more than one cursor can be used to represent

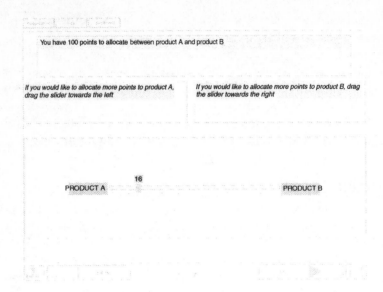

You have 100 points to allocate between product A and product B

If you would like to allocate more points to product A, drag the slider towards the left

If you would like to allocate more points to product B, drag the slider towards the right

16

PRODUCT A   PRODUCT B

Figure 5.9   *Slider scale on electronic questionnaire*

different brands, or brand logos can be used in place of cursors. Then each respondent can place a number of brands along the scale, so that they are positioned relative to each other as well as to the scale ends, according to the respondent's perceptions. This is quicker for respondents than rating each brand individually, is more interesting for them when logos are used, and provides better relative measures of the attitude variation between brands.

Although the data collected are continuous, the measurements will be assigned to categories and treated as interval data for analysis purposes. It is possible to have a large number of very small intervals, but the researcher must decide at what level the apparent accuracy of the data becomes spurious. That will depend on the length of the line used, the accuracy with which respondents are able to place the cursor, and the degree of accuracy to which respondents are likely to have tried to place the cursor.

The questionnaire writer may wish to apply labels to the scale. The scale can be numerically labelled, so that one end is 0 and the other 100. The position of the cursor can then be indicated as a number between 0 and 100, which allows the respondent to place the cursor accurately. In some instances, a centre-point label might be added, for example if

	Just right	
Too sweet _____		Too bitter
Too fruity _____		Not fruity enough
Too runny _____		Too solid

Figure 5.10   *Graphic rating scale with labelled mid-point*

the technique is being used to evaluate reactions to a new product. This scale could have just the verbal descriptors (see Figure 5.10), or these could be combined with numeric values, either shown on the line or appearing with the cursor. Here a numeric scale would have a zero point at 'Just right' extending to -50 for each of the end points, as they always represent a move away from the preferred positioning.

Pictorial scales

In many instances, it is desirable to avoid using semantic scales in favour of pictorial representations. This may be desirable:

▓ where the target population is children who are unable to relate their responses to verbal descriptors;
▓ where there are cultural differences between sub-groups of the target population that may mean that they interpret descriptors differently;
▓ with multi-country studies where translation of descriptors may alter shades of meaning;
▓ where there is a low level of literacy among the target population.

A common solution to this is the use of smiley or smiling face scales. A range of smiles and down-turned mouths is used to indicate that the respondent agrees with or is happy with the statement, or disagrees with or is unhappy with the statement.

A pictorial version of the continuous rating scale is the thermometer scale. With this the respondent 'colours in' a depiction of a thermometer so that colouring to the top is positive and not colouring it is negative. As with other types of continuous scale it is difficult economically to

Figure 5.11 *Smiley scale*

measure and code responses, except with electronic self-completion questionnaires.

Anchor strength

With all semantic scales, the wording of the 'anchor statement' is crucial to the distribution of data that is likely to be achieved. A five-point bipolar scale that goes from 'Extremely satisfied' to 'Extremely dissatisfied' is likely to discourage respondents from using the end points and to concentrate the distribution on the middle three points. If the end points were 'Very satisfied' and 'Very dissatisfied', the end points would be used by more respondents and the data would be more widely distributed across the scale. This can make the data more discriminatory between items.

As a general rule, the stronger the anchors, the more points are required on the scale to obtain discrimination.

RATING SCALES IN CUSTOMER SATISFACTION RESEARCH

Deciding which scale to use

Using rating scales in customer satisfaction research presents the questionnaire writer with a number of choices for the most appropriate scale.

Rating scales are commonly used in customer satisfaction research interviews for very good reasons. They provide a relatively easy way in which a customer can assess the service on a number of different items in a way that allows comparisons to be made between the items. The interval nature of the data makes it appropriate for the production

Figure 5.12   Hotel questionnaire

Seen in print

1 = Excellent	2 = Very good	3 = Good	4 = Fair	5 = Poor				
Cleanliness of your guest room upon entering			1	2	3	4	5	
Cleanliness and servicing of your room during your stay			1	2	3	4	5	
Overall cleanliness of bathroom			1	2	3	4	5	
Cleanliness of bathtub and tiles			1	2	3	4	5	
Condition of duvet cover			1	2	3	4	5	
Overall guest room quality			1	2	3	4	5	
Overall maintenance and upkeep			1	2	3	4	5	
Condition of grounds			1	2	3	4	5	
Condition of the lobby area			1	2	3	4	5	
Condition of the lounge and restaurants			1	2	3	4	5	
Functionality of guest room			1	2	3	4	5	

of mean scores, and for carrying out correlation or regression analyses using other data such as overall satisfaction or behavioural data.

Scales such as these are commonly found on questionnaires left in hotel rooms. The questionnaire that Figure 5.12 was taken from continued with 53 attributes in total to be rated on this scale, and 12 other questions. It contained no instructions other than to define the points of the scale, thus assuming that its clients had a reasonable level of familiarity with questionnaire completion. This is probably not an unreasonable assumption. In today's climate of customer service, you may be asked to complete a customer satisfaction survey if you:

- use a bank;
- subscribe to a telephone company;
- take out an insurance policy;
- book a holiday;
- travel by train or air;
- buy computer software;
- buy a car;

- have a car serviced;
- visit a hotel or any number of other places.

Customer satisfaction questionnaires abound, from short one-sided cards left for the client to complete, to many-paged very detailed studies conducted by telephone. And most of them use rating scales.

The researcher, though, needs to decide what is the appropriate scale to use. Should it be a rating of absolute performance, as in Figure 5.12? This is sufficient to allow us to track any changes over time, but how does the reported performance relate to expectations? A rating of 'Very good' may be wonderful news for a two-star hotel but a poor score for a five-star hotel where everything is expected to be 'Excellent'. Do customers bear that in mind when completing customer satisfaction questionnaires? Would the same level of service be rated as 'Excellent' in the two-star hotel but 'Poor' in the five-star hotel because expectations are different? Nor can it be assumed that these factors will remain constant over time. The ratings may start to decline despite the level of service remaining constant because a new competitor has entered the market with an improved service that has changed customers' expectations.

The questionnaire writer therefore needs to consider other scales as well. A scale may be devised to monitor performance relative to expectations. One such scale might be:

Much better than I expected
Better than I expected
As I expected
Worse than I expected
Much worse than I expected

Achieving a high score on this scale would demonstrate both that customers are delighted with the level of service, which they did not expect, and that there is possible over-delivery, which could be cut back.

In some circumstances, meeting customers' needs rather than their expectations may be more appropriate.

The level of service was:

A lot more than I needed
A little more than I needed
Exactly what I needed
A little less than I needed
A lot less than I needed

The provision of hotel services – the swimming pool, the trouser press, the range of restaurants, for example – may have been excellent, and may have been what was expected from a five-star hotel, but was more than was needed by clients, who will go elsewhere next time where they can get what they need for a lower price.

THE DIMENSIONS

Determining the attributes to measure

No matter which scale is used, one crucial factor to get right is the wording of the items against which the attitude is to be measured. As with all questionnaire research, if the item is not measured it cannot be analysed, and if important attributes are not included then the analysis could be totally misleading.

If there is no existing set of attitude or attribute dimensions that have been proven to represent the issues in the market under consideration, then they will need to be developed.

Ideally the dimensions should be developed through a preliminary stage of qualitative research, designed specifically to determine the range of emotions, attitudes and perceptions that exist and that are relevant to the study and its objectives. The principal purpose of the preliminary study is to provide the attitude dimensions that are to be measured for strength of agreement in the quantitative survey. This stage can also be used to develop some preliminary hypotheses about attitudinal segments that might exist in the market, which the quantitative survey can then test.

If it is not possible to carry out a preliminary stage, the dimensions must be collated from elsewhere. Previous studies in the same area are the best place to start even if not designed to answer precisely the same objectives. Any similar work carried out previously by the client should be examined.

Sometimes, though, it comes down to experience and brainstorming, in an effort to try to generate every possible attitude, emotion or image perception that might exist and might need to be included in the questionnaire. This approach has obvious dangers:

▨ New attitudes that have not yet been identified will be omitted, which will tend to lead to a continuation of the existing perceptions of the market, rather than providing new insight.

▓ Something important may be overlooked completely.
▓ The wording used may not be that used by the respondents.
▓ In the absence of any information as to what is and what is not important, there will be a tendency to produce too many dimensions in an attempt to ensure that everything is covered.

To counter this last point it is not unusual for a preliminary survey to be conducted that concentrates principally on the large set of attitude dimensions that have been initially generated. Most other questions are omitted from this questionnaire in order to make it manageable for the respondents. Care most be taken, though, not to alter the context of the attitude question by omitting preceding questions such as the respondent's behaviour in relation to the topic. Techniques such as principal component or factor analysis are then used to reduce a large battery of attitude dimensions to a smaller, more manageable set that can be included in the questionnaire. There is a danger here, though, that small differences in attitude dimensions that were specifically introduced in the brainstorming because they are important get excluded because the purpose of the factor analysis is to produce broader, underlying attitude dimensions. It is important, therefore, to follow any reduction process by a further review of the dimensions and reinstate those of particular importance or that show particular nuances of difference, which have been removed.

There exist sources such as *The Handbook of Marketing Scales* (Bearden and Netemeyer, 1999) that provide lists of dimensions for a range of different attitudinal subject areas that have been used in published studies. They are a useful starting point for someone compiling an attitude battery, when looking for standardized wording or for checking that the compiler has not overlooked an important dimension. Before adopting a complete set of standardized scaling dimensions, however, users should ensure that they cover all aspects of the topic under consideration in their study.

Number of attributes

If the number of statements exceeds the respondent's boredom threshold, the likelihood of pattern responding is increased.

The size of the statement battery is something that the researcher should consider carefully. Clearly there must be a sufficient number of statements to address adequately all of the attitudes under consideration. If possible, there should be several statements for each attitudinal dimension to enable the researcher to cross-check responses for consistency within respondents. The number of statements before fatigue sets in will vary according to the level of interest of the respondent in the subject. However, the maximum number in one battery is rarely more than about 30 before a respondent's attention begins to wander. If questionnaire writers are unsure, they should ask themselves whether they could themselves maintain concentration throughout a battery of 200 statements about, say, greetings cards.

If, despite all attempts to reduce the number of statements, it is not possible to cover the required attitudinal dimensions without producing a formidable battery of statements, it can sometimes be possible to split the statements into two batteries that are located at different points in the questionnaire. The statements should be split so that the two batteries cover different sets of underlying attitudinal dimensions, and, if possible, this should be explained in the introduction to the question. Without this precaution, there is a danger that respondents will believe when they are presented with the second battery that they are being asked the same questions again and will not take sufficient care.

Nevertheless, with a battery of statements of any size it is inevitable that some respondent fatigue will set in. Statements at the beginning of the battery will be given more careful consideration than those towards the end. The dangers of this type of response order bias and how to deal with it are discussed in Chapter 6.

Providing examples

It is generally wise to provide an example to show respondents how to complete the questionnaire. Questionnaire writers frequently forget that respondents may not be familiar with these techniques, and helping them to understand how to complete a battery of scales can avoid ruined questionnaires or abandoned interviews. It is probably less important to provide examples with electronic questionnaires, as they can be programmed to accept responses only in the specified format, one answer to each statement. It is also usually possible and easy with electronic self-completion questionnaires for respondents to go back and alter their responses if they realize that they have misunderstood something. It is rather more difficult with paper questionnaires to alter responses without ruining the questionnaire, and it is less likely that respondents would attempt to correct their misunderstanding.

COMPARATIVE SCALING TECHNIQUES

Paired comparisons

With paired comparisons, respondents are asked to choose between two objects based on the appropriate criterion, eg that one is more important than the other or preferred to the other. This can be repeated with a number of pairs chosen from a set of objects, such that every object is compared against every other object. Summing the choices made provides an evaluation of importance or preference across all of the objects. This can be easier and sometimes quicker for respondents than being asked to rank-order a list of objects, because the individual judgements to be made are simpler.

By careful rotation of the pairs, some of the order bias inherent in showing lists can be avoided.

The disadvantage of this technique is that it is limited to a relatively small number of objects. With just six objects, 15 pairs are required if every object is to be assessed against every other one, and the number of pairs required increases geometrically. With 190 possible pairs from a list of 20 items, clearly no respondent can be shown all of them. A balanced design of the pairs shown to each respondent can provide sufficient information for the rank order of each item to be inferred.

Constant sum

With a constant sum technique, respondents are asked to allocate a fixed number of points between a set of options to indicate relative importance or relative preference. The number of points given to each option reflects the magnitude of the importance, from which we can also deduce the rank order of the options for each respondent (see Figure 5.14).

Some respondents are likely to have problems with a constant sum question, as it requires some effort and mental agility on their part, both to think simultaneously across all of the items and to do the mental arithmetic.

**For each pair of flavours of yoghurt shown below,
please indicate which one you prefer.**

Black Cherry	○		Mandarin	○
Apricot	○		Pineapple	○

Raspberry	○		Raspberry	○
Strawberry	○		Mandarin	○

Blackcurrant	○		Pineapple	○
Peach	○		Black Cherry	○

Gooseberry	○		Peach	○
Peach	○		Pineapple	○

Figure 5.13   *Paired comparison*

It is easier with electronic questionnaires, where the scores allocated can be automatically summed and the respondent not allowed to move on until exactly 100 points have been allocated. The need to make simultaneous comparisons between a number of different objects still remains, though. As the number of items increases, so it becomes more difficult to think through and to mentally keep a running total of the scores.

Another way of asking this is to use a constant sum approach combined with paired comparisons. In Figure 5.15 the task for respondents has been reduced to making comparisons between 10 pairs of objects. Dealing with pairs is usually easier for respondents to manage.

Following is a list of items that might or might not be important to you when choosing a new car. I would like you to take 100 points and allocate them across the five items depending on how important each one is to you when choosing a new car. So if something is very important to you, you should give it a lot of points, but if it is not important you should give it relatively few points. Remember the total number of points must add to 100.

The engine size	☐
The colour	☐
Manual or automatic gearbox	☐
Quality of the radio/CD player	☐
Country of manufacture	☐
	100

Figure 5.14 *Constant sum technique*

In this example we have chosen to ask respondents to allocate 11 points between each pair. An odd number has been chosen so that the two objects in any pair cannot be given the same number of points. This forces a distinction between them. This technique can equally well be used for comparing preferences for products, when forcing even small distinctions can be important to the researcher. Had the respondents been asked to allot 10 points per pair, this would have allowed objects in a pair to be given equal weight of five points each.

Both the paired comparison and direct point allocation approaches have difficulties as the number of items increases, either because of the increased mental agility required in the direct approach or because of the increasing number of pairs that are generated.

Card sorting

When the number of objects is large, say more than 30, then a different approach is required to obtain a rank ordering or rating of each object. One such approach is card sorting.

In face-to-face interviews each object is described on a card. The card needs to be relatively small but not so small that respondents cannot read it. Larger cards are then laid out, marked as itemized rating scales,

Following is a list of pairs of items that might or might not be important to you when choosing a new car. For each pair please allocate 11 points depending on how important each is to you. So if one is very important and the other not, you would give one 10 points and the other 1. If they are of similar importance you would give one 5 and the other 6 points.

Engine size	Colour	
☐ +	☐	=11

Manual or automatic gearbox	Quality of radio/CD player	
☐ +	☐	=11

Country of manufacture	Engine size	
☐ +	☐	=11

Colour	Manual or automatic gearbox	
☐ +	☐	=11

Quality of radio/CD player	Colour of manufacture	
☐ +	☐	=11

Engine size	Manual or automatic gearbox	
☐ +	☐	=11

Colour	Quality of radio/CD player	
☐ +	☐	=11

Country of manufacture	Colour	
☐ +	☐	=11

Quality of radio/CD player	Engine size	
☐ +	☐	=11

Manual or automatic gearbox	Country of manufacture	
☐ +	☐	=11

Figure 5.15 *Constant sum combined with paired comparisons*

for example from 'Very important' to 'Not at all important'. Respondents are then asked to sort the cards into piles according to the rating scale laid out in front of them. Once that task is completed each pile is returned to and the objects in the pile put into rank order.

With electronic self-completion questionnaires, respondents first go through the list of objects, rating them against the itemized rating scale. They are then presented with the objects they have placed in each category in turn and asked to rank-order them.

The data obtained are thus a combination of rating and rank ordering. Complex scoring systems can then be used to provide mean scores for each object. If a five-point rating scale is used, from 'Very Important' to 'Not at all Important', the scoring structure may be as follows:

Very important – scores between 81 and 100
Quite important – scores between 61 and 80
Neither important nor unimportant – scores between 41 and 60
Not very important – scores between 21 and 40
Not at all important – scores between 1 and 20

The exact score given to each object for each respondent depends on the number of objects that the respondent has placed in the category.

This technique is relatively simple for respondents to cope with, either with face-to-face or Web-based interviewing, and provides a sensitive scoring system for a large number of objects.

Q sort

A similar approach designed for larger numbers of attributes is Q sorting. This might be used where there is a very large number of objects, in the region of, say, 100.

The objects are sorted by respondents into a number of categories, usually 11 or 12, representing the degrees on the scale, such as appeal or interest in purchase. Respondents may be instructed to place a specific number of objects on each point of the scale so that they are distributed approximately according to a normal distribution. They are asked to put a few objects at the extremes of the scale, with increasing numbers towards the middle of the scale. Objects placed in the two extreme positions can then be rank-ordered by the respondent for increased discrimination.

This technique is only suitable for face-to-face interviewing and for small numbers of respondents and is not frequently used in commercial research.

MEASURING BRAND IMAGE

Scalar approaches

Scales are frequently used to measure the brand image, or perceptions of the brands held by people in the market. Each brand is evaluated on a number of dimensions, defined as those being the key dimensions that discriminate between brands. Each brand is evaluated monadically, with the sequence of evaluating rotated between respondents. The rotation of the sequence order is important here, as the way in which respondents rate one brand can affect how they rate any following brands. How they rate the first brand on, say, 'quality' sets a benchmark for all subsequent brands. A slightly generous rating for the first brand, even though they think it might only be of average quality, requires increasingly positive ratings for any subsequent brands thought to be of better quality.

Respondents are only asked to evaluate brands that they are aware of from a preceding or earlier prompted (aided) brand awareness question.

Figure 5.16 is typical of the self-completion question to evaluate brand image using an agree–disagree scale. Note that this is technically not a Likert scale. As we are not measuring attitude, but perception, there is no necessarily positive or negative position for each dimension, only different brand positionings. Being traditional and serious is different from being modern and fun (or even traditional and fun), but the individual respondent scores cannot be summed in order to provide an overall attitude score.

The question in Figure 5.16 could equally have been posed as a bi-polar semantic differential scale. Care then has to be taken in defining the pairs of statements so that they have truly opposite meanings.

The scalar approaches to measuring brand image provide strong interval data that can be used in a variety of ways, including the calculation of mean scores and standard deviations and analytical techniques such as correlation, regression, and factor analysis.

They do though suffer from two drawbacks. First, because they are completed monadically it is difficult for respondents to reference brands against each other. As discussed earlier, respondents may rate a

Below are a number of statements that have been made about Crianlarich whisky. For each statement please indicate how much you agree or disagree that it applies to Crianlarich whisky.

	Disagree strongly	Disagree slightly	Neither agree nor disagree	Agree slightly	Agree strongly
High quality	❐	❐	❐	❐	❐
Traditional	❐	❐	❐	❐	❐
For younger people	❐	❐	❐	❐	❐
For older people	❐	❐	❐	❐	❐
A fun brand	❐	❐	❐	❐	❐
A modern brand	❐	❐	❐	❐	❐
To be taken seriously	❐	❐	❐	❐	❐

Figure 5.16 *Evaluating brand image using an agree–disagree scale*

brand for a particular attribute, only to find that for the following brands they have not left themselves sufficient space on the scale to express properly the differences that they perceive between them.

The second disadvantage is that they can take a long time for respondents to complete. A list of 20 attributes for each of six brands requires respondents to complete 120 scales if they are aware of all six brands. At an estimated 15 seconds for each attribute for the first brand, and 10 seconds for subsequent brands, this can take over 20 minutes to complete. This adds to the potential fatigue and boredom of the respondents, the length of the interview and the cost of the study.

Attribute association

An alternative approach is the brand-attribute association grid.

Respondents are shown a list of brands and asked to say which brand or brands they associate with each of a series of image attributes. The image attributes are either read out by an interviewer or appear on the questionnaire or screen for self-completion.

This is quicker because respondents only have to go through the list of attributes once. They also do not have to make such complex decisions about how well each brand performs on each attribute, only that it applies or that it does not.

I am now going to read out a number of words and phrases that have been used to describe different brands of whisky. For each one I would like you to tell me to which, if any, of the brands on this card (SHOW CARD) you think it applies. Each phrase could apply to any number of the brands, all of them or none of them.

READ OUT.

	Brand A	Brand B	Brand C	Brand D	Brand E	None of them
High quality	1	1	1	1	1	1
Traditional	2	2	2	2	2	2
For younger people	3	3	3	3	3	3
For older people	4	4	4	4	4	4
A fun brand	5	5	5	5	5	5
A modern brand	6	6	6	6	6	6
To be taken seriously	7	7	7	7	7	7

Figure 5.17 *Assessing a set of brands*

Brands of which they are not aware will usually not be nominated as possessing any of the characteristics. Some respondents may nominate brands that they have previously said that they are unaware of to have certain characteristics (particularly for attributes such as 'not well known') but these can be identified at the analysis stage. If respondents really are responding with an image of a brand of which they are hearing for the first time, that can tell the researcher a great deal about the image attributes of the name alone.

Another advantage is that respondents can assess the full set of brands together. This makes it easier for them to make comparisons between brands and determine that an attribute is or is not associated with one brand rather than another.

Figure 5.17 is taken from an interviewer-administered questionnaire from which the data have to be manually entered, but the arrangement of the layout could equally be from a self-administered questionnaire.

The coding numbers here have been arranged vertically rather than horizontally. This is for two reasons. First, if respondents should see the questionnaire, there is no suggestion of an order of priority among the brands. A horizontal arrangement would have Brand A always as code 1 and Brand F as code 6. Where coding is shown on self-completion questionnaires this can be a potential source of bias.

Secondly, it helps the researcher to think in terms of brand image profiles for each brand, and the data-processing spec-writer to write tables to produce that. It is more likely to be of value to the analyst to be able to see the image attributes associated with each brand rather than the brands associated with each image attribute. It also makes it easier to be able to analyse by respondents who have heard of the brand, brand users and non-users, those aware of the advertising, etc.

The disadvantage of attributing image statements in this way is the loss of the degree of discrimination that would have been obtained had scales been used. It may be found, for example, that most respondents think that all brands possess certain attributes, whereas a scalar approach would have shown variation in the strength with which each brand is seen to possess them.

The level of discrimination can be increased through a bipolar version of the question. For each attribute, opposite positions are asked. 'High quality' would be complemented with 'Poor quality', 'For younger people' with 'Not for younger people'. ('For older people' is not necessarily the opposite of 'For younger people', as the brand could be seen to be for both.) This doubles the number of attribute statements that need to be included, although it probably does not double the time taken to administer them. It effectively creates a three-point scale, with each brand nominated either for the point at each end of the scale, or not mentioned at all, which can be taken as the mid-point of the scale. The extent to which the brand is associated at all with the dimension, that is the proportion of all respondents who mention it in relation to either of the two attribute statements, is sometimes referred to as the 'strength of the brand image'. The proportion of respondents who associate the brand with the positive of the two statements, divided by the number who associate it with either, is then known as the 'quality of the brand image'.

An alternative way to increase discrimination is to ask which brand or brands respondents would choose if they were looking for one that possessed the successive image attributes. Respondents then tend to nominate only brands that are strongly associated in their minds with the attribute. This reduces the number of brands associated with each attribute, and demonstrates 'ownership' of attributes by brands more clearly.

A disadvantage of the technique is that the levels of association are dependent on the brand set shown. This acts as the reference set against which each brand is judged. The choice of which and how many brands are included is thus an important decision that can affect apparent brand positionings. Should the number of brands or choice set change over time, on repeat studies or tracking studies, there is a danger that comparability will be lost. A study may, for example, ask respondents to associate brands from a set of five airlines. If the number of airlines were to be increased to six in a later study, then we should expect to see the levels of association for all brands decrease. This is because the average number of brands associated with each attribute tends to remain reasonably constant, so that with more brands the average number per brand decreases.

Had one of the attributes been 'innovative' and the new brand introduced been Virgin Atlantic, a brand known for its innovation, then a substantial change in association for the remaining brands should be expected on this attribute. The frame of reference on this attribute for many respondents would have changed, and brands that were previously thought to be innovative, in the context of the set asked about, would now appear to be less so. A similar change on this attribute would have been expected had Virgin Atlantic been substituted for another brand in the set, so that the total number remained the same. The levels of association recorded are not absolute, but are relative both to the number of brands asked about and to the actual brands in the set.

When deciding upon the brands to use, it can be important to relate them to the attributes to be asked about. Thus, an attribute should not be included without very good reason if the brand set does not include the brand that has the strongest associations with the attribute. The false conclusion that a brand performs strongly on that attribute could easily be arrived at, because it only does so in the context of worse-performing brands.

The data generated by this approach allow correspondence mapping, as well as correlation analysis and, with some transformation, regression analysis.

Indirect techniques

The difficulty that people have in recognizing let alone accurately articulating their emotions and feelings about brands has led to a number of techniques that approach the issue indirectly. For example, instead of respondents being asked to associate image dimensions with brands, there are now techniques established that associate the brand with picture stimuli, which in turn are established as having certain emotional associations. The respondents' feelings towards the brand can then be evaluated, even if the respondents do not consciously recognize those feelings themselves.

Most of the techniques of this type, however, are proprietary and have a specified set of questions. They are therefore outside the scope of this book.

6 Writing the questionnaire

INTRODUCTION

In the previous chapters, we have examined the different types of question and technique that are available to the questionnaire writer. These represent the tools in the armoury that can be used to compile a questionnaire. A number of other issues, though, need to be considered in the process of writing the questionnaire. These issues include:

* the language and style of language in which it is written;
* ensuring that there is no ambiguity in the questions or the responses;
* whether pre-codes will be used or responses recorded verbatim;
* if pre-codes are to be used, what they should be;
* the use of prompt material and the choice between verbal and pictorial prompts;
* bias that can be caused by the order of the questions;
* bias that can be caused by the order of prompted responses.

This chapter considers these issues.

USE OF LANGUAGE

When writing the questionnaire it is the questionnaire writer's job to ensure that the respondents will understand the questions and that the respondents will not feel intimidated, challenged or threatened by the questions.

Writing questionnaires is about helping respondents to give the best information that they can. Questions should be clear and unambiguous, and the respondent should be put at ease by the tone of the questions and not made to feel challenged by the words and phrases used. Respondents who feel challenged because they don't understand the questions will quickly become alienated from the interview process and make little effort to respond accurately. They may become fatigued earlier than they would have done and fail to complete the interview.

Therefore, we must ensure that the questions are phrased in everyday language to which the respondents can relate. The interview can be seen as a conversation by proxy between the researcher and the respondent. The questionnaire should be suitably conversational in tone, while not seeking to be too familiar or condescending. In transactional relationship terms the questionnaire should be 'adult to adult', but clearly understood.

Researchers are frequently given briefs by clients that are expressed in technical terms that relate to the client's business. They may talk of 'channels of distribution' or 'above-the-line advertising'. It is the job of the questionnaire writer to turn this into phrases that will be part of the everyday speech of respondents, or at least readily understood by them.

Seen in print

In a study about aircraft noise, respondents were asked to indicate how important they thought it was that:

'Cash compensation should be offered to those households that suffer a significant increase in noise to a level greater than 57 decibels but less than 63 decibels, and who therefore do not qualify for insulation.'

This question falls down on two counts. Firstly, it is difficult to understand what the question means because it is phrased in technical terms. Secondly, even if someone understands it, few people would be competent to answer it accurately. How many respondents understand exactly how loud 57 or 63 decibels is?

Getting rid of technical terms is not always easy to achieve. They exist because they are needed. Some sympathy must be felt for the writer of the question in the box above. How do you convey to respondents precise noise levels? But equally, how usable is any response to this question? Anyone using the data generated must be concerned about how well the question was understood.

Because technical terms are often the everyday language of the commissioners of the study, they do not always appreciate that others outside of their industry or profession might not understand them, or might understand something different by them.

Sometimes technical terms are used in order to describe something, or to differentiate between objects or services, with far greater subtlety than the non-specialist can appreciate. To most motorists a petrol pump is a petrol pump, and they would not distinguish between a 'high line fast flow' and a 'grouped hose blender'. Researchers must ask themselves if it is necessary for the respondent to be able to distinguish between them in the interview. If it is, then the differences must be clearly explained, if possible without reference to the technical terminology.

Some technical terms are words that have a different everyday use. Market researchers will use the terms 'random' and 'significance' with specific meanings that are different to they way that they are used by most people. The danger here is that researchers might think that respondents understand the terms in the same way that they do. The respondents, though, understand these terms differently, and so answer a different question to the one that the researcher thinks is being asked.

Seen in print

Q1. What do you think of Big Oil?
PROBE FULLY.

This was the opening question in the survey. The term 'Big Oil' was well understood by the questionnaire writer, who worked in the oil industry, but meant nothing to respondents.

The interview as conversation

Previously in this chapter, the interview was described as a conversation by proxy between the researcher and the respondent. However, it is not the sort of conversation that two people who know each other would have.

Schober (1999) points out two key differences between having a conversation with your aunt and carrying out an interview with a structured questionnaire, known as 'audience design' and 'grounding'.

Audience design

When one person who knows another asks the second person a question or makes a statement, it is framed to be heard specifically by that other person, and draws on the knowledge that each has of the other. This is known as 'audience design'. The person to whom it is said is the addressee. Addressees are likely to give different interpretations and responses to the question 'How many hours a week do you work?' depending on whether it is asked by their aunt, their boss or someone from the tax office. Addressees will use their knowledge of the relationship to determine what type of response the questioner expects to hear. Other people may hear the question – side participants, bystanders and eavesdroppers – and some of these people may have been intended to hear by the questioner, who may have framed the question partly with side participants and bystanders in mind. But their interpretation of it may well be different from that of the addressee because they have to interpret it by making assumptions regarding the common ground that is shared by the two principal participants. Schober writes that 'side participants, bystanders and eavesdroppers have all been shown to understand the references in utterances less accurately than addressees'.

In a survey questionnaire, the questions are not framed for specific respondents, but to have general applicability to as many people as possible. Interviewers are specifically instructed neither to deviate from the question script nor to tailor the question to the individual. In quantitative research, as hard as questionnaire writers may try, they cannot write a questionnaire to be one side of a conversation.

Grounding

Grounding occurs in a conversation when the participants establish that each has understood what one of them has said, and that it has entered their common ground. This can come from an acknowledgement of the question or statement ('uh-huh', 'okay') or a request for elaboration as to what is meant from the addressee, or clarification volunteered by the questioner if it is clear that the addressee has not understood.

Some level of grounding is available in an interview, but interviewers are deliberately restricted in the procedures that they can use in order to avoid introducing bias. Often when asked for clarification, all the interviewer can do is to repeat the question, or describe the type of response that is needed, or ask for a best estimate. Elaboration of individual words in the question is to be avoided as, apart from potentially introducing bias, the interviewers themselves may not understand precisely what is meant and present a misinterpretation of the question to respondents.

These difficulties in audience design and grounding can lead to a number of response effects from prompt material, question ordering and interpretation of questions.

Minority languages

There are many different types of question that can be asked and in many different ways. What is common to all questions, though, is that they must be worded in a way that is understood by the respondents and to which respondents can relate. This means ensuring that there are minority-language versions of the questionnaire if the sample is likely to include people who speak a language other than the majority language, or whose command of that language is unlikely to be sufficiently good to be able to complete an interview in it. By denying sections of the survey population the opportunity to participate in the study, the questionnaire writer is effectively disenfranchising them from influencing the findings.

For many studies commissioned by the public sector in many countries, it is important that the interview is capable of being conducted in any language that is spoken by a significant number of people in the survey population to avoid the danger of disenfranchisement. In the UK many government studies require questionnaire versions in Welsh, Urdu, Hindi and other languages, and in the USA a Spanish-language version will often be required.

The relevance of minority-language speakers to the study will naturally vary by the subject of the study and the degree of accuracy required in the data. For a study of housing conditions it is likely to be important that recently arrived immigrant communities are represented in the sample in their correct proportions. If the questionnaire is not available in a language that they understand, they will be effectively excluded and hence under-represented.

For many commercial studies, the issue of minority languages can be mostly ignored in many countries, although a Spanish version of the questionnaire is frequently necessary in the USA. This is because for most commercial studies the difference that a minority of non-majority-language-speaking consumers is likely to make to the findings is small, particularly in comparison to the variation caused by sampling error, non-response rates and even interviewer error.

AVOIDING AMBIGUITY IN THE QUESTION

Ambiguity is to be avoided at all costs. If a question is ambiguous, then the respondent may be presented with the dilemma of hearing or seeing two different questions and will not know which to answer. With an interviewer-administered questionnaire the respondent may seek help from the interviewer. The interviewer may be able to assist with the knowledge of the context of the question in relation to other questions, but this may not always be the case. With self-administered questionnaires, respondents have to make their own decision as to what the question means. Either way, the researcher does not know which way the respondent has understood the question, except in the occasional instances where either the interviewer or respondent has recorded it. This rarely happens, though, except in pilot studies.

Ambiguity in the question can make it impossible for a respondent to know how to answer. Consider the following question:

'Do your parents work full time?'
   Yes
   No

There is no difficulty for the respondent if both parents work full time or if neither parent does (although a definition of what constitutes 'full-time working' would be helpful). If, however, one works full time and the other does not, what is the respondent to answer? The question would be better asked:

'Do either or both of your parents work full time, that is more than 30 hours a week?'
   Both
   One
   Neither

There still remain the issue of what constitutes 'work', and whether it should include unpaid work, such as charity work, or only paid work.

While some respondents may see the ambiguity and make a decision which way to answer, others may not see it and understand it only in the sense in which it was not intended. Then the answer given will not be the one that would have been given to the intended question and, again, the researcher is unaware of this.

If the ambiguity in the question is not spotted until the data have been collected, then the researcher has no way of knowing which respondents answered the question as intended and which answered the alternative meaning. This can render the data from that question incapable of interpretation and therefore useless.

Ambiguity is obviously to be avoided in questions, but is not always easy to spot. This is because it is not always possible to anticipate every respondent's circumstances, and a question that may not be ambiguous to most respondents may, because of their circumstances, contain an ambiguity for a few. For example, 'How many bedrooms are there in this property?' is a simple question apparently incapable of more than one possible answer for most people. But what is meant by a bedroom? If someone has a study that doubles as an occasional bedroom, should that be included?

In most instances this level of ambiguity will not be a major issue. Where the number of bedrooms is collected as classification data to provide a cross-analysis of data by approximate size of house, then this degree of ambiguity may be acceptable to the researchers.

Where this information is central to the data collected, then the ambiguity must be addressed. In the example of the number of bedrooms, such ambiguity would be unacceptable in, say, a study of housing conditions. Then the question would require expanding, possibly to ask the number of rooms currently used as bedrooms, the number occasionally used as bedrooms and the number that could be used as bedrooms, or as required by the study.

DETERMINING THE PRE-CODES

The pre-codes that are used on the questionnaire determine what data are collected. If the pre-codes have insufficient accuracy or are incomplete, then data will be lost that may be important to answering the objectives. In many instances the responses will be obvious – yes–no,

---

Seen in print

From a hotel customer satisfaction questionnaire:

Level of satisfaction:	Low		Average		High
Friendly and efficient service at reception	❏	❏	❏	❏	❏

Some of the friendliest receptionists are often the least efficient, and vice versa. How does the guest answer this question if that is the case? It is possible that the guest who wants to indicate that the service was friendly but not efficient, or that it was efficient but not friendly, will give up at this point and not complete the rest of the questionnaire.

Figure 6.1   *An ambiguous question*

male–female – but in others care must be taken to ensure that they are:

* mutually exclusive;
* as exhaustive as possible;
* as precise as necessary;
* meaningful.

Unless they are mutually exclusive, it will be possible to code the same response against more than one response code. This is confusing for the interviewer (or respondent with a self-completion questionnaire) and makes the output ambiguous and impossible to interpret (see Figure 6.1).

The pre-codes need to be as exhaustive as they can in order to minimize the number of 'other answers' written in. If there are a lot of 'other answers' written in, the question would better have been recorded as an open-ended one.

Recording values

When recording answers that are values, the level of detail needs to be as precise as is necessary to meet the research objectives without demanding more detail than respondents can accurately give. Sometimes it is possible to record precise values (eg the number of times the respondent has visited a pub or bar in the past week), but frequently we do not want to record that level of detail, and nor can

Q. Into which of these ranges did the cost of your holiday fall, per person?
SHOW CARD.

UP TO £200	1
£201 TO £400	2
£401 TO £600	3
£601 TO £800	4
£801 TO £1,000	5
£1,001 OR MORE	6

Figure 6.2 *Determining the level of detail*

respondents be expected to provide it. Then the answers will be recorded in value bands.

In Figure 6.2, the questionnaire writer has determined that bands of £200 are sufficiently accurate to meet the demands of the study. Bands of £50 would have given the researcher greater accuracy in calculating the average cost of a holiday and in making comparisons between sub-groups, but may have been difficult for respondents to recall accurately. This could have led to an increase in the proportion of 'Don't know' responses. In this example the response categories are exclusive. If someone had paid exactly £400, it is clear where the answer should be coded. Had either the bottom or top category been left out, then the response list would not have been exhaustive, and someone who paid less than £200 or more than £1,000 would not have been able to answer.

The pre-code response categories must also be meaningful to both respondent and researcher if the first is to be able to answer and the second to interpret. Precise wording is important in achieving clarity. Words such as 'often', 'frequently' and 'occasionally' are best avoided, as their interpretation varies between situations and between people.

Constructing ranges

Wherever possible, values should be recorded as absolute numbers. However, if values are to be recorded in ranges, the ranges should usually be constructed such that the most popular values occur in the middle of the ranges. For example, if the question is 'How much did

---

Seen in print

Q. And, on average, how much do you pay for these text alerts, per text?
INTERVIEWER, IF DON'T KNOW, PROBE FOR AN ESTIMATE BEFORE CODING DK.

FREE OF CHARGE	1
1–5 PENCE	2
5–10 PENCE	3
11–15 PENCE	4
16–20 PENCE	5
21–25 PENCE	6
26–30 PENCE	7
31–35 PENCE	8
36–40 PENCE	9
41–45 PENCE	10
46–50 PENCE	11
50–75 PENCE	12
75 PENCE – £1	13
MORE THAN £1	14
DON'T KNOW	15

In this case, the duplications at 5, 50 and 75 pence were all spotted by the agency's checking procedures before the questionnaire went live. It is because this type of error is so easy to make that most agencies have strict checking procedures.

Figure 6.3 *Duplications in the values*

you pay for the paperback novel that you are currently reading?', we know that most answers, if accurately given, will be £x.99. However, it would not be unusual to see the following ranges given for this question:

Under £4.99
£5 to £5.99
£6 to £6.99

Seen in print

Qa. How often do you make local telephone calls on your home line?
Qb. How often do you make national telephone calls on your home line?
Qc. How often do you make international calls on your home line?
Qd. How often do you make calls to mobile phones on your home line?

	(a) Local calls	(b) National calls	(c) International calls	(d) Calls to mobiles
VERY OFTEN	1	1	1	1
OFTEN	2	2	2	2
OCCASIONALLY	3	3	3	3
SELDOM	4	4	4	4
NEVER	5	5	5	5

Respondents may or may not have had difficulty in interpreting what each code was intended to mean, but the researcher would have had serious problems analysing the resulting data. 'Frequently' used in relation to local calls is likely to mean several calls a day to most respondents. The same word applied to international calls may well be just one or two a week. So what framework have respondents used in giving their answers? Has the frequency been judged against a common standard, with one type of call (possibly the local call, as that is asked first) being used to define what is frequent for all four types of calls, or have the response codes been interpreted independently for each type of call, so that the meaning of 'frequent' varies between types of call? The researcher cannot know. Even if the researcher did know, he or she could not know how what is considered 'frequent' varies between respondents. These answers would have been better recorded as frequency values.

Figure 6.4 *Imprecise wording*

£7 to £7.99
£8 to £8.99
£9 or more

This can cause loss of accuracy. A book costing £6.99 will be reported by some respondents as costing that amount precisely. Other respondents will round it up to £7, and the response will be recorded in the category above the one it should be in. Other respondents may say 'about £7', leaving the interviewer unsure as to where it should be coded. As importantly, in the analysis of these data we may want to produce an average price paid. Having collected the data in these ranges, we would normally allocate the value of the mid-point of each range to calculate the average. However, if nearly all of the actual values are at the top end of each range, the calculated average price paid will be around 50p below what it should be.

USING PROMPTS

Show cards are frequently used to provide the respondents with prompted answers in face-to-face interviews. In self-completion interviews the prompts are provided with the question, either on a paper questionnaire or on-screen with a Web-based questionnaire. With telephone interviews the prompts are frequently read out or, if they are to be repeated, as with a scale, respondents are sometimes asked to write them down.

Prompts can be scale points, attitudinal phrases, image dimensions, brands, income ranges or anything that the questionnaire writer wants to use to guide the respondents or to obtain reaction to. They can be purely verbal or they can utilize pictures, illustrations or logos. However, it is important to be clear about the different jobs that verbal and pictorial stimuli do.

Picture prompts

Pictures can be used in a number of different ways as prompts. If they are to be used, then questionnaire writers must be careful to ensure that they know exactly what role the pictures are playing.

Brand awareness

One use of picture prompts is to show brand logos or icons instead of a list of brand names, in order to measure prompted brand awareness. With CAPI and Web-based interviews this is easy to do, and is often included in order to make the interview more interesting for the respondent. However, questionnaire writers should be aware that they might be changing the question.

Prompted awareness is a question of recognition. If a list of names is used, then the respondents are being asked which of the names they recognize. If brand logos are shown, then the question becomes which of the logos they recognize. The researcher infers awareness of the brand through recognition of the logo. This is likely to be higher than simple name recognition, as the logo gives more clues. The improvement in apparent brand awareness is likely to be stronger for the smaller brands in a market. Prompted awareness of Coca-Cola does not require the use of a visual prompt in order to be very high amongst carbonated drink users. There is little opportunity for visual prompts to make an improvement. But for smaller brands, the opportunities for improvement offered by visual prompts are much greater. The total average number of logos recognized per respondent is usually likely to be greater than the average number of brand names from a simple list. Neither approach is necessarily incorrect, but each is likely to give a different level of response.

Likelihood to purchase

When asking likelihood to purchase, much more information is given to respondents if a pictorial stimulus is used. Rather than show a list of brands and prices, a mocked-up shelf can be shown as in Figure 6.5. The cues and information that are given by the pack shots mean that respondents do not have to rely on memory and recall of the brands when making their decision. Price information can easily be excluded, included or changed as required.

Brand image

Showing logos can also alter the responses to questions about brand image. It is normal to establish prompted brand awareness before asking about images of certain brands. If prompted brand awareness is established using a list of names, then the mental picture taken into the image question is the image of the brand as it exists in isolation within the respondents' minds. The image is purely what the brand name stands for and the images that are associated with it.

After prompting with a logo or pack shot, however, respondents are given clues and reminders of what the brand is trying to stand for. The logo or pack will have been designed to reflect the desired brand positioning and may well communicate something of those values to

Figure 6.5 *A mocked-up shelf*

the respondents in the interview, or at least act as a reminder of them. The image question is therefore also prompted with at least a partial reminder of the brands' desired postionings, which is likely to yield slightly different responses.

Again it is not a question of one approach being incorrect. Using a brand list may be described as giving a 'purer' measure of image. This is an image, it can be argued, that the potential purchasers have in their minds before leaving home to go shopping, and it will act upon their intent to purchase the brand. But it can be equally argued that most brands are rarely seen without their logos, and that it is the image in the purchasers' minds at the point of purchase, when there are likely to be many visual cues, that is important.

The questionnaire writer should consider which is the more appropriate approach for the market in question, and decide which approach to use accordingly.

Advertising recognition

Showing advertising to establish recognition is a particular case of showing picture prompts. Except for radio advertising, it is difficult to establish advertising recognition without the use of picture prompts. These often consist of a series of stills taken from the advertisement in question, known as a storyboard. This may or may not include the script of the characters or voice-over. It also may or may not have all references to the brand removed, depending on whether being able to name the correct brand is to be asked. With CAPI and Web-based interviewing, however, there is a choice between showing a storyboard and showing the actual ad as film. The two methods will generally lead to different responses, with higher awareness recorded among respondents shown the film.

For press and poster ads, copies of the actual ad can be shown. It may be necessary to use a reduced format from the actual size (particularly for posters), in which case there should be an explanation that it has been reduced.

ORDER BIAS AND PROMPTS

The order in which prompts are presented to respondents, whether on the questionnaire or screen, shown on a card or read out, can have a significant effect on the responses recorded. Such bias can occur with the presentation of:

- scalar responses;
- monadically rated batteries of attitude or image dimensions;
- lists from which responses are chosen.

The questionnaire writer must consider how to minimize the order bias for each of these.

Scalar responses

A considerable amount has been written about the effect that the order of presentation of prompted alternative answers has on responses. Artingstall (1978) showed that when respondents are given a scale from which to choose a response in face-to-face interviewing they are significantly more likely to choose the first response offered than the last. Of 72 end items that were offered in his test, 62 were given greater endorsement when offered first. This is known as 'the primacy effect'.

Thus if the positive end of a scale is always presented first a more favourable result will be found than if the negative end of the scale is always first. The finding held for any length of scale, and was independent of the demographic profile of the respondents. The difference was shown to be an increase of about 8 per cent to the positive responses.

What this and other work show is that the order of presentation has an effect. It does not say which order gives the best representation of the truth. However, it underlines the need to be consistent in the order in which scales are shown if comparisons are to be made between studies.

One approach to dealing with the bias is to rotate the order of presentation between two halves of the sample. This does not remove the bias but at least has the effect of averaging it.

In new product development research, it is not uncommon always to have the negative response presented first on scales rating the concept or the product. This then gives the least favourable response pattern, thereby providing a tougher test for the new product and ensuring that any positive reaction to the idea of the product is not overstated.

When visual prompts are used, the primacy effect is noticed, as demonstrated by Artingstall, as respondents notice and process the possible responses in the order that they are presented. Where prompts are read out, a recency effect is more marked, as respondents remember better the last option or last few options that they have been given. This effect has been demonstrated by Schwarz, Hippler and Noelle-Neumann (1991). With telephone interviewing, therefore, a recency effect should be expected, unless respondents are asked to write down the scale for reference before answering the question.

Batteries of statements

Fatigue effect

Where there is a large battery of either image or attitude statements, each of which is to be answered according to a scale, there is a real danger of respondent fatigue. This can occur both with self-completion batteries and where the interviewer reads them out. As discussed in Chapter 5, the precise point at which respondent fatigue is likely to set in will vary with the level of interest that each respondent has in the subject. However, it should be anticipated that, where there are more than about 30 statements, later statements are likely to suffer from inattention and pattern responding. To alleviate this type of bias, the presentation of the statement should be rotated between respondents. With electronic questionnaires, statements can often be presented in random order, or in rotation in a number of different sequences.

With paper questionnaires, rotating the order requires producing a number of different versions for self-completion, or careful instruction to interviewers if they are to read them out.

In the latter case it is common for the starting point on the battery for each respondent to be ticked or checked at the time of printing the questionnaires or before they are sent out to the interviewers. Ideally, the start point can be rotated between questionnaires so that the reading out starts at each statement an equal number of times. However, it may not always be possible to print this on automatically. It requires as many different versions of the page to be printed as there are statements in the battery. With possibly up to 30 statements the potential for error is considerable. Printing the questionnaire with no marked start points and marking each questionnaire by hand can be time-consuming where there are thousands of questionnaires. An alternative, which is usually acceptable, is to have a limited number of start points, and these can be printed using different versions of the page. Thus if there are 30 statements, six different start points can be used, spread throughout the battery. The statements are still reasonably well rotated and, with only six versions of the page to be printed, the scope for error is much reduced.

Where the battery of statements is to be read out by the interviewer using a paper questionnaire, it is important that every interviewer understands the process of rotating start points. In particular, interviewers must understand that every statement must be read out. It has been known for interviewers to read out only the statements from the designated start point to the end of the battery, and not to return to the beginning of the battery for the remaining statements. This is more likely to occur where the battery is on more than one page and the start point is not on the first page.

Statement clarification

The order in which statements are presented to respondents can sometimes be used to clarify their meanings. If there is a degree of ambiguity in a statement that would require a complex explanation, a preceding statement that deals with the alternative meaning can clarify what the questionnaire writer is seeking.

For example:

How would you rate the station for:
The facilities and services at the station

On its own, it could be unclear to respondents whether car parking should be considered as one of the facilities or services at the station. If, however, this statement is preceded by one about car parking:

Facilities for car parking
The facilities and services at the station

or, even better:

Facilities for car parking
Other facilities and services at the station

then respondents can safely assume that the facilities and services are not meant to include car parking as that has already been asked about.

Where random presentation of statements is used, care must be taken to ensure that such explanatory pairs of statements always appear together and in the same order.

Response lists

Showing a list of alternative responses is a common form of prompting in order to make respondents choose from a fixed set of options. For example:

Thinking about the advertisement that you have just seen, which of the phrases on this card would you say describes it? You can mention as many or as few phrases as you wish.

A   It was difficult to understand
B   It made me more interested in visiting the store
C   I found it irritating
D   It's not right for this type of product
E   I quickly got bored with it
F   I did not like the people in it
G   It said something relevant to me
H   I will remember it

I	It improved my opinion of the store
J	It told me something new about the store
K	It was aimed at me
L	I enjoyed watching it
M	None of these

The respondent is expected to read through all of the options and select those that apply. In this question, respondents can choose as many statements as they feel are appropriate. In other questions, they may be asked to choose one option or any other specified number.

Primacy and recency effects

Similar primacy effects as are seen with scales should be expected. The effects have been demonstrated by Schwarz, Hippler and Noelle-Neumann (1991), even where there are a small number of possible responses, down to three or even two if they are sufficiently complex to dissuade respondents from making an effort to process the possible answers in full. Duffy (2003) confirms the existence of primacy effects and adds that a significant minority read the list from the bottom. This would suggest that a recency effect can also be expected.

Indeed, both primacy and recency effects have been demonstrated by Ring (1975). He showed that with a list of 18 items there is a bias in favour of choosing responses in the first six and the last four positions. The implication is that those in the middle of the list either are not read at all by some respondents or are not processed as possible responses to the same extent.

Where a list is of such size, then reversing the order and presenting one order to half of the sample and the reverse order to the other half does not adequately address the problem. Ring's experiments showed that with a list of 18 items the first 14 should be reversed and the last four reversed. The items that were fourteenth and fifteenth in the initial list then become first and last in the alternative list. This asymmetrical split better balances the bias across the items than simply reversing them. For further reduction in order bias Ring suggests additional splits after the seventh and sixteenth items, but for most research purposes these are not necessary.

In practice, many, if not most, researchers satisfy themselves with two or at most four rotations. With electronic questionnaires, statements can often be presented in random order, or in rotation in a larger number of different sequences. This does not eliminate bias but spreads it across the statements more evenly.

Table 6.1 *Asymmetrical rotation of positions on the list*

| | Two-way split | | Four-way split | | | |
| | Position in: | | Position in: | | | |
Item	List 1	List 2	List 1	List 2	List 3	List 4
A	1	14	1	14	7	8
B	2	13	2	13	6	9
C	3	12	3	12	5	10
D	4	11	4	11	4	11
E	5	10	5	10	3	12
F	6	9	6	9	2	13
G	7	8	7	8	1	14
H	8	7	8	7	14	1
I	9	6	9	6	13	2
J	10	5	10	5	12	3
K	11	4	11	4	11	4
L	12	3	12	3	10	5
M	13	2	13	2	9	6
N	14	1	14	1	8	7
O	15	18	15	18	16	17
P	16	17	16	17	15	18
Q	17	16	17	16	18	15
R	18	15	18	15	17	16

After Ring (1975)

Satisficing

Some people when buying items such as a washing machine, stereo system or car will spend a great real of time researching which of the available models best meets their needs and requirements. Other people will buy one that satisfactorily meets their needs and requirements, and are not prepared to invest the time in researching all of the available models to determine whether there is one that is marginally better. The latter approach is known as 'satisficing', and occurs when choosing attitude statements from a list.

The satisficers will read the list until they find an adequate answer that they are happy reasonably reflects their view, rather than reading all of the statements to find the optimal answer that best reflects their view. This is another source of order bias, which will tend to reinforce the primacy effect and is a further reason for ensuring that lists are rotated.

QUESTION ORDER

There are certain rules regarding the ordering of questions that must always be borne in mind. These have been covered in Chapter 3 and include:

* There must be no prompting of any information before spontaneous questions on the same subject.
* The interview should normally start with the more general questions relating to the topic and work through to the more specific or detailed subject matter.
* Behavioural questions should be asked before attitudinal questions on the same topic.

These issues should have been considered when the questionnaire was planned, but still need to be thought about as the detailed questionnaire is written.

Funnelling

Funnelling sequences are used to take respondents from general questions on a topic through to questions that are more specific without allowing the earlier questions to condition or bias the responses to the later ones.

Typically in the funnelling sequence, whether respondents are asked a question depends on their response to the previous one. This means that people for whom questions are irrelevant can be routed round them. Because people are routed out without knowing what the cri-teria are for continuing the question sequence, we can be more confident that the response that we obtain to the final question is not biased. In the example in Figure 6.6, we would have little confidence that there

133

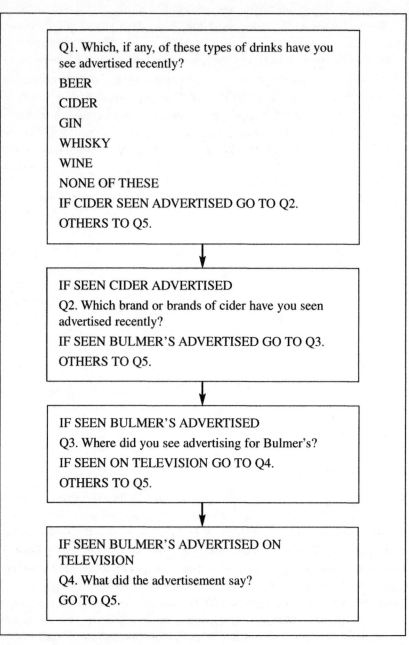

Figure 6.6 *Funnelling sequence*

was no bias had we asked the one question 'If you have seen any advertising for Bulmer's cider on television recently, what did it say?' This question would lead to overclaiming of having seen advertising, because there is an assumption that Bulmer's cider has been advertised on television recently. Some respondents would then claim to have seen it, even though they had not.

Funnelling sequences can be complicated for respondents to follow on paper self-completion questionnaires because of the routeing, and are best avoided. However, they can be used with any interviewer-administered questionnaire and work very well with electronic or Web-based self-completion questionnaires where the routeing is hidden.

Question order bias

Priming effects

Where there is a key question to be asked, such as approval of a proposal, response to a new concept or rating of an issue, the act of asking questions about the respondent's feelings regarding the proposal, concept or issue prior to the key questions can have an effect on the response to it.

This can be desirable, as the researcher will want respondents to give an answer that takes into account their considered view. However, the researcher can suggest to respondents what they should answer. McFarland (1981) reported that asking a series of specific questions about the energy crisis led to a higher rating of the severity of the crisis than when the questions were not asked.

Questionnaire writers need to be aware of the influence that prior questions can have, and write the questions and interpret the responses accordingly.

Consistency effect

A particular type of priming effect is the consistency effect. This can occur because respondents are led along a particular route of responses to a conclusion to which they can only answer one way if they are to appear consistent.

Consider the sequence in Figure 6.7.

Now compare Figure 6.7 with the sequence in Figure 6.8.

It should be expected that the responses to Q2 will show significant variation between Figures 6.7 and 6.8. By using statements that reflect

Q1. Please indicate whether you agree or disagree with each of the following statements, and how strongly, by ticking one box for each statement.

	Agree strongly	Agree	Neither agree nor disagree	Disagree	Disagree strongly
Delays at airports in this country are becoming unacceptable.	❑	❑	❑	❑	❑
There is insufficient capacity at this country's airports.	❑	❑	❑	❑	❑
Airports in this country are dangerously overcrowded.	❑	❑	❑	❑	❑
There is a shortage of jobs in this region.	❑	❑	❑	❑	❑

Q2. Do you support the government's proposal to build a new airport in this region?

YES ❑

NO ❑

DON'T KNOW ❑

Figure 6.7 *The consistency effect (first sequence)*

one side of an argument, in this case for and against the building of a new airport, respondents are led to Q2 along different paths. Most people like to appear to be consistent. If they agree with the statements in Q1, it is then very difficult not to answer 'yes' at Q2 in the first example or 'no' in the second example.

To be even-handed, the preliminary question should contain statements that relate to both or all sides of an argument. The researcher may want to put questions to respondents about the issues before asking the key question, in order to help them to give a considered answer to that question. However, the preliminary questions must fairly represent all the issues if they are not to bias the response to the key question.

Q1. Please indicate whether you agree or disagree with each of the following statements, and how strongly, by ticking one box for each statement.

	Agree strongly	Agree	Neither agree nor disagree	Disagree	Disagree strongly
The countryside round here is disappearing too quickly for my liking.	❐	❐	❐	❐	❐
There is too much building on green-field sites.	❐	❐	❐	❐	❐
I would not want to see this country's plant and animal life killed off.	❐	❐	❐	❐	❐
Noise pollution is a major nuisance round here.	❐	❐	❐	❐	❐

Q2. Do you support the government's proposal to build a new airport in this region?

YES ❐

NO ❐

DON'T KNOW ❐

Figure 6.8 *The consistency effect (second sequence)*

STANDARDIZING QUESTIONS

Where a question has been asked in a previous study it is usually to the advantage of the researcher to ensure that, unless there is a good reason otherwise, the same question should be used and the same pre-codes. Doing this allows the researcher to build up a body of knowledge about how this question is answered, and so spot any response pattern that deviates from this.

It also means that results from different studies can be compared more easily.

Many major manufacturers and some research companies have standard ways of asking particular questions that allow them to build up this body of knowledge.

The benefits of standardizing certain questions, and not just within individual organizations, have long been recognized. In 1973 the UK Market Research Society produced a booklet entitled 'Standardised questions' in order to encourage harmonization of questions throughout the industry.

TRACKING STUDIES

Consistency of question wording is important in ongoing or tracking studies, in order to ensure that changes in data over time are not due to wording changes.

To ensure data consistency, it is also important to maintain the order in which the questions are asked, so that any order bias that exists is itself consistent. Keeping the question order means that adding new questions can cause problems, and the positioning of them must be considered very carefully. If possible, new questions should be added to the end of the questionnaire so as not to affect responses to any of the earlier questions. For the sake of the interview flow, though, this is not always possible.

For example, in an ongoing customer satisfaction survey, respondents were asked to give a rating of their overall satisfaction with the service received on their most recent visit to the client company. This has then been followed with questions rating various staff and service attributes, including one on efficiency. After a while, a competitor introduces a guarantee that all transactions will be completed within 10 minutes or customers get their money back. To measure the impact of this, the client now asks that, on the next wave of the survey, a new question is inserted between the overall satisfaction question and the service attribute ratings, on how quickly the customers perceive their transaction to have been handled and how satisfied they were with that. The introduction of these questions at this point could influence the way in which respondents rate the individual service attributes, in particular the one relating to efficiency, as the speed of transaction has been raised higher in their consciousness than in previous waves of the study. Researchers must alert the client to the potential impact of such a change in the questionnaire on the comparability of the data with previous waves, and endeavour to find an alternative solution, such as a less sensitive position.

If no alternative solution can be found and the question changes are to be included for the foreseeable future, then it may be worth considering having a split run for one wave. For this, the sample is split randomly into two. One half is asked the existing questionnaire, the other the new questionnaire with the changes incorporated. Differences in results on the affected questions between the two halves of the sample can then be attributed to the changed questionnaire. An assessment of the impact of the changes can thus be made.

OMNIBUS STUDIES

An omnibus survey is a particular type of study on which clients buy space for their own questions. The questionnaire can therefore cover a number of different subject areas for a number of different clients. The cost of sampling and contacting these respondents is effectively shared between all of the clients, making this a cost-effective way of asking a limited number of questions of a large sample or one that is expensive to sample.

Several different topics are asked about, and the question writer will not know what has been previously covered. The first question should therefore include a bridging phrase or sentence to indicate that a change of subject is about to occur.

Omnibus surveys are normally charged by the number of questions; whether they are pre-coded or open-ended; whether they use prompts or not; and the proportion of the sample of which they are asked. To keep down the cost, question writers must decide what are the most essential questions they need to cover, in order to limit the number.

The order of the questions may also be affected by the desire to keep down the cost. For example, we may be interested in asking some questions of people who have visited or considered visiting a particular resort. Normally we might ask:

Q1. SHOW CARD.
Which of the resorts on this card have you ever visited?

Q2. SHOW CARD.
And which others have you ever considered visiting?

Both questions would be asked of all respondents.

However, if the number who have visited or have considered visiting is a minority, the cost can be reduced by reversing the questions:

Q1. SHOW CARD.
Which of the following resorts have you ever considered visiting, regardless of whether you have actually visited them?

Q2. SHOW CARD.
And which have you actually visited?

The first question is still asked of all respondents, but the second one is only asked of people who say that they have considered the resort in which we are interested. We can still classify all respondents into the three categories – visited, considered but not visited, and not considered – but, because the second question is only asked of a minority of the sample, we have saved money.

7 Laying out the questionnaire

INTRODUCTION

The way in which the questionnaire is laid out is very important to its success as an instrument of accurate data capture. If the layout is not clear to any of the various users of the questionnaire, the wrong responses may be recorded or the wrong questions asked.

There are two types of user, the respondents themselves in the case of self-completion questionnaires, and interviewers. The two user groups have different needs and requirements of a questionnaire. The two main media distinctions of paper and electronic questionnaires also present different issues to the questionnaire writer.

Non-electronic questionnaire formats also have a third user group – the data entry team. They must also be considered when laying out the questionnaire in order to minimize data entry errors.

INTERVIEWER-ADMINISTERED PAPER QUESTIONNAIRES

If a paper questionnaire is being used, the primary concern with regard to layout is that the interviewer can follow the questionnaire sequence easily, asking the correct questions for each respondent and accurately recording the answers. This is the case for both face-to-face and telephone interviews. If the interviewer has difficulty following the questionnaire or finding the correct question to ask, the flow of the interview can be lost, together with the interest and attention of the respondent. The wrong questions may be asked, which may be entirely inappropriate for the respondent and so lose the respondent's confidence that the survey is worth the time taken to complete it. And, of course, relevant data will be lost.

Most research companies adopt a set of conventions and standardized templates for questionnaire layout that are designed to help the interviewer.

Font size and formats

It may be tempting to use a small font size in order to fit more questions on to each page. This is particularly the case with face-to-face interviews that are relatively long. It may be thought that response rates will be harmed if the potential respondent can see that the questionnaire is the size of a small book. In practice, this is not usually the case, however, and a crowded layout may just lead to interviewer error.

A questionnaire that is printed in a small-sized font will be difficult for interviewers to read. They are more likely to make mistakes both in determining which questions they are supposed to ask and in recording the responses accurately. The quality of the data therefore suffers. They are also more likely to lose respondents during the course of the interview if they make mistakes and ask inappropriate questions, or if there are long pauses between questions whilst the next question is found.

In any case, the likely length of the interview should be told to the respondent as accurately as possible at the outset, so the physical size of the questionnaire should not affect the respondent's decision to cooperate.

It is usual to adopt a general font size of 10, 11 or 12 points, although of course larger font sizes can be used for key instructions.

Bold and italic formats can also be used to draw attention to instructions and key points, or to emphasize particular words in a question where that is necessary. It is important that formatting is used consistently (eg instructions to interviewers are always in bold and underlined; anything to be read aloud is in lower case) so that interviewers can distinguish clearly between instructions, directions, etc and what is to be read out.

A question should never be allowed to go over two pages, so causing interviewers to turn the page to see all of the possible responses. This is likely to lead to errors as the interviewers turn the pages backwards and forwards trying to match the respondents' answers to the given pre-codes.

Upper and lower case

It is common to use upper and lower case to distinguish between questions that need to be read out and instructions for the interviewer that should not be. Most companies adopt the convention of upper case for instructions and lower case for items in the questionnaire that should be read out. This helps interviewers to distinguish quickly between instructions and questions and to see to whom they are meant to put a question and to whom they are not. Some agencies also embolden all instructions to help the interviewer to distinguish them. Others underline instructions for additional emphasis, or use selective underlining for important instructions.

This upper and lower case convention is often extended to the responses to pre-coded questions, which are given in upper case if they not to be read out and lower case if they are meant to be. Other agencies use lower case for all pre-coded responses. The former approach may distinguish better between what is and is not meant to be read out, so helping to avoid unintended prompting, while the latter may be easier and therefore faster for the interviewer to read and to code, so helping to maintain the flow of the interview.

Pre-coded responses

With pre-coded questions the responses are listed on the questionnaire. The order in which they are given can help (or hinder) the interviewer in finding the correct response code quickly. Usually, lists of brand names or simple categories would be given in alphabetical order. However, sometimes it is preferable to group them by categories or sub-categories, if that makes it quicker for the interviewer to find them.

Q12. What was the main method of transport you used to get here today?

BICYCLE	1
BUS	2
CAR	3
MOTORCYCLE	4
TRAIN	5
WALKED	6
OTHER ANSWER (WRITE IN)	7

Figure 7.1   *Inclusion of an 'Other answers' code*

Note in Figure 7.1 the inclusion of an 'Other answers' code, together with an instruction that the interviewer should write in what that 'other' is. It is rare that the questionnaire writer can assume that all possible responses have been thought of and included in the pre-coded list. It is therefore generally prudent to allow for other answers to be given and recorded. Space should be left for the answer to be written in.

When there are a significant number of other answers, the researcher should look to see what they are. It may be that an important response has been overlooked or that there is an ambiguity in the response codes. A respondent to the question in Figure 7.1 may have travelled by tram. That this was not included in the pre-codes may have been an oversight because the researcher was unaware that the tram was an option, or it may have been that the researcher intended to include trams with buses, but failed to make this clear on the response list. If the missing response has been written in, the researcher has the option to create a new code for tram or to recode those who said tram into the bus category.

Single and multiple responses

Frequently it is clear from the question whether the anticipated response is a single answer or whether each respondent could give more than one. In the question about how the respondent travelled (Figure 7.1), the use of the term 'main method of transport' indicated to both respondent and interviewer that only one answer was expected.

Q12. Which method or methods of transport did you use to get here today?
RECORD ALL THAT APPLY.

BICYCLE	1
BUS	2
CAR	3
MOTORCYCLE	4
TRAIN	5
TRAM	6
WALKED	7
OTHER ANSWER (WRITE IN)	8

Figure 7.2   *Possibility of multiple responses*

Had the question been asked as in Figure 7.2, more than one answer would have been possible. Now an instruction to accept multiple responses has been included to ensure that the interviewers recognize that this is permissible.

Wherever there is any possibility of ambiguity as to whether only one response or more than one is permissible, an instruction to the interviewer should be used to make it clear what is expected.

Common pre-code lists

It often happens that successive questions use the same list of pre-codes. When that occurs a single set of responses can be used with the codes for each question next to each other, as in Figure 7.3. This arrangement saves space on the questionnaire, but also allows the interviewer to see what was coded for the first question and to ensure that the same answer is not coded for the second one. Clear instructions and headings are needed so that the interviewer can easily see to which question each column of code applies. Note the inclusion of a 'No others' response category for the second question.

'Don't know' responses

The example of the method of transport used does not include a 'Don't know' category in the list of possible responses. In this instance that is

Q12. What was the main method of transport you used to get here today?
SINGLE CODE ONLY.

Q13. And what other methods of transport did you use, if any?
MULTIPLE CODES ALLOWED.

	Q12 MAIN METHOD	Q13 OTHER METHODS
BICYCLE	1	1
BUS	2	2
CAR	3	3
MOTORCYCLE	4	4
TRAIN	5	5
TRAM	6	6
WALKED	7	7
OTHER ANSWER (WRITE IN)	8	8
NO OTHERS	–	9

Figure 7.3 *Common pre-code list*

justified because respondents are being interviewed shortly after arriving at the place of interview and it is reasonable to assume that they will remember how they travelled there.

However, had the question been about which brands of grocery products they had bought most recently, then a 'Don't know/Can't remember' category should have been included. It is not reasonable to assume that everybody will remember an event that may have taken place some time ago, particularly if it is an event that they see as being of little importance.

A fuller discussion of this is given in Chapter 4.

'Not answered' codes

Some researchers argue that every question should include a 'Not answered' pre-code, so that, should it not be answered for any reason, there is a record that it has been asked. The argument against this is that having such a code could encourage interviewers to accept a refusal to reply too easily.

Occasionally respondents will refuse to answer or are unable to answer a question. If this occurs it is most likely to be because the question is sensitive in some way or because the response options are inadequate for the answer they wish to give. An example of the latter might be that the question asks for a single response but the answer given is a genuine multiple response. If the question asks which *brand* was most recently bought, but two different *brands* were bought at the same time, the interviewer or respondent may consider a multiple response as being contrary to instructions, and leave the question unanswered or coded 'Don't know'.

Where questions go unanswered, that is generally a shortcoming on the part of the questionnaire writer. Sensitive questions should be recognized as such and a 'Refused' category included on the list of pre-codes.

With paper self-completion questionnaires, it is not normal to include a 'Not answered' response. We must assume that the respondent has read all of the questions and has chosen not to answer any that have been left blank.

Show cards

Show cards are commonly used to prompt respondents with lists of possible responses. These can be lists of brands, time periods, behaviour, activities or attitude scales. It is important that interviewers show the correct card at the correct time. The most common practice is for cards to be identified by letters (Card A, Card B, etc) and for the instruction to show a particular card to appear at the appropriate question.

Sometimes the questionnaire writer wants to ensure that the card is removed from the respondent's sight before subsequent questions are asked. This may occur when the card contains the description of a new product concept or an advertising idea and the researcher wants to establish which parts of it have stuck in the respondent's mind. Then an instruction to remove the card from sight should be included.

Read-outs

Where an interviewer is to read out a number of response options, this should be clearly indicated as an instruction at the appropriate place.

Reading out is frequently used where respondents are asked to react to a list of attributes by associating them with brands, or to a list of attitude dimensions to which they indicate strength of agreement. The questionnaire writer should instruct interviewers as to whether or not the question should be repeated between each attribute or statement being read out. The initial question might be: 'Which of these brands do you think is...? READ OUT.' It may be unclear to interviewers whether they should read out that question at the front of each phrase, or whether it is only necessary to read it out once. If the questionnaire writer intends that it should be read out before each phrase, then this should be made clear.

Grids

Where a large grid is used to record responses, visual aids should be included in order to help the interviewer or respondent to record the responses correctly. A commonly used format is to have a number of brands across the top of the grid, which appear on a card shown to the respondent, and a list of attributes down the side of the grid that the interviewers read out. It can be difficult for interviewers to read across a large grid, and they may miscode an answer on to the wrong line, particularly when standing on a doorstep or in a mall.

Sight lines going across the page and shading of alternate lines are simple but effective ways of helping interviewers to avoid this type of error.

Routeing

Clarity of routeing is one of the key aspects of an interviewer-administered paper questionnaire. If interviewers get lost in deciding which questions they should or should not be asking, the credibility of the survey is damaged in the eyes of the respondent and it is almost certain that questions will not be asked that should have been, so data will be lost.

Where routeing is dependent on the responses given to a question, the number of the subsequent question to be asked should be indicated alongside. In Figure 7.4, respondents who answered 'car' at Q12 are routed to Q13, whereas all others are routed to Q14. The heading at

---

Q12. What was the main method of transport you used to
get here today?

BICYCLE	1	
BUS	2	Q14
CAR	3	Q13
MOTORCYCLE	4	
TRAIN	5	
WALKED	6	
OTHER ANSWER (WRITE IN)	7	
————————————		Q14

Q13. ALL WHO TRAVELLED MAINLY BY CAR.

Were you the driver of the car or a passenger?

DRIVER	1	
PASSENGER	2	Q14

Q14. ASK ALL.

Will you mainly use the same method of transport
for your return journey?

YES – USE SAME METHOD	1	
NO – WILL USE DIFFERENT METHOD	2	
DON'T KNOW/NOT DECIDED	3	Q15

Figure 7.4 *Routeing in a questionnaire*

Q13 confirms to interviewers that this is the correct question to be
asked of people who travelled mainly by car, and the heading at Q14
confirms that everybody should be asked this question. Note the inclusion of a 'Don't know' option at Q14.

Occasionally routeing can become very complex, with respondents
coming to a question from a variety of routes, or with routes that are
dependent upon the responses to more than one question. In these
circumstances, the questionnaire writer should consider including the
same question more than once in the questionnaire if doing so makes
it less likely that routeing errors will be made.

Open-ended questions

Open-ended questions should be laid out with sufficient space for full responses to be written in. Interviewers will often stop probing once they have filled the space available to record the answer. More space can mean fuller responses.

Responses to open-ended questions will be coded into a number of categories depending on what answers are given and what answers are being looked for. The practices for recording these codes for data entry vary. Some companies leave a blank space for the coder to write in the appropriate code for the data enterer to use. Others print the codes on the questionnaire and the coder then circles the appropriate code in the same way as the interviewer records responses.

Thanking and classification questions

Interviewers rarely need reminding to thank respondents for their time and cooperation, especially if they have built up a rapport with them. However, it is good practice to include a line on the questionnaire thanking respondents for their time. It demonstrates that the questionnaire writer is also grateful to respondents for their help.

It is the practice in some research companies to record all classification details on the front page of the questionnaire even though they may not be asked until the end of the interview. This is to facilitate the checking of quota controls and demographic details when the questionnaire is returned to the office. If this is the case, it is prudent to include a reminder at the end of the questionnaire for the interviewer to return to the front page and complete the classification questions. Again, few interviewers will need reminding, but it is an indication of the questionnaire writer's concern to help them if it is included.

Administrative information

Each study will require an identification code if you are carrying out, or are likely to carry out, more than one similar study. Each questionnaire will require a unique identifier or serial number so as to be able to distinguish between respondents. Study and respondent identification are required for all questioning media, and allowance must be made on the questionnaire for them. Interviewer-administered questionnaires should also include an interviewer identification code. Interviews can then be analysed by interviewer in order to determine any between-interviewer effects, or to identify interviewers who may have made errors in their interviews.

If there is more than one version of the questionnaire, the different versions will also usually need to be identified for analysis purposes.

Data entry

The format and layout for data entry will depend on the way in which the data are to be entered and the program that will be used to analyse them. The examples in this book generally use the column format. This has one or more columns allocated to each question, depending on the number of response codes required. Each column has 12 positions (1 to 9, 0, X, V), one of which is allocated to each response code. This is the format used by analysis programs such as those from Pulse Train and SPSS MR. Other programs use different formats.

If data are to be scanned in, using optical mark reading, there will be specific instructions regarding the layout, depending on the type of scanning equipment used. This usually involves having fixed points on each page from which the position of the marks made by the inter-viewer or respondent is measured. In Figures 7.5 and 7.6 the fixed marks are the diamonds in the four corners of the page. Note that the job identification and page numbers must also be included on each page in order to identify the scanned data correctly.

SELF-COMPLETION PAPER QUESTIONNAIRE

Much of the success of a paper-based self-completion survey depends on the appearance of the questionnaire and the ease with which respondents can use it. An unattractive questionnaire that is difficult to follow will reduce the response rate, increasing the risk of an unac-ceptably low level of response. An unattractive or shoddily produced questionnaire suggests to the respondents that you don't really care about the project, so why should they?

J.012345

Q11. You said that you had switched energy company recently. Which energy supply did you switch to Powerplus?

| Both gas and electricity | ☐ | Gas only | ☐ | Electricity only | ☐ |

Q12. Why have you decided to switch to Powerplus?

Tick one main reason in the first column and any other reasons in the second.

	Main	Other
To have both gas and electricity supplied by one company	☐	☐
They said they could offer lower prices	☐	☐
No standing charge	☐	☐
Moved house	☐	☐
They offered me Internet account management	☐	☐
I was unhappy with the customer service at the previous company	☐	☐
I did not receive bills in a timely manner before	☐	☐
I was unhappy with the accuracy of my bills	☐	☐
Bills were not easy to understand before	☐	☐
Too many estimated meter readings	☐	☐
Inaccurate estimated meter readings	☐	☐
They offered me green energy	☐	☐
Other (tick box and write in space below)	☐	☐

Q13. If Powerplus said they could offer lower prices, what were the approximate savings per year you expected?

Up to £20 per year	☐
£21 to £40 per year	☐
£41 to £60 per year	☐
£61 to £80 per year	☐
£81 to £100 per year	☐
More than £100 per year	☐
Not sure	☐

Q14. Which supplier were you with before?

Powergen	☐
British Gas	☐
EDF Energy	☐
Npower	☐
TXU Energi	☐
Scottish Power	☐
Other	☐

03

Figure 7.5 *Questionnaire for scanning (1)*

J.012345

(OFFICE USE ONLY)   SERIAL NO

Dear Research Club Member

Thank you for taking the time to complete this questionnaire. Please answer all the questions by putting a cross ✍ in the appropriate box or by writing in the boxes provided.

Q1.   Are you male or female?

        PLEASE GIVE ONE ANSWER ONLY

                        Male ....□

                        Female ....□

Q2.   Into which of the following groups does your age fall?

        PLEASE GIVE ONE ANSWER ONLY

                        18–25 ....□

                        26–29 ....□

                        30–34 ....□

                        35–39 ....□

                        40–44 ....□

                        45–49 ....□

                        50–54 ....□

                        55–59 ....□

                        60–65 ....□

                        Over 65 ....□

Q3.   How many times a week do you brush your teeth, if at all?

        PLEASE WRITE IN BOXES – USE LEADING ZERO IF NECESSARY

Q4.   What is your regular brand of toothpaste, the one you use more than any other brand nowadays?

        PLEASE WRITE IN BOXES – USE 3-DIGIT CODE FROM OVERLEAF

Q5.   Would you be willing to take part in surveys where we send you a tube of toothpaste to try?

        PLEASE GIVE ONE ANSWER ONLY

                        Yes ....□

                        No ....□

Q6.   If you are not the Research Club member to whom this questionnaire was addressed, please write in your name here. Otherwise leave this blank.

| First Name | | | | | | | | | | | | | | | |
| Surname | | | | | | | | | | | | | | | |

THANK YOU FOR COMPLETING THIS QUESTIONNAIRE.

PLEASE NOW RETURN IT TO US USING THE REPLY-PAID ENVELOPE PROVIDED.

01

Figure 7.6   *Questionnaire for scanning (2)*

153

Making it attractive

There are many ideas about how to make a questionnaire attractive to potential respondents. However, it is almost certainly true that time, effort and money spent on improving the appearance are rarely wasted.

Printing should be of good quality and it is preferable for the paper to be a slightly heavier weight than for an interviewer-administered questionnaire. The paper should always be of sufficient quality that the printing on one side cannot be seen from the other side through the paper. Using different colours in the printing can increase the attractiveness if used sparingly. Colour can be used to distinguish instructions from questions, or to provide borders to questions. Coloured paper, though, should be used with care. Pale or pastel colours can be used, particularly if there are different versions of a questionnaire that have to be easily distinguishable. Darker colours and gloss-finish paper, either of which makes the print difficult to read, should always be avoided.

If the budget allows, the questionnaire is best presented in the form of a booklet. This looks more professional and is easier for respondents to follow. With a questionnaire printed on both sides of the paper and stapled in one corner it is easy for respondents to miss the reverse pages, and it is possible that some back pages will become detached or inadvertently torn off. The booklet format avoids both of these potential problems. It does, however, create its own problem of forcing the number of sides to be four or a multiple of four. When the questions fit neatly on to five pages, this means that the researcher has to decide whether to use a less optimal question layout, or to drop some questions, or to accept a significantly greater printing cost.

To help make the respondents feel that the survey is worthwhile, the study should have a title, clearly displayed on the front page of the questionnaire, together with the name of the organization conducting it. The address of the organization should also be included. Even if a return envelope is provided, it may get mislaid by respondents, so an address on the questionnaire gives them an opportunity to return it.

Use of space

Little is more daunting for potential respondents than to be confronted with pages crammed full of print that they have to struggle to find

Seen in print

Q8. Do you think the property will require any of the following repairs or improvements in the next five years?

Please tick all that apply.

Additional ☐   Improved ☐   Rewiring ☐   Damp- ☐   Roof ☐   Window ☐
security   heating   proofing   repairs   repairs

Q9. Do you intend to carry out any of the following repairs or improvements in the next five years?

Additional ☐   Improved ☐   Rewiring ☐   Damp- ☐   Roof ☐   Window ☐
security   heating   proofing   repairs   repairs

Figure 7.7   *Horizontal listing*

their way through. Lay the questions out sparingly. If the booklet form of questionnaire is used this can lead to a need to squeeze more questions on to a page than is ideal. However, the questionnaire designer should be aware of the consequences of trying to get too much on to a page.

Dividing the questions into sections with a clear heading to each section helps respondents understand the flow of the questionnaire and focuses their attention on the topic of each section. It also helps give them a small sense of achievement when a section is completed, particularly if the questionnaire is long. Vertical listing of responses should be used in preference to horizontal listing, as it is easier to follow and creates a more open appearance. However, it does require more space.

Figures 7.7 and 7.8 show the same questions with responses listed horizontally and vertically, respectively. The original questionnaire used the horizontal listing.The vertical listing uses more space on the page but is easier to see, and makes the page more attractive.

Never allow questions to go over two pages, or over two columns if the page is columnated. If a response list continues on another page it may not be seen. Avoid, if possible, a short question being placed at the bottom of a page, preceded by a question with a large response grid. The short question is likely to be overlooked.

Q8. Do you think the property will require any of the following repairs or improvements in the next five years?

Please tick below all that apply.

Q9. Do you intend to carry out any of the following repairs or improvements in the next five years?

	Q8	Q9
Additional security	☐	☐
Improved heating	☐	☐
Rewiring	☐	☐
Damp-proofing	☐	☐
Roof repairs	☐	☐
Window repairs	☐	☐

Figure 7.8 *Vertical listing*

Open-ended questions

Open-ended questions can be a deterrent to respondents, depending on their interest in the subject matter. If the level of interest is low then open-ended questions tend to be at best poorly completed and at worst can damage the response rate. If possible, keep open-ended questions until the latter part of the interview. The questionnaire can be read through before being completed, so the respondents must be assumed to be prompted by any information that is on the questionnaire. There is thus no issue of having to ask an open-ended question before one that shows pre-codes that might prompt the open responses.

Avoid, if possible, starting the interview with an open-ended question, as this can be a deterrent for many people even to start to complete it.

Routeing instructions

Routeing should be kept to a minimum. Where they are necessary, routeing instructions must be clear and unambiguous. If the questions can be ordered such that any routeing only takes respondents either to the following question or to the next section, both of which are easy to find, errors of omission are more likely to be avoided.

Covering letter

When the questionnaire is to be completed unsupervised or if it is a postal or mail survey, a covering letter and instructions will be required. The covering letter may be printed on the front page of the questionnaire if the layout allows sufficient space. There is then no danger of it becoming separated from the questionnaire. This also simplifies the production process if you wish to print a respondent identifier (eg customer type) on the questionnaire, as this can be printed on to the latter page, avoiding the need to match the letter to the questionnaire when mailing out.

Data entry

With a paper questionnaire, data entry will be required. Data entry instructions and codes should be kept as unobtrusive as possible. Where numeric codes are used to identify the responses, there is a danger of suggesting to respondents that there is a hierarchy of responses, which have been numbered from one onwards. For this reason circling of codes, in the way that is often used with interviewer-administered questionnaires, should be avoided. Ticking or checking boxes should always be preferred to avoid any such bias, and response codes should be kept as small as is possible while still compatible with accurate data entry.

Where data are read by optical scanning, data entry codes can often be completely removed or confined to the margins of the questionnaire. This has the benefit of removing some of the visual clutter from the page, so making it more attractive to the respondent. It also removes any concerns that the responses may be biased by the data entry number codes.

ELECTRONIC QUESTIONNAIRES

All forms of electronic questionnaires, for face-to-face, telephone or Web-based interviewing, have a number of advantages over paper questionnaires. Electronic questionnaires from all of the major software suppliers can:

- cope with complex routeing;
- rotate or randomize the order in which questions are asked;
- rotate or randomize the order in which responses are displayed;

157

- adapt questions, depending on answers to previous questions;
- adapt response lists, depending on answers to previous questions.

The programs generally offer a range of standardized formats, which can be customized to the research organization's conventions and layouts. This means, however, that many of the issues of layout are predetermined and thus taken out of the hands of the questionnaire writer.

The issues that remain are not dissimilar to those encountered with paper questionnaires, namely ensuring that all of a question and its responses appear on one page or screen and, for self-completion questionnaires (usually Web-based), ensuring that the appearance is attractive and that the questionnaire is easy to navigate.

However, electronic questionnaires should not just be seen as paper questionnaires transferred to screen. They offer many opportunities for questionnaire writers to be more creative in the way in which they ask questions, to ask more complex questions without the questions appearing to be so, and to use prompt material that would not otherwise be possible.

Presenting scales in electronic questionnaires

Electronic questionnaires, either online Web-based or self-completion CAPI, provide alternative means of presenting scales and recording responses to those available on paper questionnaires. The layout of paper questionnaires can be replicated, with statements displayed down one side (or both sides if bipolar) and the response options given as 'radio buttons' across the page. This is a familiar layout to most questionnaire writers.

For electronic questionnaires, though, it has the drawback of being heavy on space. The questionnaire writer does not want to overcrowd the screen and deter or confuse the respondent, so it is usual to limit the number of items to 10 or fewer, whereas twice that number may be given on one page of a paper questionnaire. This means that the number of screens required is greater than the corresponding number of pages in the paper version, increasing the possibility of drop-out by the respondent. Also, when ratings are requested for two or more objects, brands, etc, the layout of the screen can become cluttered.

Electronic questionnaires present two options, one of which is not available and the other rarely used with paper questionnaires. The

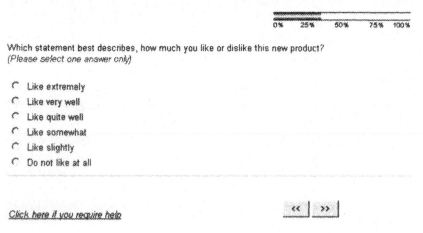

Figure 7.9 *Scale using radio buttons*

rarely used option is a write-in box, in which respondents are asked to write a number, say from 1 to 5, to represent their response on a scale where the end points have been defined for them. The likelihood of error in misreading many different styles of handwriting is a major deterrent for this approach with paper questionnaires. However, with electronic questionnaires it is straightforward and accurately recorded. There is slightly more effort involved for the respondents than with radio buttons, which only require them to move a mouse and click on the button. Care must be taken to ensure that respondents know what each point on the scale means by showing the full scale with descriptors on the page, most likely above the relevant response boxes. A full semantic scale can be shown with each point labelled, or anchors used only for the end points. The space saved means that more items can be included on the same page, and brands can be rated more easily alongside each other.

The option that is not available with paper questionnaires is drop-down boxes. A drop-down box following the statement can contain the full scale. Respondents only have to click on their choice of response for it to be displayed and recorded. Again a little more effort is required than with radio buttons. There might also be concerns that the direction in which the scale is displayed, with either the positive or negative end of the scale at the top of the drop-down box, will introduce a bias. This bias could be expected to be greater than that associated with the

Which statement best describes how you feel about the believability of the claims made about this new product? *(Please select one answer only)*

Figure 7.10 *Scale using drop-down box*

direction of the scale when using radio buttons, as respondents may not read all the way down the complete scale.

However, work carried out by Hogg and Masztal (2001) has demonstrated that this is not the case. Their study, which compared radio buttons with write-in boxes and drop-downs, showed that both write-in boxes and drop-downs gave greater dispersion of responses across a five-point scale than did radio buttons. With radio buttons there was a greater likelihood of respondents using one point of the scale repeatedly (pattern responding). This suggests that both of the other two methods may result in respondents giving more consideration to each response. The more deliberate process of choosing a response option with these methods could mean that more consideration is given to what that response should be.

Their results for the two versions of the drop-down, one with the positive end of the scale at the top of the box, the other with the negative end at the top, were almost identical, indicating that order is not a crucial issue, at least for five-point scales. However, it may become more so for longer scales, and as a precaution the order should be rotated between respondents to balance any bias.

There may be a concern that the additional time taken to complete the questionnaire could result in an increased rate of drop-out. Hogg and Masztal found that, although there was a small increase in the time taken, there was no evidence of any increased drop-out as a result.

'Don't know' and 'Not answered' codes

CAPI and CATI questionnaires will tend to have 'Don't know' or 'Not answered' codes for most questions. The interviewer may not be able to proceed to the following question without entering a response, and the respondent may refuse any answer other than a 'Don't know' or refusal. Where the answer is used for quota purposes or the responses are to be used for routeing, these codes may be omitted. Even then, the questionnaire writer should have a strategy for routeing the genuine 'Don't knows' from such questions.

With electronic self-completion questionnaires there are other issues. No researcher can force respondents to answer every, or indeed any, question on a questionnaire. However, many Web-based surveys do not permit the respondent to continue to the next question until an answer has been provided. Several companies have carried out their own investigations, which show that very few respondents terminate an interview because of the lack of a 'Not answered' or 'Don't know' code, nor does it significantly alter the distribution of responses. Against this it can be argued that there is an ethical issue that respondents should be allowed not to answer a question without having to terminate the interview or provide a random answer.

An alternative approach adopted by some companies is to have a screen or a pop-up that appears if respondents try to continue without having answered a question. This screen points out that they have not answered the previous question and gives the opportunity to return to it and complete it. The respondents must actively click to say that they do not want to or cannot answer the question before being allowed to continue to the next one. This approach, although it requires more complex programming, provides the researcher with full information about respondents' abilities to answer questions and avoids them inventing answers just to proceed.

Questions that demand a response in order to route the respondent to the next question would normally treat a 'Not answered' as a 'Don't know' and route accordingly.

The inclusion of a 'Not answered' category on all questions as a matter of course is a question of individual preference, but the author's view is that it is likely to lead to interviewers accepting refusals and ambiguities in response too readily, with a consequent increase in lost data.

Checking the questionnaire

The questionnaire layout should always be thoroughly checked from the standpoint of the interviewer, the coder, the data enterer, the data processor and, if self-completion, the respondent.

Checking for sense and usability will be repeated as part of the pilot survey (see Chapter 8). Before the pilot survey is reached, though, the questionnaire should be thoroughly proofread, and all interviewer and routeing instructions double-checked. Routeing instructions in electronic questionnaires should be checked and checked again.

8 Piloting the questionnaire

INTRODUCTION

It is always advisable to pilot the questionnaire before the survey goes live. Whether it is a new questionnaire written to meet a set of specific objectives or a set of questions that have been used before and adapted or arranged for a new study, testing it out before committing to a large-scale study is an essential precaution. Questionnaires are rarely the best that they could be at the first attempt. They need revising and testing until all concerned, researcher and client, are happy that they have the best questionnaire that they can get. Piloting the questionnaire should be an integral part of that process.

Unfortunately, it is very common with commercial studies for piloting time not to be built into the project schedule. This stage in the process is often seen as expendable in the light of the pressure for information to be delivered as fast as possible. The experience of the researcher is relied upon to get it right first time. But even the most experienced researchers cannot be expected to do that every time. Failure to pilot the questionnaire represents a serious risk to the success of the project.

WHY PILOT QUESTIONNAIRES?

There are a number of good reasons why questionnaires should be piloted, and a pilot survey should address the following points:

- *Do the questions sound right?* It is surprising how often a question looks acceptable when written on paper but sounds false, stilted or simply silly when read out. It can be a salutary experience for questionnaire writers to conduct interviews themselves. They should note how often they want to paraphrase a question that they have written to make it sound more natural.
- *Do the interviewers understand the questions?* Complicated wording in a question can make it incomprehensible even to the interviewers. If they cannot understand it there is little chance that respondents will.
- *Do respondents understand the questions?* It is easy for technical terminology and jargon to creep into questions, so we need to ensure that it is eliminated.
- *Have we included any ambiguous questions, double-barrelled questions, loaded or leading questions?*
- *Can respondents answer the questions?* We must ensure that we ask questions to which respondents are capable of providing answers.
- *Are the response codes provided sufficient?* Missing response codes can lead to answers being forced to fit into the codes provided or to large numbers of 'other' answers.
- *Do the response codes provide sufficient discrimination?* If most respondents give the same answer, then the pre-codes provided may need to be reviewed to see how the discrimination can be improved, and if that cannot be achieved queries should be raised regarding the value of including the question.
- *Does the interview retain the attention of respondents throughout?* If attention is lost or wavers, then the quality of the data may be in doubt. Changes may be required in order to retain the respondents' interest.
- *Can the interviewers or respondents understand the routeing instructions in the questionnaire?* Particularly with paper questionnaires we should check that the routeing instructions can be understood by the interviewers or, if self-completion, by respondents.
- *Does the interview flow properly?* The questionnaire should be conducting a conversation with the respondent. A questionnaire that unfolds in a logical sequence, with a minimum of jumps between apparently unrelated topics, helps to achieve that.

▓ *Do the questions and the responses answer the brief?* We should by this time be reasonably certain that the questions we think we are asking meet the brief, but we need to ensure that the answers that respondents give to those questions are the responses to the questions that we think we are asking.

▓ *How long does the interview take?* Most surveys will be budgeted for the interview to take a certain length of time. The number of interviewers allocated to the project will be calculated partly on the length of the interview, and they will be paid accordingly. Assumptions will also have been made about respondent cooperation based on the time taken to complete the interview. The study can run into serious timing and budgetary difficulties, and may be impossible to complete, if the interview is longer than allowed for. Being shorter than allowed for does not usually present such problems, but may lead to wasteful use of interviewer resources.

▓ *Have mistakes been made?* Despite all the procedures that most research companies have in place to check questionnaires before they go live, mistakes do occasionally still get through. It is often the small mistakes that go unnoticed that have a dramatic effect on the meaning of a question or on the routeing between questions. Imagine the effect of inadvertently omitting the word 'not' from a question.

▓ *Does the routeing work?* Although this should have been comprehensively checked, illogical routeing sequences sometimes only become apparent with live interviews.

▓ *Does the technology work?* If unusual or untried technology is being used, perhaps as an interactive element or for displaying prompts, this should be checked in the field. It may work perfectly well in the office, but field conditions are sometimes different, and a hiatus in the interview caused by slow-working or malfunctioning technology can lose respondents.

TYPES OF PILOT SURVEYS

Informal pilots

An informal pilot represents the minimum that any questionnaire should undergo. In the informal pilot, the questionnaire writer should carry out the interview with a number of colleagues. At the minimum, this will give an indication of the length of time taken to complete the interview. It must be remembered though that an interview undertaken in the calm conditions of an office will usually take less time than one in the field when the respondent may be subject to a number of distractions and interruptions. Because colleagues are familiar with the conventions of questionnaires and they know it is not a 'real' interview, they will also tend to answer more quickly and without the same pauses for thought that occur with respondents.

Ideally, the colleagues interviewed should meet the eligibility criteria for the study, so that they can answer as respondents. This may highlight incomplete sets of pre-codes when a colleague's responses don't fit those provided, or an inadequacy in the routeing or in the questions when key information is not elicited.

If colleagues do not fit the eligibility criteria, then they must be asked to pretend to. This is less likely to identify problems such as incomplete code lists, as the pretend respondent, who may not know the market well, will tend to give the same sorts of responses that the questionnaire writer has already anticipated. Nevertheless, this type of interview may well identify issues of timing, wording and routeing errors.

It is often worthwhile asking a colleague to pretend to be someone in the market with particular characteristics or a particular minority pattern of behaviour. If there is complex routeing in the questionnaire, this approach can be used to test it. If the colleague can be as obstructive as possible, challenging questions and providing the most difficult responses that he or she can think of, this will give the questionnaire a further test. Remember that the questionnaire has to work not just for most respondents but for all respondents.

The questionnaire writer should conduct these interviews, and it may be that no more than two or three such interviews are required. The questionnaire writer is the best person to understand the intent of each question and therefore to identify if it is misunderstood. However, if possible, a colleague who has not been involved in the questionnaire design can also be used as an interviewer. This will give the questionnaire some degree of testing as a tool to be used by someone not familiar with it.

Colleagues may not be thought to be the ideal sample for testing questionnaires, but it has been shown that people with a knowledge of questionnaire design are more likely to pick up errors in questions than are people who are not (Diamantopolous, Schlegelmilch and Reynolds, 1994), so they are good place to start.

Self-completion questionnaires should be given to a small number of colleagues to complete. These colleagues should be asked to make notes about any questions or routeing instructions with which they have difficulty.

Accompanied interviewing

Testing questionnaires amongst colleagues may identify some issues with the questionnaire, but cannot properly replicate what will happen in the field with real respondents and, where necessary, with real interviewers. For interviewer-administered questionnaires, the next stage should be for the questionnaire writer to listen in to a small number of interviews carried out by members of the interviewing team who will conduct the main survey.

The questionnaire writer should be listening for:

* mistakes by the interviewer in reading the questions;
* misunderstandings of the question by the respondent;
* failures in the questionnaire to cope with the respondent's situation;
* mistakes made by the interviewer in following routeing instructions;
* errors in the routeing instructions that take the respondent to the wrong question.

There is also the opportunity here for the questionnaire writer to talk to respondents to find out what they understood by certain questions or why they responded as they did. The researcher should make notes throughout the interview of points that he or she wishes to return to.

The researcher can interrupt the interview at any point to ask for clarification, but this risks ruining the flow of the interview for the respondent and the interviewer alike. It could also give the interviewer additional time to review routeing instructions in the questionnaire, which then goes unnoticed by the researcher.

It is possible to ask the respondents to 'think out loud' as they answer the questions, but this runs the danger of altering the way in which they think about the questions and how they respond.

One question always worth asking is whether the respondents felt that the questionnaire allowed them to say all they wanted on the subject. It is not uncommon to find that one of the main things that a respondent wanted to say on the subject was not asked about. It may not have been asked because it was not seen as relevant to the objectives of the study. Nevertheless, the impression left with the respondent is that the study was incomplete and that decisions would be made without full knowledge of the facts. This perception can be damaging to the image and reputation of market research, and could affect the willingness of the respondent to take part in future surveys. If there is an issue that consistently comes through as important to respondents that is not asked about, then consideration should be given to including it in the interview regardless of its apparent relevance to the study objectives.

Respondents should be chosen to represent a broad range of the types of people to be included in the main study. Any particular subgroups amongst whom it is thought that there might be some difficulties with the questionnaire should be represented.

Questionnaire writers should also conduct some interviews themselves in order to be able to understand any difficulties that the interviewers have with following the questionnaire instructions or in reading out the words of the questions as they have been written.

This type of pilot survey should allow the researcher to amend the questionnaire so that there can be confidence in it that it works in asking respondents questions that they can understand and can cope with the answers that they give.

Self-completion questionnaires, either paper or electronic, can be tested by asking a small number of eligible respondents to complete a questionnaire, and then talking them through what they understood from the questions and the way in which they responded to them.

Large-scale pilot survey

With completion of the small-scale pilot survey, it may be possible to move to a larger-scale exercise. The objective here is to extend the pilot exercise to a larger number of interviewers and to a broader range of respondents, and for there to be a sufficient number of respondents for some analysis to be carried out to confirm that the questions asked are delivering the data required to answer the project objectives.

Some commentators suggest that the interviewers used should be the most experienced interviewers available, who are capable of determining ambiguities and other errors in the questions. Others suggest that a mix of interviewer ability is more appropriate, as it reflects the ability range of interviewers likely to be used on the main study. This range of views suggests that the principal purpose of the pilot study should be determined and the interviewers chosen accordingly. Thus if the interview is straightforward in terms of routeing and instructions, and the focus of the pilot is more on the wording of the questions, more experienced interviewers may be more appropriate. If the focus, however, is equally on how well the interviewers can cope with a complex questionnaire, then a range of abilities would appear to answer the needs better.

This type of large-scale pilot is likely only to be carried out with large-scale studies, where the cost of failure is high if the study is unable to meet its objectives.

Upwards of 50 interviews may be carried out in this pilot, which should be designed to cover different sections of the market and possibly different geographical regions. It is at this stage that small regional brands may be discovered that should be added to brand lists, or unanticipated minority behaviour that had not been catered for. (The small-scale pilot survey is only likely to clarify anticipated minority behaviour.)

It is it at this stage that unusually high numbers of 'Don't know' or 'Not answered' responses may indicate an issue with a question.

The questionnaire writer is unlikely to be able to be present at all of the interviews. Indeed, doing so could be counterproductive, as it would be difficult not to give guidance to an interviewer consistently making an error. Interviewers should therefore be asked to write notes on each interview. They should be provided with note sheets on which to record comments – their own and the respondents' – as they go through the interview, which can later be referred to.

A debriefing of the interviewers should be held if possible, where they are brought to a central location to discuss their experiences with the questionnaire. The questionnaire writer should have seen all of the completed questionnaires before the debrief so as to have determined where there might still be issues with some questions, including issues that the interviewers themselves might not be aware of. If, for example, they all consistently misinterpret a question, they are unlikely to identify that as a problem. It will require the questionnaire writer to do so.

Should significant changes be made to the questionnaire as a result of the pilot testing, then, of course, another round of pilot testing should be carried out.

Although not part of the questionnaire development process, a further use to which the large-scale pilot survey can be put is to give an indication of the incidence of minority groups within the research universe. If it is intended that the study should be capable of analysing specific sub-groups, the incidence of which is unknown, the pilot sample can give a first indication of this and so suggest whether the intended sample size of the main study is sufficient for this intended analysis. This may lead to revision of the sample size or sample structure for the main survey.

Dynamic pilot

The dynamic pilot is a type of pilot exercise that can be very useful where a questionnaire is experimental. This is similar in scale to the small pilot survey. However, instead of the questionnaire writer listening in to a number of interviews and then deciding what is and is not working, the questionnaire is reviewed after each interview and rewritten to try to improve it. The client and researcher will often do this together. The improved questionnaire is then used for the next interview, after which it is reviewed again.

This is a time-consuming and possibly costly process, particularly if a central location has to be hired to accommodate it. However, where there is real concern about the sequence of questions or the precise wording of questions, it can be the quickest way to achieving a questionnaire that works, particularly if the client is part of the dynamic decision-making process.

An example of where this might be appropriate is if we wish to test the reaction to a complex proposed government policy. In this situation, it may be important to ensure that respondents understand some of the detail of the policy. A key component of the questionnaire design would be how to explain a number of different elements of the policy and gain reaction to each one. So we may need to test the wording of the descriptions of the different elements in order to judge how clearly it correctly conveys the policy; and to assess any order effects dependent on the sequence in which the components are revealed. By observing the reaction of the pilot respondents and where necessary asking them questions regarding what they understand from the descriptions, the questionnaire writer can adjust the wording and the order of the questions between interviews until a satisfactory conclusion is reached.

9 Ethical issues

INTRODUCTION

The ability of the market research industry to continue to use sample surveys as sources of primary data depends upon the willingness of members of the public to give their time and cooperation to answer our questions. There is frequently little, if any, obvious reward for them (although we regularly employ the argument that research helps to improve products and services on the market), and they are rarely paid. In order to be able to continue, market research needs to maintain this goodwill.

The level of goodwill and cooperation has declined in most countries over the past 30 years. Possible reasons for this include:

- Direct marketing has increased, which makes potential respondents distrustful that market researchers are not trying to sell them something.
- Potential respondents do not distinguish between market research and activities such as database marketing. Indeed in one study three-quarters of respondents said that they could not distinguish between them (Brace, Nancarrow and McCloskey, 1999).
- Many people lead busier lives than they used to or than their parents used to. Many genuinely have less time for non-rewarding activities such as market research.
- There are more market research studies than there used to be, and

consequently many people are asked to participate in research surveys more often. Some markets are very over-researched, particularly business-to-business and medical markets.

▓ Our demands on respondents have increased. Interviews have got longer and more tedious as demands for information from client management have increased. Many potential respondents have been bored by a market research interview once before, or know someone who has been, and are not prepared to go through the same tedium again.

There is little that the questionnaire writer can do to free up more time in people's lives or to prevent markets becoming over-researched. However, by treating respondents honestly, openly and respectfully when writing the questionnaire, the questionnaire writer can help to distinguish genuine market research from direct marketing. And by creating involving and interesting interviews, he or she can improve the standing of market research interviews. Potential respondents may then be more willing to participate in surveys in the future.

This is one of the reasons why codes of conduct exist. There are three main codes: those of the Market Research Society (MRS) in the UK, the Council of American Survey Research Organizations (CASRO) in the USA, and the European Society for Opinion and Marketing Research (ESOMAR). All market researchers should make themselves familiar with the code that is appropriate to them. The codes can be found on the organizations' Web sites: www.mrs.org.uk, www.casro.org and www.esomar.org. Membership of any of these bodies requires adherence to their code. The current MRS Code of Conduct is given in Appendix 2.

In addition to their code, which provides an overall set of principles to be followed, some organizations provide more detailed guidelines on specific aspects of research. As an adjunct to its code, the MRS has produced 'Questionnaire design guidelines', which are regularly updated and can be found at www.mrs.org.uk/standards/quest.htm.

Many countries now have laws, usually in the form of data protection laws, that define certain points of information that questionnaire writers are required to give to respondents. These laws take precedence over codes of conduct, should there be any conflict.

In the UK, the relevant law is the Data Protection Act 1998. There is variation in these laws between countries with, for example, the laws of Germany and the UK being more prescriptive than the corresponding laws in many other countries. Again, it is the responsibility of questionnaire writers to ensure that they comply with the laws of the country in which they work, as well as with the laws of the country or countries in which they are carrying out the survey if they are different.

RESPONSIBILITIES TO RESPONDENTS

The introduction

What is said in the introduction to an interview is crucial in securing the cooperation of respondents. This is true for both interviewer-administered surveys and self-completion studies.

From an ethical standpoint the introduction should include:

- the name of the organization conducting the study;*
- the broad subject area;
- whether the subject area is particularly sensitive;
- whether the data collected will be held confidentially or used at a personally identifiable level for other purposes such as database building or direct marketing, and if so by whom;*
- the likely length of the interview;
- any cost to the respondent;
- whether the interview is to be recorded, either audio or video, other than for the purposes of quality control.*

The items marked * are required by the Data Protection Act 1998 in the UK.

This gives respondents or potential respondents the information that they require in order to be able to make an informed decision about whether or not they are prepared to cooperate in the study.

Sometimes it is not easy to comply with these requirements, but the questionnaire writer should make every effort to do so.

Name of the research organization

The name of the organization carrying out the study would usually be the research company that is responsible for writing the questionnaire if that is the same as the company that will be responsible for analysis of the results. (In UK Data Protection Act terms, this is the Data Controller.) If part or all of the fieldwork is to be subcontracted, then the name of the subcontracting agency need not be mentioned, providing that it is passing on completed interviews to the main agency for processing, and it is possible to identify individual interviewers in case of a complaint being made.

Subject matter

The broad subject area should be given so that the respondent has a reasonable idea of the area of questioning that is to follow. Frequently we do not wish to reveal the precise subject matter too early as this will bias responses, particularly during the screening questions. However, every effort should be made to give a general indication. For example, a survey about holidays could be described as being about leisure activities, although such a description may be inadequate for a survey about drinking habits. 'Leisure activities' would certainly be an inadequate description for a survey about sexual activity, which is regarded as a sensitive subject.

In the UK sensitive subjects are defined as including:

- sexual activity;
- racial origin;
- political opinions;
- religious or similar beliefs;
- physical or mental health;
- implication in criminal activity;
- trade union membership.

This list, though, is not exhaustive in terms of what respondents may find sensitive, and the questionnaire writer should examine the study for any possible sensitive content. Anyone working in areas dealing with drugs and medication, or illness, or conducting studies on financial topics should be particularly alert to this issue.

Confidentiality

One of the key distinctions between market research surveys and surveys carried out for direct marketing or database building is that the data are held confidentially and are for analysis purposes only. No direct sales or marketing activity will take place as a result of the respondent having taken part in the study. If this is the case, this should be stated in the introduction on the questionnaire or in the covering letter in the case of a postal survey. It is then the responsibility of the research organization to ensure that the data are treated solely in this way.

Sometimes, research organizations carry out studies that are not confidential research. Some customer satisfaction surveys utilize individual-level data to enhance the client company's customer database or to allow selective marketing to customers, dependent on their recorded level of satisfaction. Or research may be used to identify respondents who show an interest in a new product or service that the client can follow up with marketing activity. The latter may occur particularly in small business-to-business markets, where most or all of the potential market is included in the study. Such studies are not confidential research and the questionnaire must not represent them as such.

Apart from it being against the Data Protection Act in the UK to represent such studies as confidential research, it is morally wrong to mislead respondents. It is also bad for the image of market research if respondents are wrongly led into thinking that nothing will occur to them as result of participating in the study. It can only damage response rates for future surveys if respondents become disillusioned about the reassurances that they are given.

Interview length

How long the interview is likely to take is another area where a respondent once misled is unlikely to trust future assurances. One of the most common causes of complaints received by the Market Research Society from members of the public is that the interview in which they participated took significantly longer than they were initially told. Sometimes they were not told how long the interview would take, and wrongly assumed that it would be only a few minutes. On other occasions, though, they were told the likely duration of the interview, which was then significantly exceeded.

Sometimes it is straightforward to estimate the length of the interview. When the study has a questionnaire with a simple flow path and little routeing, the pilot survey will have demonstrated how long it will take, and that is likely to be about the same for all respondents.

The time required to complete the interview can vary considerably between respondents as the questionnaire becomes more complex. It can depend on the speed with which respondents answer the questions and the amount of consideration that they give to each. It can also vary significantly depending on the answers that they give. The question- naire may contain sections that are asked only if the respondent displays a particular behaviour, knowledge or attitude at an earlier question. The time taken to complete the interview can increase or decrease con- siderably, depending on whether or not such sections are asked. The eligibility of any individual respondent for these sections cannot be predicted at the outset of the interview, with the consequence that the interview length could vary between, say, 15 minutes and 45 minutes for different respondents.

If there is likely to be a significant variation in interview length between respondents, then the questionnaire writer should try to reflect this in the introduction.

The introduction must never deliberately understate the likely time required. It is better to be vague about the interview length than deliberately to mislead.

Source of name

Respondents have a right to know how they were sampled or where the research organization obtained their name and contact details. For surveys using non-pre-selected samples, this does not usually present any difficulties, although explaining how random digit dialling works to someone who is ex-directory can sometimes be difficult.

Where the names have been supplied from a database, this can sometimes present more of a problem. With customer satisfaction sur- veys, we shall often want to say in the introduction that respondents have been contacted because they are customers of the organization. Frequently, clients will see the customer satisfaction survey as a way of demonstrating to their customers that the organization cares about the relationship between them. Then it is not uncommon for the introduc- tion to state this and for postal or Web-based satisfaction questionnaires to include client identification and logos.

However, sometimes we do not wish to reveal the source at the beginning of the interview because that may bias responses to questions where the client organization is to be compared against similar organizations. If, in a personal interview, the interviewer is asked the source before these questions arise, the respondent can be asked to wait until later in the interview or until the end of the interview for that to be revealed. An explanation of why the respondent is being asked to wait until then should also be given. If the respondent refuses to continue unless he or she is told, then the interview must be terminated. Instructions to interviewers to this effect may appear on the questionnaire, or may be included in their training or in separate instructions.

Web-based surveys can carry a similar promise to reveal the name of the client at the end of the interview if it is thought that not to do so might reduce response rates. For postal surveys, this is not possible.

Cost to respondent

If taking part in the interview is going to cost the respondents anything other than their time, this must be pointed out. In practice it is usually only Internet or Web-based interviews that are likely to incur cost for the respondent (Nancarrow, Pallister and Brace, 2001) and then only if they are paying for their Internet connection on a per-minute basis. Occasionally, though, respondents will be asked to incur travel costs in order to reach a central interviewing venue such as a new product clinic. These costs, though, would normally be reimbursed.

During the interview

Right not to answer

Researchers must always remember that respondents have agreed to take part in the study voluntarily. Should they wish not to answer any of the questions put to them, or to withdraw completely from the interview, they cannot be compelled to do otherwise. Part of the art of the interviewer is to minimize such occurrences by striking up a relationship so that respondents continue for the sake of the interviewer even when they would rather not.

However, if a respondent refuses to answer or continue, then this must be respected.

In Chapter 4 we examined the pros and cons of including 'Not answered/refused' codes at every question and concluded that they should not be included as a matter of course. However, it should be possible to identify the questions that are most likely to be refused and to include a code for refusals as appropriate. Such questions are likely to be the sensitive questions listed above, and personal questions such as income and questions about family relationships.

With paper questionnaires the interview can progress even if a question is not answered, unless an answer is required for routeing purposes.

In Chapter 7 the issue of electronic self-completion questionnaires was discussed and whether or not the researcher should build in an ability to move on to the next question following a refusal to answer. The alternative to allowing this can be that the respondent terminates the interview rather than answer the question. Different research organizations take different views on whether to accept termination of the interview or to provide another mechanism that allows respondents not to answer. Sensitive questions, though, should always include an option not to answer.

Maintaining the interest

It could be considered an ethical issue that respondents must not be put through a process that is boring and tedious.

The ethics of, for example, a telephone survey questionnaire that consists almost entirely of 200 rating scales that would take most people nearly an hour to answer, and on a topic that is of low interest to most respondents, must be questioned. This may be an extreme (although true) example, but questionnaire writers must look out for any tendency towards this.

Creating a boring interview is not just bad questionnaire design, which leads to unreliable data. It is also ethically questionable, fails to treat the respondents with respect, and damages the reputation of market research.

Long and repetitive interviews should be avoided. This sometimes means that the questionnaire writer must find a creative way of asking what would otherwise be repetitive questions. Banks of rating scales, in particular, can cause problems because of the desire to maintain a common format for analysis purposes.

RESPONSIBILITIES TO CLIENTS

Ethical behaviour does not just extend to the relationship between questionnaire writer and respondent, however. The questionnaire writer also has a responsibility to behave ethically towards the client.

Much has been written in previous chapters about designing questions that are unbiased and strive to capture the best and most accurate data. This is not just a matter of good questionnaire design. There is also an ethical and moral duty to provide clients with data that are the best that can be obtained in order to meet their objectives and answer their questions.

The questionnaire writer has an ethical duty to ensure that the questionnaire is fit for the purpose of the study. Deliberately introducing bias in order to support a particular point of view is unethical and is rarely of value to the client's organization.

The client should always be given the opportunity to comment on the questionnaire. Most quality control procedures require that the client signs off the questionnaire as having been agreed. It is the questionnaire writer's responsibility to ensure that the client has sufficient time to consider the questionnaire and any implications for the data to be collected before being asked to agree it.

By implication, questions should not be included to which the client has not agreed. It can be tempting to add questions on a different topic, possibly for a different client, where the sample definition for the two subject areas is the same. It is unethical to do this without the agreement of both clients.

10 Social desirability bias

RESPONSE BIAS

No matter how carefully the questionnaire writer constructs the questions, the data collected are only as accurate as the responses that are elicited. Respondents give inaccurate answers for a number of different reasons. They give inaccurate answers both consciously for reasons of their own, and also without any conscious realization that the information they are giving is inaccurate. The researcher must be aware of these inaccuracies, try to minimize them and, where necessary, take into consideration the bias and inaccuracy in the data.

In Chapter 1 some of these biases were examined, including the problems of memory, inattention by the respondent and deliberate lying. This chapter examines a particular category of response bias known as 'social desirability bias'.

SOCIAL DESIRABILITY BIAS

Social desirability bias (SDB) arises because respondents like to appear to be other than they are. This can occur consciously, because respondents want to manage the impression that they are giving of themselves in terms of social responsibility, or subconsciously, because they believe themselves to be other than they are, possibly a form of denial. Thus SDB can manifest itself both in stated behaviour, with, say, an over-claiming of environmentally friendly behaviour, or in the attitudes that someone expresses.

Sudman and Bradburn (1982: 32–33) identified the following topics as being desirable and therefore areas in which behaviour is likely to be over-reported:

- *Being a good citizen:*
  - registering to vote and voting;
  - interacting with government officials;
  - taking a role in community activities;
  - knowing the issues.
- *Being a well-informed and cultured person:*
  - reading newspapers, magazines and books, and using libraries;
  - going to cultural events such as concerts, plays and exhibitions;
  - participating in educational activities.
- *Fulfilling moral and social responsibilities:*
  - giving to charity and helping friends in need;
  - actively participating in family affairs and child rearing;
  - being employed.

They also quote examples of conditions or behaviour that may be under-reported in an interview:

- *Illness and disabilities:*
  - cancer;
  - venereal diseases;
  - mental illness.
- *Illegal or contranormative behaviour:*
  - committing a crime, including traffic violations;
  - tax evasion;
  - drug use;
  - consumption of alcoholic products;
  - sexual practices.
- *Financial status:*
  - income;
  - savings and other assets.

Until relatively recently, SDB was seen as an issue mainly affecting social research, as the above list suggests. Thus, it has been a problem in health care, where people might claim to lead a healthier lifestyle than is the case. It has been an issue for social researchers in a range of issues such as immigration, attitudes to minority groups, housing, public transport and the environment. If it has affected market researchers, it has been an issue mainly for a small number of specific categories in which there is a perceived element of social responsibility, or perceived social irresponsibility. In certain markets, such as tobacco, alcohol and gambling, both attitudes and behaviour are likely to be misrepresented. Many respondents will deliberately under-report their consumption in these markets in order to appear socially responsible, while others may over-report their consumption, particularly in the alcohol market, in order to appear more 'macho' to the interviewer. Researchers working in these fields have learnt that they cannot ignore SDB as an influence on the data that they collect.

More recently, though, the rise in the association between many types of businesses and the impact that they have on both the physical and social environments has meant that this has become an issue for researchers working in many more fields:

- For consumer goods companies and retailers it can arise with consumer concerns about the impact on the environment of excess or inappropriate packaging.
- The social responsibility of food and confectionery manufacturers to their customers has become a global issue, highlighted by activist groups at economic summit meetings.
- For manufacturers of consumer durables the impact of the disposal of their products can be a social concern.
- Cause-related marketing has been adopted by many organizations in recent years, in which the brand is linked to a good cause, such as supporting schools.
- Issues such as 'fair trade' products arise in individual markets.

It can no longer be assumed that SDB is an issue only for social researchers. Researchers in commercial markets now have to be equally aware of it.

In many areas of commercial market research, if the questionnaire writer and researcher fail to recognize that SDB may be influencing responses, then they may come to false conclusions from the research data.

Types of SDB

Impression management

Possibly the most common form of SDB is the need for approval, known as 'impression management'. This is partly a function of the individual and partly a function of the question, and its occurrence varies depending on a combination of the two. Some people will answer honestly certain questions but will not do so other questions where they feel the need for approval. The questions or topics on which people feel the need for approval may vary between respondents. However, within any one study it is most likely that if impression management occurs, it will do so on a small and consistent set of questions.

Ego defence and self-deception

Maintaining one's own esteem is a further cause of bias. Here respondents' intentions are not to manage the impression that they give to someone else, such as the interviewer or the researcher, but to convince themselves that they think and behave in socially responsible ways. This is less likely to be a conscious activity than is the need for approval, but can result in the same exaggeration of claimed socially responsible behaviour and attitudes. This type of behaviour may particularly affect future projections of likely behaviour, where the respondents convince themselves that they will behave in a responsible fashion in the future even if they do not do so currently. When this is carried out consciously it is known as 'ego defence'; when it is carried out subconsciously it is known as 'self-deception'.

Instrumentation

A further type of bias, and one that is totally conscious, is instrumentation (Nancarrow, Brace and Wright, 2000). This means that respondents give answers designed, in their own view, to bring about a socially desirable outcome. Respondents may say that they will participate in a scheme or purchase a product, for example, although they know that it is unlikely that they will. They do so because they believe the introduction of that scheme or product is desirable. A survey of attitudes to how lottery money should be divided between good causes and lottery administrators may suffer from this effect, for example. Respondents may deliberately give low estimates of the proportion that should be allocated for administration because they believe that if it is seen that the public wants a higher proportion to go to charities this could have an impact on the decisions of the regulatory body. This may be in addition to or in place of impression management, in which the respondent wishes to be seen by the interviewer to be generous to charities. Many respondents are relatively sophisticated with regard to marketing and to market research, and know that they have an opportunity to influence decision making through their responses to the survey.

DEALING WITH SDB

When writing the questionnaire care must be taken to identify question areas that are possible sources of SDB. If the questions ask about attitudes or behaviour on any subject that has a social responsibility component, then consideration should be given to how best to minimize any possible bias. Simply asking respondents to be honest has very little effect (Phillips and Clancy, 1972; Brown, Copeland and Millward, 1973).

Research carried out under the MRS or ESOMAR or CASRO code of conduct should anyway tell respondents that their responses will be treated confidentially. This could be reinforced with a restatement of confidentiality as part of the introduction to the sensitive questions. However, the effect of this appears to be slight (Singer, Von Thurn and Miller, 1995; Dillman *et al*, 1996) or even to reduce the level of cooperation (Singer, Hippler and Schwarz, 1992). This reduction in cooperation could be because the additional emphasis on confidentiality highlights to respondents that the questions are particularly sensitive, and so increases their nervousness about answering them. And, except for self-completion surveys, there is still the interviewer, who will be aware of the responses. Appealing for honesty and assurances of confidentiality are insufficient. Measures that are more positive are therefore required.

Removing the interviewer

With face management, respondents are trying to create an impression that they are more socially responsible than they already are. They may be trying to create that impression for the interviewer or for the unseen researcher. Many respondents will not appreciate that their responses are likely to be seen at an identifiable level by only the interviewer and, if using a paper questionnaire, by the person entering or editing the data. That may not matter in the sense that they just want to be 'known' as responsible people. However, the most obvious person for whom they want to create a good impression is the interviewer. Using a self-completion questionnaire, by removing the interviewer from the interface, should therefore eliminate much, but probably not all, of this particular problem. However, it will not eliminate ego defence/self-deception or instrumentation. Work published on this topic (Lautenschlager and Flaherty, 1990; Booth-Kewley, Edwards and Rosenfeld, 1992) has been inconclusive regarding whether removing the interviewer reduces SDB. More recently, Kellner (2004) reports that in self-completion surveys, both online and paper, only 2 per cent and 3 per cent of respondents claimed to be aware of a fictitious brand of bottled water, compared to 22 per cent in face-to-face interviews and 29 per cent in telephone interviews. This would seem to suggest that removal of the interviewer does remove some pressure on respondents to appear knowledgeable.

Self-completion questionnaires are good to use where the subject is potentially embarrassing for the respondent, and they eliminate much of the bias that would otherwise occur. However, the researcher should be aware that there might be other biases in the data that have not been eliminated. Both mail surveys and Internet-based surveys benefit in this respect, with Internet-based surveys possibly being seen by respondents as the most anonymous form of interview.

Random response technique

The randomized response technique was first developed by Warner (1965). It provides a mechanism for respondents to be truthful about embarrassing or even illegal acts without anyone being able to identify that they have admitted to such an act.

This is achieved because the respondent is presented with two alternative questions, one of which is sensitive and the other not sensitive. No one other than the respondent knows which question has been answered.

To achieve this, two questions with the same set of response codes are presented for self-completion. One of these is the sensitive or threatening question, and the other is the non-threatening and innocuous one. Respondents are allocated to answer one of these questions in a random way, the outcome of which is unknown to the interviewer. This can be by having balls of two different colours in a bag and asking the respondent to draw one out without showing it to the interviewer, or tossing a coin out of sight of the interviewer. However, this can be a cumbersome process in most interview situations.

An alternative method, which would also work in online self-completion interviews, is presented in Figure 10.1. We know from other sources that 17 per cent of the population have their birthday in November or December and, given a sufficiently large sample, we can reasonably apply this proportion.

So, of a sample of 1,000, it can be assumed that 830 will have answered the threatening question and 170 the non-threatening question. Of the 170, half (85) will have answered 'Yes' to the question about their telephone number.

Below, there are two questions with only one place to record the answers. Please answer question A if you were born in November or December, and question B if you were born in any other month of the year. Don't tell me which question you are answering. As I do not know, and will not ask you, which month you were born in, no one will know which question you have answered. Please be honest about which question you answer and how you answer it.

A. TO BE ANSWERED IF YOUR BIRTHDAY IS IN NOVEMBER OR DECEMBER
Does your home telephone number end with an odd-numbered digit, 1, 3, 5, 7, 9? Answer YES if it does, NO if it does not.

B. TO BE ANSWERED IF YOUR BIRTHDAY IS NOT IN NOVEMBER OR DECEMBER
Have you used marijuana at all in the last 12 months?

YES ☐
NO ☐

Figure 10.1   *Random response question example*

If X out of the total sample have answered 'Yes' at all, we can deduce that, of the people who answered the threatening question, $X - 85$ answered 'Yes' to the threatening question. We can therefore arrive at an estimate of the proportion of the population who have used marijuana in the last 12 months, which is $(X - 85)/830$.

It is a risky assumption that respondents are honest, both about which question they choose to answer and about the way in which they answer the threatening question. If people wish to avoid answering the threatening question, they only have to pretend to themselves that their birthday falls when it does not, and there is nothing to stop them simply ignoring the instruction and answering the non-threatening question. Some people may not be convinced that the researcher will not be able to determine which question they have answered and so lie about their behaviour anyway. Whether respondents have either understood or followed the instructions cannot be directly checked. Some may also judge the question to be pointless as they cannot understand how it works. They may then not answer the question or, if they do, not follow the instructions.

It has been shown (Sudman and Bradburn, 1982) that the technique works effectively for subjects that are relatively unthreatening, eg having been involved in a case in a bankruptcy court, but that with more threatening subjects, eg drunken driving, it still significantly underestimates levels of behaviour.

This approach is limited to providing an estimate of the proportions answering 'Yes' and 'No' to the threatening question among the total sample, or among sub-groups that are of sufficiently large sample size for the assumptions regarding the proportions answering the non-threatening question still to hold. As it is not possible to distinguish individual respondents who answered the threatening question, it is not possible to cross-analyse them against any other variables from the survey in order to establish, say, the profile of those who admit to the behaviour and that of those who do not.

What the technique achieves is providing an opportunity for the respondent to answer honestly. This means that, while it addresses 'impression management', it can do nothing about 'self-deception'.

This technique would therefore appear to be a useful, if limited, tool provided that the subject is not too threatening. The difficulty is in determining when a topic is too threatening for this approach to be successful.

Face-saving questions

Face-saving questions give respondents an acceptable way of admitting to socially undesirable behaviour, by including in the question a reason why they might behave in that way. For example, if the questionnaire writer wishes to measure how many people have read the new edition of the Highway Code, instead of asking 'Have you read the latest edition of the *Highway Code*?' the writer could ask 'Have you had time yet to read the latest edition of the *Highway Code*?'

The first question can sound confrontational, with an implication that respondents ought to have read the latest edition and be aware of current driving rules. This can force respondents on to the defensive, or to feel guilty about not having read it, and hence to lie and say that they have read it. The second question carries an assumption that respondents know that they ought to read it and will when they have the time. This is less confrontational, eases any guilt about not having read it and makes it easier for respondents to admit that they have not.

Work carried out in the USA (Holtgraves, Eck and Lasky, 1997) has consistently demonstrated over a series of studies that questions of this type can significantly reduce over-claiming of socially desirable knowledge (eg global warming, health care legislation, trade agreements and current affairs) and reduce under-claiming of socially undesirable behaviour (eg cheating, shoplifting, vandalism, littering). However, the work is inconclusive regarding the impact of such questions when applied to socially desirable behaviour (eg recycling, studying, attending concerts). Questionnaire writers therefore can use this technique confident that it reduces SDB where knowledge is being asked about, or where the task is to get respondents to admit to undesirable behaviour. However, caution should be applied before using this technique to reduce over-claiming of desirable behaviour.

Care must also be taken with face-saving questions so as not to create a truly double-barrelled question. The question 'Do you read a newspaper on a daily basis?' might be expected to lead to over-claiming of a socially desirable behaviour. It would then be replaced with the question 'Do you have the time to read a newspaper on a daily basis?' This, however, now contains two clear elements – reading the newspaper and having the time. Some respondents may answer positively on the grounds that, although they do not read a newspaper daily, they do have the time to do so. Other respondents might give a negative answer because, although they do read a newspaper each day, they do not feel that they have enough time.

Another technique that has the effect of reducing threat in questions of knowledge is to use the phrase 'Do you happen to know…' at the beginning of the question. Rather than ask 'How many kilometres are there in a mile?' or 'Do you know how many kilometres there are in a mile?' the question should be 'Do you happen to know how many kilometres there are in a mile?' This softens the question and makes it less confrontational and has been shown to lead to an increase in the level of 'Don't know' responses, suggesting that respondents find it easier to admit their ignorance rather than guess.

Indirect questioning

A technique sometimes used in qualitative research is not to ask respondents what they think about a subject, but to ask them what they believe other people think. This allows them to put forward views that they would not admit to holding themselves, which can then be discussed. It can sometimes be possible to use a similar technique in a quantitative research questionnaire. However, in qualitative research the group moderator or interviewer can discuss these views and use his or her own judgement as to whether or not respondents hold these views themselves or simply believe that other people hold them.

In quantitative research both the structured nature of the interview and the separation of respondents and researcher make this far more difficult to achieve. The researcher is therefore left with uncertainty as to the proportion of respondents who projected their own feelings and the proportion who honestly reported their judgement of others.

Question enhancements

The questionnaire writer can take a number of other simple steps in order to help minimize SDB.

Reassure that behaviour is not unusual

Where there is a concern that people may misreport their behaviour, statements that certain types of behaviour are not unusual can be built into the question, to reassure respondents that whatever option they choose, their behaviour will be considered by the interviewer or by the researcher to be normal. For example, 'Some people read a newspaper every day of the week, others read a newspaper some days a week, while others never read a newspaper at all. To which of these categories do you belong?'

Extended responses on prompts

In a similar way, extended responses on prompt material can suggest that extreme behaviour is not unusual and encourage honest responses. For example, when asking the amount of alcohol that people drink, the researcher can use prompts with categories that go well beyond normal behaviour, so that categories of mildly heavy drinkers appear midway on the list. This helps heavier drinkers to feel that their consumption might be of a more normal level than it actually is, and they may be more likely to be honest and not under-report. Care needs to be taken not to make light drinkers feel inadequate and so feel forced to over-report their weight of drinking. Having relatively small gradations at the lighter end of the scale, thus helping the lighter drinkers to see that they have more options, can help this (see Figure 10.2).

An alternative approach is to have broad categories, probably no more than three in total, so that respondents do not have to identify the amount too closely.

The second approach is likely to be preferred by respondents because they do not have to specify closely, which they may be reluctant to do either because they do not want to admit it or because they find it difficult to calculate. However, for most research purposes the broad categories supply insufficient data to the researcher for the required analyses.

This approach can be used as a first part of a two-part question. The first question is used to identify which of the three broad categories the respondent falls into and a second question is used to identify the amount more precisely within the category.

Identifying responses by codes

So that respondents do not have to articulate the response to the interviewer, code letters can be used against each of the prompted response categories and the respondent asked to read out the appropriate code letter. Respondents therefore do not have to read aloud the answer,

Using one of the phrases on this list, please tell me how many units of alcohol you drink in an average week.

Approach A	Approach B
None	None
1 to 2 units	1 to 14 units
3 to 5 units	15 to 39 units
6 to 8 units	40 units or more
9 to 12 units	
13 to 17 units	
18 to 24 units	
25 to 34 units	
35 to 54 units	
55 to 74 units	
75 to 94 units	
95 to 134 units	
135 to 184 units	
185 units or more	

Figure 10.2 *Two approaches to categories*

which helps them to feel that a degree of confidentiality is being maintained. The interviewer of course knows to which response category each code applies, but respondent and interviewer do not have to share the information overtly (see Figure 10.3).

Bogus pipeline

One other approach should be mentioned, though it has little application in normal market research surveys: that is the bogus pipeline.

Respondents are physically connected to an apparatus that they are told can detect their true feelings and emotions. There is therefore no point in them not giving wholly truthful responses to the questions asked. This is, of course, not true, and the apparatus is bogus. This approach has been used and has been shown to reduce social desirability bias. There is concern though that, although the technique

ASK ALL IN PAID EMPLOYMENT.

SHOW CARD.

What is your personal annual income before tax or other deductions? Please read out the letter on this card next to the band in which your income falls.

J	UP TO £8,000
N	£8,001 TO £12,000
D	£12,001 TO £16,000
P	£16,001 TO £20,000
W	£20,001 TO £24,000
K	£24,001 TO £35,000
G	£35,001 OR ABOVE

Figure 10.3 *Use of code letters*

does affect responses, it may be because respondents answer more carefully and with more thought rather than because they are trying to be truthful.

However, because of the ethical issues it poses of deceiving members of the public about the capabilities of the apparatus and because of both the difficulty and cost of applying it, this is generally not an appropriate technique to use in market research surveys.

DETERMINING WHETHER SDB EXISTS

It can be difficult to determine whether or not the responses to a question have been influenced by SDB.

Matched cells

One approach to determining whether or not there is a problem is to use one of the techniques described above and to have part of the sample as a control cell that is asked the same question but in a direct form.

The control cell must be matched on all relevant criteria to the rest of the sample and must be sufficiently large to enable reasonably sized differences to be statistically significant. If the responses from the control cell differ significantly from the rest of the sample, then this may confirm that SDB exists and that the questionnaire writer was correct to take the appropriate precautions.

This approach is likely to mean sacrificing a significant part of the sample on the appropriate questions, and the uncertainty resulting if no difference in responses is found. It is unlikely in most commercial studies that this technique can be justified. It is a better use of resources to assume that SDB does exist and to use an appropriate question technique that will minimize it.

Matching known facts

Where it is possible to cross-check responses against known data from other sources, then this can highlight differences that may be due to SDB. The cross-checkable facts will tend to be factual or behavioural data, such as volume of product sold. Attitudinal questions cannot be checked in this way. Even with factual data it is frequently difficult to match external data sources with survey data because of differences in definitions, time periods and so on. Survey data can sometimes provide their own internal cross-checking. Pantry checks, to see what is actually in a respondent's store cupboard, can be used as a check against what the respondent has previously claimed to be there.

It has been suggested that, to check the level of SDB in attitudinal data, friends of the respondents might be interviewed and asked to evaluate their perceptions of the respondents' attitudes. This seems fraught with difficulties regarding both the accuracy of the friends' evaluations and their motivations. The scale and complexity of such a study is, anyway, likely to make it impracticable for commercial market research projects (Sudman and Bradburn, 1982).

Checking against measures with known SDB

For attitudinal questions it is possible to design a battery of scales that measure a sample's tendency to SDB. Such a battery would include: behaviours that are common (majority of the population) and socially undesirable; and behaviours that are not common (minority of the population) but are socially desirable.

Consistently low scores on the first group (indicating low levels of undesirable behaviour) and a high score on the second (indicating high levels of desirable behaviour) would suggest that the respondent either falls into a small and angelic minority of the population or that SDB exists in the responses. Individual respondents with these response patterns can be identified, and if on another topic the sample has a higher-than-expected level of claimed desirable behaviour or a lower level of claimed undesirable behaviour, then the researcher knows that there is an SDB problem with the sample as a whole.

There are several published batteries of scales to help the questionnaire writer, including the Edwards (1957), Crowne–Marlowe (1960) and Paulhus (Paulhus and Reid, 1991) batteries of scales. In addition, shortened versions of the Crowne–Marlowe scale have been tested by Strahan and Gerbasi (1972) and by Greenwald and Satow (1970) that may be more suited to market research interviews.

Rating the question for social desirability

Questions can be included that directly ask the respondents to assess the attitude or behaviour for social desirability (Phillips and Clancy, 1972). This can indicate the relative problem between different scales or questions. However, there must be doubt about whether such questions do not suffer from SDB themselves.

Noting physiological manifestations of unease

It is likely that there will be physiological signs that a respondent is trying to mislead an interviewer, such as facial muscle movement, galvanic skin response and pupil dilation. However, interpreting these even in laboratory conditions is problematic and outside of laboratory conditions is likely to be impossible and outside of the skill set of most market research interviewers.

It will be seen that there are few ways of eliminating SDB with certainty. However, if researchers recognize the possibility or even probability of its existence, this may help them to design questionnaires that minimize its occurrence and to avoid misinterpretation of the data.

11 International surveys

INTRODUCTION

This chapter looks at the issues facing international surveys. The term 'international' is used to mean a study that is being carried out in one or more countries different to that of the originator. This can include multinational studies that cover many countries, or it could be a study in one country only.

International surveys encounter all of the issues discussed in previous chapters, together with a number of problems that do not arise when the study covers only the home country of the researcher. In the home country, the questionnaire writer should understand the conventions, nuances and subtleties of the language that are used in that country. They might not, though, understand these issues in another country, even though it uses the same language.

There are many issues regarding coordination of fieldwork and analysis that will not be gone into in depth here, except in so far as they impinge upon the writing of the questionnaire. Similarly, reporting issues will not be discussed in detail here.

Where an international study has been conducted for a number of years, the questionnaire is likely to be already written, tried and trusted in all of the appropriate languages. Similarly with proprietary techniques administered by research companies, the wording of questions will be largely predetermined and is likely to have been tested in most major languages. However, the survey coordinator should still be aware of the issues relating to questionnaires in multiple languages, as there are invariably some variations between every study. If these variations are mishandled or mistranslated, they could jeopardize the remainder of the study.

CLIENT PRESENCE

If you are conducting a multinational study, then it is possible that the commissioning organization, or client, has a presence in most if not all of the countries that are to be covered. However, the extent and expertise of that presence may differ between countries, depending on the size and the nature of their operation there. If the research is to assist in determining whether or not the client should enter the country, then there may be no presence.

This is significant because the extent of the client's knowledge of each country and its market will affect the information that the questionnaire writer has about each country, and how it is similar to or different from the same market in other countries.

With a strong presence in each country it is likely that much is already known about the market, and certain assumptions can be made when writing the questionnaire. If little is known, then the questionnaire may need to be more open in the way it addresses topics, because of the danger of making wrong assumptions.

The amount that is known about each market will have an impact on the way in which the same approach can be adopted across countries.

COMMON OR TAILORED APPROACHES

When faced with the prospect of conducting a study across a number of countries the first issue is whether to write a separate questionnaire for each country or a single questionnaire that varies only on items such as brand lists.

This can only be answered by examining the objectives of the study and the known or likely differences between the markets. Downham (Worcester and Downham, 1978) lists the following differences that can have an effect upon the questionnaire:

- *Language.* There may be different languages not only between countries but also within countries. Is it necessary to include all minority languages in all countries? Apparently common languages may have different usages, eg English in the UK and the USA.
- *Ethnic differences.* Different ethnic groups may speak different languages. Where they don't, they may have different consumer habits and attitudes.
- *Religion.* This may be associated with ethnic differences, but may have implications for attitudes, lifestyle, and consumption of products such as alcohol and meat, for which different questions will be required both to make sense and not to offend.
- *Culture and tradition.* It would be wrong to ignore cultural differences, and questions must allow for the machismo culture in some Latin countries, the issue of 'face' in the Far East, and the different levels of importance given to gifting in different cultures.
- *Literacy.* Literacy levels vary between countries, and even official statistics can overstate it. Low literacy levels among the sample mean that aids such as verbal prompt material cannot be used, let alone self-completion questionnaires.
- *Geography and climate.* Differences in climate can mean that product usage patterns are different, particularly with regard to food products that are suited to either a warmer or cooler climate, such as butter and olive oil. Issues such as water hardness can also create different usage patterns for the same product.
- *Institutional factors.* Different market backgrounds often require different questions to be asked. Baths are more common than showers in some countries but rarely taken in others; approaches to clothes washing, savings and credit cards all vary between countries for reason of history and market development.
- *Distribution.* Supermarkets, hypermarkets and shopping malls dominate distribution of many goods in some countries but are unknown in others, where different questions may be needed.
- *Media and advertising.* The media that carry advertising vary between countries, and, even more so, the access to the media may vary.

To this list can be added:

- *Infrastructure.* Different infrastructures may have an impact on usage and attitudes. The greater use of communal heating systems in some countries than others, different transport systems, different stages of development in telecommunications, and different approaches to health care may all affect the way in which the questionnaire is written for different countries.

It may be relatively easy to have a common format for a brand awareness and image study in the pasta sauce market across a number of European countries, for example. The same spontaneous and prompted brand awareness questions can be used, and the same format used to determine brand images. The brand list will almost certainly vary between countries in most markets and the image dimensions measured may need sensitive adaptation, but the structure of the questionnaire can remain the same. There are a number of reasons, though, why the questionnaire approach may need to be different.

Different usage of product

In some product fields and markets a study may require completely different approaches for different countries. Some products are used in completely different ways in different parts of the world. For example, milk-based products that are used as night-time drinks in Europe are frequently used as aphrodisiacs or body-building products in parts of Africa and the West Indies, and razor blades are used to shear sheep in some parts of the world. It is unlikely that a single questionnaire could be used that would adequately describe the usage patterns of these products in all regions.

Different market segments

Market segments that exist in one country may not exist in another. Low and mid-priced Scotch whisky segments, which can account for the majority of the market in Western countries, may not exist in some Asian countries where only luxury brands are available. The usage questions and image dimensions that are appropriate for a market segment with a strong mid-priced segment of many brands may not be of any use in countries where the competitive set is not just Scotch but other high-priced luxury drinks.

Brands in different segments

Brands may be in different segments in different countries. This can happen in any market and is quite likely to happen in countries where distributors are used who are independent of the manufacturer and who have historically been given the authority to position the brand as they wish. Brands that in one country would be considered mid-priced may elsewhere be luxury brands. Good market data and local knowledge should identify this type of problem.

For most clients and researchers, the more the same questions can be asked in all countries under study, the easier it is to manage, analyse and report the study and the more likely it is that the client can adopt a common marketing approach. There can therefore sometimes be considerable pressure on the survey designer and questionnaire writer to adopt a common approach and set of questions. The client may want to adopt a common marketing strategy, but the researcher would not be doing his or her job if the client was led to believe that the markets possessed only a number of common characteristics and was left unaware of the differences because they were not asked about.

The biggest danger is the assumption that because a questionnaire has been used successfully in one country it can be used in any country.

Comparability

Where a common research approach is adopted across countries, then, there are many reasons to try to make the questionnaires, and hence the data output, as comparable as possible. Downham (Worcester and Downham, 1978) again suggests that:

- time and money are saved by using a standardized approach;
- life is simplified for the researcher;
- end-users often have greater confidence in a standardized approach, rather than one that has many variations;
- absolute uniformity is essential in some cases, particularly in the data required for the technical development of products.

Having a common questionnaire is also likely to lead to fewer errors in survey administration than if there are a number of different ones.

Given these reasons, most organizations would agree that a standardized questionnaire is always preferable and should be used unless there are good reasons that can be demonstrated why it would not be suitable for a particular country or group of countries.

One approach to writing questionnaires for a multi-country study is to start by writing the questionnaire with one country in mind. Once that has been refined, it should be tested for its appropriateness in every country in which it is to be used, even those sharing a common language. Amendments should then be made in order to accommodate differences between markets. This may require changes only in the brand lists, but it may also require changes in image dimensions, advertising media and prompts used, methods of distribution in the market, absolute prices, relative prices, the competitive product set, frequency of use bands, or completely different behavioural questions. The researcher reaches a point where the changes are so significant that it becomes a different questionnaire.

Coordinating common elements

Even if a study is able to use a standard questionnaire across a number of different countries, there will nearly always be minor variations to be accommodated.

Brand lists

Almost invariably the brand list will change in most consumer markets. There may be local brands that are available only in that country or region, and the multinational companies may sell different brands in different countries. Some brands of Scotch whisky, for example, are sold only in the Asia Pacific region. Others only have a significant level of distribution in a small number of European countries. The brand list in many product sectors is unlikely to be the same in any two countries.

The questionnaire writer needs to be aware of these differences, which will affect the brand lists used both as pre-codes and as prompts for questions such as brand awareness, purchase and usage.

Brand image

Brand image questions are frequently asked of a small number of brands deemed to be important either in the market or in the direct competitive set to the client's brand. Even if the long list of brands available is similar in two countries, the short list of brands that are the most relevant to be asked about in image and brand-positioning questions may vary between countries.

Frequently the client will be able to advise on the appropriate brands for each country both for the long and the short lists. This may come from the company's marketing plans for each country and from the company's office or representatives or distributors. It is always worthwhile to check the list with local representatives, who may be aware of new local brands that have not yet made it into the company's global marketing strategy. It is also worthwhile for the research agency to ask its own representatives in each country for their views on the brand lists, for the same reason.

Image dimensions

Frequently the objective is to produce a single, global, brand image map on which variations between countries can be plotted. If insufficient care is taken in choosing the image dimensions relevant to each country, this can result in a misleading picture being produced for some countries because the brand position has been measured using a set of image dimensions developed for a different country and a different competitive brand set.

To achieve the ideal set of image dimensions the researcher should determine all the relevant image dimensions for each country, bearing in mind that the positioning and the competitors could be different. A preliminary stage of qualitative research to explore the way in which consumers in each country perceive the market and the brands in it can be used to give the most appropriate image dimensions for each country. For studies across many countries, however, this is frequently too costly and time-consuming to carry out. Findings from qualitative research that has already been conducted in a country for other purposes can often be used to provide a consumer-led picture of the market structure and brand perceptions. If that does not exist, reliance will sometimes be placed on qualitative research carried out in a few countries that are thought to be representative of a group of countries. Where this occurs, it is particularly important to pilot the questionnaire in the countries in which no qualitative research was carried out.

However it is arrived at, a distillation of all relevant image attributes across the countries in the study can be compiled to form a 'master set' of image dimensions.

If the intention is to use a technique such as correspondence analysis to produce a global map, then all image dimensions may have to be used in all countries regardless of their relevance. There is a danger that the list, in trying to accommodate the key points for each country without becoming overlong, will contain too many compromises. While it will provide a global overview, it will not be sufficiently detailed to provide an accurate positioning in any one country. Supplementary questions specific to each country may be required for that to be achieved.

Attitudinal questions

Attitudinal questions can sometimes be difficult in maintaining comparability between countries. Not only may consumers have different attitudes to a market or product area in different countries, but what is important to them in arriving at those attitudes may also be completely different.

Frequently, the attitude dimensions to be measured should be the same in each country, although with the expectation that response patterns will be very different between countries. If a battery of attitudinal rating scales is to be used, the wording of each dimension must be appropriate for each country, and care must be taken to avoid offence, in relation to both cultural and religious attitudes.

TRANSLATING THE QUESTIONNAIRE

Accurate translations are, of course, essential. But an accurate translation is not simply one that is literally accurate. Translations must be carried out sensitively so that meanings, shades of meaning and nuances are accurately retained.

Possibly the most difficult to translate are brand image and positioning statements and attitude dimensions. There may be fine but clear distinctions in one language that cannot be translated into another. In English there is a clear difference of understanding between 'old-fashioned' and 'traditional'. In some languages this distinction cannot be made. Other words for which there may be no direct equivalent in certain languages include 'arrogant', 'rigid', 'proud' and 'ordinary'.

The word 'warm' is frequently used as a brand image descriptor in English, to describe the warmth and affection of the relationship between brand and consumer. However, it is not infrequently translated into other languages as something equivalent to 'mildly hot'.

Even interviewer instructions can be ruined by a translator who is too literal, and inexperienced in the language of market research. The instruction to 'Skip to Q5' has been seen translated as 'Run to Q5', and 'Probe fully' turned into an instruction to poke the respondent with a stick.

For all of these reasons initial translations should be carried out by people who understand the research process and the importance of capturing the sentiment rather than a literal translation. Oppenheim (1992) quotes the case where a question asking whether a house had 'running water', although translated literally into other languages, was taken in some countries to mean having a stream or river running through the house. Wright and Crimp (2000) quote how 'out of sight, out of mind' became 'invisible, insane' in Mandarin Chinese.

Using native speakers

There are a number of different routes to achieving a good translation. Probably the most important step is for the first translation to be carried out by a native speaker of the language who also understands the research process. Native speakers are the most likely to understand the nuances of the language as they are understood by other native speakers. Many multinational research companies employ multilingual research executives or other members of staff who are from other countries.

However, native speakers living abroad may, depending on how long they have lived there, be out of touch with changes in the language as it is spoken locally. Subtle changes of meaning can occur with fashion or with a new usage. It is therefore important to have the translation checked by someone living in the country. The most likely candidate for this is someone in the agency that is going to be responsible for the fieldwork, provided that the person also has a good knowledge of the language in which the questionnaire was originally written.

A study is at a disadvantage if there is no fieldwork to be carried out locally, because it is being carried out online or by telephone from another country, as there is then a lack of opportunity for local input.

For such studies, it is worth finding someone resident in the country who will check the translation for usage of current language. This is becoming an increasingly common issue, with the growing use of multi-country and multi-language Web-based Internet studies. The multinational research companies, with offices around the world on which they can call for this, have an advantage in this respect.

Using the client's representative

If possible, the local representative of the client in each country should also check the translation. Local representatives may have had direct or indirect input to the questionnaire writer's understanding of the structure of the market in the country. They should be aware of any variations in technical terminology relating to the local market that the research-led translator may not know about. It may also be important to get local representatives' 'buy-in' to the questionnaire, if they are going to be responsible for implementing action that arises as a result of the research project. If they are not happy with the questionnaire, they may be less willing to implement the study's findings. However, be aware that local representatives may try to influence the wording of questions for their own purposes.

Back-translation

Finally, the questionnaire should be back-translated into the original language. This can show up changes in meaning, although it has to be determined whether they arise from the original translation or from the back-translation.

The process described here is what should ideally happen. However, it is quite possible for some of these steps to be omitted, depending on the ability of the translators and whether the question-naire has been used before.

It must not be overlooked that in some countries translation into a number of different languages and dialects will be required. Advice should be taken from the local client and research organizations as to how many and which languages are required. In a country such as India, for example, this can be a complex issue.

DEMOGRAPHIC DATA

One area that often causes difficulty is the classification of demographic data. Many countries subscribe to a social-grade classification system, which uses a grouping system described as A, B, etc. There the similarity often ends, with the number of groups and their definitions differing widely. The UK has a six-grade system (A, B, C1, C2, D, E), Ireland a seven-grade system (A, B, C1, C2, D, E, F) and India an eight-grade system (A1, A2, B1, B2, C, D, E1, E2). Many developing countries have no commonly acknowledged system of social-grade classification, and local researchers may all have their own approach. Level of education may be used as a surrogate for social grading or to complement it, but education systems similarly vary between countries. Terminal education age is something that can be measured in a consistent way between countries, but its implications are likely to be very different.

Alternatively, a measurement of living standards can be obtained by asking about ownership of durables. That too must be tailored to the local situation. Ownership of a moped, fridge or television might indicate a very different level of social grade in, say, Vietnam and Germany.

CULTURAL RESPONSE DIFFERENCES

In some cultures, people are more prepared to criticize than in others. In India, for example, it is considered rude to be critical of someone else's work. Responses to rating scales therefore tend to be more positive than in many other countries. Within Europe, as a rule people in Latin countries will tend to give higher ratings than in Nordic countries.

Corrections can be introduced to allow for this at the analysis stage.

Some researchers, though, prefer to address the issue in the questionnaire, particularly where there are strong differences because the study includes both Western and Asiatic countries. One way is to use scales that have positive responses only. Thus a scale might run from 'very good' to 'fair', or a set of smiley faces might have five positive smiles of different sizes and no frowns or negative smiles. Alternatively, scales can be extended to 10 or 11 points with five positive responses to increase the discrimination, or extended numeric scales can be used to try to minimize the sense of criticizing by avoiding negative words.

Another approach, cited by Wable and Pall (1998), is to use a 'warm-up' statement that distances the researcher from the product or advertisement being researched, so allowing the respondent to feel more able to criticize. This is a technique commonly used in qualitative research that they have transferred to quantitative questionnaires. They quote a typical warm-up as: 'I would like your frank opinion about this ad. You don't have to necessarily say nice things about it. Please feel free to give us any positive or negative opinion. We have not made this ad, so we will not feel bad if you don't have nice things to say about it.' They have shown that in India this has a measurable effect in reducing the level of positive comment, although it is not known whether it is sufficient to make the results directly comparable with all other countries.

LAYING OUT THE QUESTIONNAIRE

Where paper questionnaires are to be used the issue arises of how differences between the layouts can be minimized. This is generally desirable if the questionnaire is broadly common to all countries.

Layout conventions

However, it is also important that local agencies use their own layout conventions where these differ. Mistakes are more likely to be made by interviewers if they are presented with an unfamiliar layout. Where a coordinating agency e-mails a laid-out questionnaire to the local agency, it may be necessary to instruct the local agency staff to lay it out in their own format. Because it is easy to use the coordinating agency's file and simply type over the text in the local language, the interviewers may be presented with a completely unfamiliar style of layout. A further disadvantage of this is that the local agency executives do not become as familiar with the questionnaire as they would have done if they had had to lay it out for themselves. They are then less likely both to spot unsuitable wordings and to be able to answer questions that may arise in the field.

Question numbering

A common question numbering scheme helps comparisons to be made easily for the same questions across countries. When the same question is being referred to there is a potential source of error if that question has a different number in each country. Checking of routeing instructions is also more straightforward if the same question numbers are used. However, a common question numbering scheme can mean that some question numbers are not used in some versions of the questionnaire. For example, where an additional question needs to be asked in one country only, that question number will not appear on questionnaires for all the other countries in the study. This must be clearly marked on the questionnaires or it can cause confusion amongst interviewers. If there are so many missing question numbers that it creates difficulties for the interviewers to follow instructions, then consideration must be given to abandoning common question numbering for the sake of minimizing interviewer error.

Similar issues arise where manual data entry utilizes a column-based format. In order to minimize data-processing errors, a common column-number and response code format is desirable. That decision, though, needs to be balanced against the likelihood of it leading to data entry errors.

Appendix 1:
Example
questionnaire

INTRODUCTION

The following, fictitious, case study is designed to demonstrate some of the techniques used in questionnaire design. The questionnaire has been written for this purpose rather than to meet precisely the objectives of the study, and deliberately includes examples of poor practice. It therefore should not be taken as a template for this particular type of project.

The output includes a flow diagram to show how the questionnaire is constructed, a discussion of each question, and the questionnaire itself. A copy of the paper questionnaire together with electronic examples of the questionnaire and a link to the Web site containing the Web-based version of the questionnaire is contained on the CD ROM that accompanies this book.

Setting the scene

Crianlarich Scotch Whisky is positioned as a brand for the off-trade, ie to be sold through off-licences and supermarkets and drunk principally at home. It has recently launched a marketing initiative to break into the on-trade business. The company is planning a press advertising campaign in England and Wales that will run for six months, appearing in a variety of newspapers and magazines. The aim of the campaign is to back a marketing initiative where pubs and bars are being encouraged to sell Crianlarich.

It is sold as a cheaper brand on the proposition that it is the brand drunk by the Scots, which is believed to be a key motivator of brand choice in this market, although this has not previously been researched. The main competition is thought to be Grand Prix (another fictitious brand), which is expected to be advertising at the same time as Crianlarich.

The company wishes to conduct a study that will measure the position of the brand in the market and provide feedback on the success of the advertising campaign.

A pre-post advertising study has been designed. The research sample definition is all adults who have drunk whisky in the past month and who drink it at least once every three months.

The objectives of the research are defined by the Marketing Director of Crianlarich as:

- to determine awareness of Crianlarich;
- to determine whether awareness of the brand changes over the course of the advertising campaign;
- to determine the perceptions of the brand on key product and image dimensions, and any change in those perceptions over the course of the advertising campaign;
- to determine the importance of the brand's key advertising proposition, that it is a brand drunk by Scots;
- to measure all of the above among both light and heavy off-trade Scotch whisky drinkers.

The same questionnaire will be used at both pre-advertising and post-advertising stages of research. The pre-advertising stage will provide an initial measure of the brand's position prior to the campaign and the post-advertising stage a measure of how that has changed over the period of the advertising.

Questionnaire planning

To meet the objectives, the key measures that we need to establish are:

▓ *Spontaneous brand awareness of Crianlarich and key competitors.* This tells us how 'front of mind' the brand is compared to other brands. As one of the objectives of the campaign is to improve awareness, this will be an important measure to compare before and after the campaign.

▓ *Prompted brand awareness for Crianlarich and key competitors.* This measure relates to how well known the brand is, and tells us how many people in the market have still not heard of it. This is an important measure for new brands in a market, as they establish recognition. For established brands prompted brand awareness is already likely to be high and so unlikely to change greatly over the course of a single campaign.

▓ *Brand image perceptions.* These need to be related to the objectives of the campaign, so that we can measure any change in image perceptions over the campaign period. They need to be measured for Crianlarich and five other brands, including several brands that are more expensive. The purpose of measuring so many other brands is so that we can map the market and determine whether or not consumers perceive Crianlarich and Grand Prix, the brand we believe to be its closest competitor, as a sector distinct from the leading brands. The approaches to be considered are:

  – monadic rating of brands either on semantic differential or Likert (agree–disagree) scales;
  – brand image association.

The brand image association technique is adopted because it is less time-consuming with this number of brands. A rating scale approach would have allowed only three brands to be rated by each respondent, Crianlarich and two competitors. Thus the competitor brands would have to have been rotated between respondents and measured on a reduced sample size, which we want to avoid.

▓ We could derive the importance of the image dimensions to brand choice by correlation analysis. However, we want to be able to cross-analyse respondents to whom price is an important factor in their choice in order to determine their attitudes to and level of use of Crianlarich. A direct approach is therefore to be used. A constant sum allocation of 11 points between two dimensions has been chosen.

▓ Behavioural information regarding weight of drinking both on- and off-licence, and whether the respondent is influential in brand choice, is required for analysis purposes. Which brand or brands are bought is also required, for measurement, to see if it changes over the course of the campaign, and for analysis purposes.

■ Awareness of Crianlarich advertising needs to be measured at a number of different levels, to determine whether or not respondents have seen or have remembered the advertising. How well the advertisement is branded will be measured by showing an unbranded ad for Crianlarich and for a competitor as a benchmark.

The question areas appear in the following order:

■ screening questions;
■ spontaneous brand awareness;
■ spontaneous brands recall seeing advertised;
■ prompted brand awareness;
■ advertising awareness prompted by brand name;
■ advertising source and content recall;
■ behavioural information – where drunk, brands bought or specified, amount drunk;
■ importance of image factors in brand choice;
■ brand image associations;
■ recognition of unbranded ads, with branding question;
■ classification data.

Spontaneous awareness questions are asked first, before there has been any prompting of brand names. Behavioural questions come before brand image questions to avoid any tendency to distort behaviour in line with image perceptions. Showing advertising material comes last, to avoid influencing responses to the brand image questions.

EXAMPLE QUESTIONNAIRE

Screening questionnaire

The wording used here is that for the paper and CAPI questionnaires. Wording for the Web-based questionnaire has some variations.

The paper questionnaire is columnated for data entry to an analysis program that uses a column-based format. While common in market research, this type of analysis format is not universal.

Good morning/afternoon/evening. I am (interviewer name) from Acme Surveys, a market research company. I am carrying out a survey about alcoholic drinks. The interview will take about 15 minutes to complete, and is carried out in accordance with the Code of Conduct of the Market Research Society.

QA. SHOW CARD A.
Do you or anybody in your household work in any of the industries or professions on this card?
ACCOUNTANCY
ADVERTISING*
COMPUTERS OR INFORMATION TECHNOLOGY
MARKETING/MARKET RESEARCH*
ALCOHOLIC DRINK PRODUCTION OR RETAILING*
BANKING OR INSURANCE
GROCERY RETAILING
NONE OF THESE

IF ANY CODED *, THANK AND CLOSE.

QA is the security question designed to screen out anyone who works, or whose household members work, in key industries, as their responses could distort responses from those of the research universe as a whole or because knowledge of the content of the survey could provide a competitive advantage.

Although we are only interested in screening out people in the three asterisked industries, a range of other industries are also offered. This disguises our interest somewhat, although as we have already said that the survey is about alcoholic drinks this is less than perfect. Just as importantly, it provides something to respond to for people who do not work in the three sensitive industries. Some people, trying to be helpful, may bend the truth somewhat and claim to have connections with one of whatever options are offered, no matter how distant or tenuous the link. Without the alternatives, they are more likely to be screened out unnecessarily, and an interview lost.

QB. SHOW CARD B.
Which of the products on this card have you drunk in the last three months either in licensed premises such as a restaurant, pub or bar, or at home or anywhere else?
ALE

LAGER
STOUT
WINE
GIN
SCOTCH WHISKY
IRISH WHISKEY
NONE OF THESE

IF SCOTCH WHISKY CONTINUE.
IF SCOTCH WHISKY NOT DRUNK, THANK AND CLOSE.

QB is the first of the screening questions proper. Again our specific interest is disguised by offering a range of drinks that might have been consumed. If we asked 'Do you drink Scotch whisky?', this would allow potential respondents to second-guess our purpose and answer on the basis that they believed they were screening themselves in or out of eligibility rather than on actual behaviour.

The list offered is not extensive or exhaustive. This is because Scotch whisky may be an irregular or occasional drink for some of our research universe. If given too many options, these people may think of their more frequently consumed drinks first and fail to mention Scotch whisky. This would result in under-representation of light Scotch whisky drinkers in the sample.

Irish whiskey is included in the list shown. This is to ensure that drinkers of only Irish whiskey do not think that the term 'Scotch whisky' is meant to cover all types of whisky and so claim to drink it when they do not.

QC. SHOW CARD C.
Which of the phrases on this card best describes how often you drink Scotch whisky?
MOST DAYS
AT LEAST ONCE A WEEK
AT LEAST ONCE A MONTH
AT LEAST ONCE EVERY THREE MONTHS
AT LEAST ONCE EVERY SIX MONTHS
LESS OFTEN THAN ONCE EVERY SIX MONTHS

IF SCOTCH WHISKY DRUNK AT LEAST ONCE EVERY THREE MONTHS CONTINUE.
IF SCOTCH WHISKY DRUNK LESS OFTEN THAN ONCE EVERY THREE MONTHS THANK AND CLOSE.

QC is an example of a scale question. Our interest is in determining whether the respondent drinks Scotch whisky more or less often than once every three months. The question could ask that directly. We don't use a direct question, partly again to disguise the precise point of our interest in order to stop people trying to opt in or out of the survey. Here, though, the subject matter could lead to some social desirability bias. Later in the interview we shall ask in more detail about how much respondents drink, and the tendency may be for heavier drinkers deliberately to understate their consumption. The categories shown in this question already begin to suggest that drinking Scotch whisky several times a week is acceptable, hopefully encouraging heavier drinkers to be honest later on.

Main questionnaire

Q1. What brands of whisky can you think of? Please name as many as you can think of. DO NOT PROMPT.
RECORD BRAND FIRST MENTIONED SEPARATELY.

BELLS
CHIVAS REGAL
CRIANLARICH
FAMOUS GROUSE
GLENFIDDICH
GLENMORANGIE
GRAND PRIX
J&B
JACK DANIELS
JOHNNIE WALKER RED LABEL
JOHNNIE WALKER BLACK LABEL
JOHNNIE WALKER UNSPECIFIED
TEACHERS
WHYTE & MACKAY
VAT 69
OTHER ANSWERS (WRITE IN)
NONE

This is a spontaneous question with no prompting. The interviewer is reminded not to prompt.

We are not interested in the precise wording used by respondents to describe the brands. If someone says 'Grand Prix', then that is all we need to know about what they have said. Therefore, the question does not have to be open-ended with verbatim recording of answers, and a pre-coded list can be supplied. This makes recording easier for the interviewer and for later processing of the data. The pre-coded list contains all of the brands that we believe are the most likely to be given. However, many more brands exist than we are able to put on the list, so space is provided for the interviewer to write in any others mentioned.

The brand Johnnie Walker has two main sub-brands – Red Label and Black Label. Respondents may specify the sub-brands or they may say just 'Johnnie Walker'. There is no prompting at this question so if someone says just 'Johnnie Walker' without specifying the sub-brand, we must accept that. A code is provided for that eventuality.

The first brand that is mentioned is recorded separately from the remaining brands. The respondent is not told this. By recording in this way we can provide a 'top-of-mind' measure as well as a measure of total spontaneous awareness.

A code is provided for 'None' but not for 'Don't know', as a 'Don't know' answer would mean 'None' in the context of this question.

Note the inclusion of Jack Daniels, which is not a Scotch whisky. We know from experience that a significant number of respondents will say this, even though it is incorrect. It is therefore included partly in order to monitor the level of misattribution, and partly to reduce the amount of coding that would be incurred if it were to be written in under 'Other answers'.

Note that for face-to-face interviews where the respondent cannot see the questionnaire we can use pre-codes in spontaneous questions; however, for Web-based questionnaires we have to treat spontaneous brand/advertising awareness questions as open-ended and ask the respondent to type in an answer.

Q2. Which brands of whisky have you seen or heard advertised anywhere recently?

This is another spontaneous question and uses the same list of pre-codes as Q1.

There are three key phrases in this question. The phrase 'seen or heard' is used and not just 'seen'. Including the word 'heard' allows respondents to include radio advertising, which might otherwise be excluded from their consideration. Advertising recall tends to be dominated by television. Including the word 'anywhere' indicates to the respondent that the advertising could have been in any media. We might have considered including the phrase 'on television or anywhere else' in place of 'anywhere', specifically to encourage respondents to think of other media. However, there is a limited amount of Scotch whisky advertising on television and this might have had the opposite effect of drawing attention to the few brands that do use that medium. The word 'recently' leaves it to respondents to define the time period to which the question refers. This can be dangerous, as some respondents may take it to mean the last six months and others the last week. However, most respondents will try to think of all the advertising for Scotch whisky that is stored in their mind, which usually (but not always) excludes anything that is very old.

Q3. SHOW CARD D.
Which of the brands of whisky on this card have you heard of? Please include any that you have already mentioned.
BELLS
CHIVAS REGAL
CRIANLARICH
FAMOUS GROUSE
GLENFIDDICH
GLENMORANGIE
GRAND PRIX
JOHNNIE WALKER RED LABEL
JOHNNIE WALKER BLACK LABEL
TEACHERS
WHYTE & MACKAY
NONE OF THESE

Here we are seeking prompted brand awareness. A shortened list of brands is used, consisting mainly of the brands in which we are principally interested as competitors to Crianlarich. Note that Jack Daniels is not included, although is in the list of pre-codes for the spontaneous question. The prompt list includes the most salient brands in the market, whether or not they are seen as direct competitors. If these were omitted, respondents might over-claim awareness of smaller brands in order to appear knowledgeable.

The brand list on the show card will be rotated between respondents or, more likely, between interviewers in face-to-face interviewing. It should be rotated four ways, so that the brands in the middle of the list are also presented at the beginning and end in some versions, in order to equalize the primacy and recency effects. On the Web-based questionnaire the order will be presented in a random order for each respondent.

Note that respondents are asked to include any brands that they have already mentioned. Without this reminder many will not mention brands that they have already mentioned. This is not necessarily a problem, as responses can be edited or recoded from the spontaneous question at the analysis stage. However, in this case, we need to take into account those who answered 'Johnnie Walker' at Q1 without specifying a sub-brand. Having given 'Johnnie Walker' once they may not say it again, but we want to encourage them to specify the sub-brands if they are aware of them.

Q4. SHOW CARD D.
Which of the brands of whisky on this card have you seen or heard advertised anywhere recently? Again please include any that you have already mentioned.

This is similar to Q3, this time asking for awareness of advertising. This question acts as a filter to route respondents to the following questions.

Q5. IF CRIANLARICH MENTIONED AT Q4
Where did you see or hear advertising for Crianlarich?
CINEMA
DIRECT MAIL SHOT
INTERNET
MAGAZINE
NEWSPAPER (INCLUDING MAGAZINE SUPPLEMENT)
RADIO
TELEVISION
OTHER
DON'T KNOW

This question is asked only of respondents who claim to have seen or heard advertising for Crianlarich at Q4. With the paper questionnaire the interviewer must follow this instruction. With the electronic questionnaires the routeing will be specified to occur automatically.

The question is not prompted in the face-to-face interview, although a list of pre-codes is supplied, but is prompted in the Web interview. This is to avoid using too many open-ended questions in the Web interview, unless they are clearly necessary (eg brand and advertising awareness). The fact that the question is not spontaneous for the Web interview may encourage respondents to code more answers, as the pre-code list jogs their memory and suggests where they may have seen or heard advertising.

In all cases there is a potential ambiguity in the response list, which must be avoided. Many newspapers include a magazine supplement once a week. If the response list included only 'Magazines' and 'Newspapers' it would be unclear as to where newspaper magazines should be coded. By including 'Newspaper (including magazine supplement)' we hope to avoid that ambiguity.

Q6. IF CRIANLARICH MENTIONED AT Q4
Please describe to me everything that you can remember about the advertising for Crianlarich. PROBE: What was it about? What did it say or show? PROBE: What else?

At Q6 we are seeking both to confirm that what the respondent remembers really was advertising for Crianlarich and was not for another brand, and to determine what the salient points are that have consciously remained with the respondent, in terms of either content or message. We should also consider whether we want to include a specific question to ask what was the main point or message the advertising was trying to convey, in case this is not elicited under probing here.

This is an open question with the answers recorded verbatim. Face to face, the interviewers will record these; on the Web, the respondents must type in the response for themselves.

Q7. IF GRAND PRIX MENTIONED AT Q4
Where did you see or hear advertising for Grand Prix?
CINEMA
DIRECT MAIL SHOT
INTERNET
MAGAZINE
NEWSPAPER (INCLUDING MAGAZINE SUPPLEMENT)
RADIO

TELEVISION
OTHER
DON'T KNOW

Q8. IF GRAND PRIX MENTIONED AT Q4
Please describe to me everything that you can remember about
the advertising for Grand Prix. PROBE: What was it about? What
did it say or show?

Q7 and Q8 repeat Q5 and Q6 for Grand Prix. This provides a benchmark for levels of advertising recall that Crianlarich should expect
from a brand believed to have a similar-sized advertising budget, and
also to determine the success of Crianlarich's main competitor in its
advertising.

Q9. ASK ALL.
Do you drink whisky only on licensed premises such as a restau-
rant, pub or bar, or only at home or someone else's home, or do
you drink it both on licensed premises and at home?
ONLY ON LICENSED PREMISES
ONLY AT HOME/SOMEONE ELSE'S HOME
BOTH ON LICENSED PREMISES AND AT HOME

Q9 is a routeing question designed to identify respondents as in-home
and/or out-of-home drinkers for subsequent questions. This question
is also the start of a funnelling process that will end in determining the
brands bought for consumption.

Note that the question does not ask about 'on-licence' and 'off-
licence' consumption, as these terms may not be understood by all
respondents, but asks about drinking 'at home'.

The question as worded presents a dilemma for the layout of the
paper questionnaire. Listing the pre-codes in the same order as they
appear in the question helps the interviewer to find the correct
response code more easily. However, the routeing from this question is
easier for the interviewer to follow if the two 'off-licence' codes and the
two 'on-licence' codes are adjacent. That could have been achieved by
having 'both' as the middle one of the pre-codes.

Q10. IF DRINKS AT ALL ON LICENSED PREMISES
How many glasses of Scotch whisky would you say you drank in

the last seven days before today in pubs, bars or restaurants? By glasses I mean single pub measures.

Q10 is a numeric question. Note that the question specifies 'the last seven days before today', rather than 'in the last week', which might have raised ambiguities as to exactly what was meant, eg this could have been interpreted as meaning since seven days ago, or since the beginning of this week, or during the whole of the last complete week.

As the sample consists of people who have drunk Scotch whisky in the last month we must expect that a significant proportion will not have drunk any Scotch whisky in the last seven days. However, we can only ask what the respondents are competent to answer, and to provide details of weight of consumption over the last month would be beyond the capacity of most people's memory for this product field (particularly if they drink a lot!).

There is a risk here of social desirability bias, with some respondents deliberately under-reporting their consumption. Rather then ask for precise numbers of glasses we could have prompted the respondent with a list of ranges, say '0; 1 to 3; 4 to 8; 9 to 15...'. This would have required less of a feat of memory from respondents and, if the ranges went sufficiently high, say to 50-plus glasses, could have encouraged heavier drinkers to be more truthful.

Precise numbers as requested are not necessary for the researcher's purposes here. Responses categorized into ranges would have given sufficient information to categorize the sample into heavy and light drinkers.

Q11. IF DRINKS OFF-LICENCE AT Q9
How many glasses of whisky would you say you drank at home, either in your own home or in anyone else's, in the last seven days?
By glasses I mean the equivalent of a single measure in a pub.

Q11 repeats Q10 for off-licence drinking.

With a respondent who drinks Scotch whisky on-licence, and has therefore answered Q10, interviewers using a paper questionnaire must check back to Q9 to determine whether they should ask Q11 or skip to Q23. An interviewer error here could mean the loss of a significant amount of data.

Q12. IF DRINKS OFF-LICENCE
Do you drink Scotch whisky in your own home, in someone else's

home or both?
OWN HOME
SOMEONE ELSE'S HOME
BOTH OWN AND SOMEONE ELSE'S

Q12 is a further funnelling question designed to identify people who drink Scotch whisky in their own home, to lead on to the brand or brands bought.

Q13. IF DRINKS AT HOME
Do you yourself usually buy the Scotch to drink at home or does someone else usually buy it for you?
USUALLY BUY IT MYSELF
SOMEONE ELSE USUALLY BUYS IT
SOMETIMES MYSELF, SOMETIMES SOMEONE ELSE
GIVEN AS GIFT
OTHER ANSWER

Q13 is another funnelling question to determine whether the respondent is the actual purchaser.

Although not included in the question, 'given as a gift' is included in the list of pre-codes in anticipation that this will be the most common 'other answer', and we wish to minimize the number of unspecified 'other answers'.

Q14. IF SOMEONE ELSE BUYS
Do you have a say in which brand of Scotch whisky they buy or do they decide, or do they always buy the same brand?
HAVE A SAY
HAVE NO SAY
ALWAYS BUY SAME BRAND

Q14 is one more funnelling question to determine whether respondents exercise any brand choice if they are not the purchaser.

There is ambiguity in the routeing here from Q13. The purpose is to identify respondents with no brand choice, so we only need to ask this where someone else usually buys the Scotch. However, 'someone else' appears in two of the responses listed at Q13. To ensure that interviewers do not make a routeing error, an additional instruction to indicate the precise code is included in the paper questionnaire.

We anticipate that there will be households where the same brand is always bought and the respondent will see this as no brand choice being exercised. Without this as an option, the list of answers would be incomplete and cause these respondents difficulty in answering within the frame of the question.

Q15. IF ALWAYS BUYS THE SAME BRAND
Which brand do they buy?
BELLS
CHIVAS REGAL
CRIANLARICH
FAMOUS GROUSE
GLENFIDDICH
GLENMORANGIE
GRAND PRIX
J&B
JACK DANIELS
JOHNNIE WALKER RED LABEL
JOHNNIE WALKER BLACK LABEL
JOHNNIE WALKER UNSPECIFIED
TEACHERS
WHYTE & MACKAY
VAT 69
OTHER ANSWERS (WRITE IN)
DON'T KNOW

Q15 is a spontaneous question, so we use the longer list of brands as used at Q1, in order to minimize the number of written-in 'other answers'. Note that Jack Daniels appears in the paper and CAPI versions where the respondent receives no prompting but it might be given, and not in the Web version where the brands are prompted, as we do not want to suggest it is a Scotch whisky.

Q16. IF KNOWS WHICH BRAND IS BOUGHT
Did you decide to always buy that brand, or was that someone else's decision, or a decision made by both of you?
RESPONDENT'S CHOICE
SOMEONE ELSE'S CHOICE
CHOICE OF BOTH
DON'T KNOW/CAN'T REMEMBER

Having established which brand is bought, we try again to determine who the original decision maker was.

The 'Don't know' code is combined with 'Can't remember'.

From this question, respondents who always buy the same brand skip to Q23.

Q17. IF HAVE NO SAY AT Q14
Which brands do they buy? Which others?
BELLS
CHIVAS REGAL
CRIANLARICH
FAMOUS GROUSE
GLENFIDDICH
GLENMORANGIE
GRAND PRIX
J&B
JACK DANIELS
JOHNNIE WALKER RED LABEL
JOHNNIE WALKER BLACK LABEL
JOHNNIE WALKER UNSPECIFIED
TEACHERS
WHYTE & MACKAY
VAT 69
OTHER ANSWERS (WRITE IN)
DON'T KNOW

Q17 is asked of those who have no influence on brand choice at Q14. More than one response is allowed here, as we want to establish the repertoire of brands bought.

Q18. IF MORE THAN ONE BRAND BOUGHT
Which brand, if any, do they buy most often?
BELLS
CHIVAS REGAL
CRIANLARICH
FAMOUS GROUSE
GLENFIDDICH
GLENMORANGIE
GRAND PRIX
J&B
JACK DANIELS
JOHNNIE WALKER RED LABEL
JOHNNIE WALKER BLACK LABEL
JOHNNIE WALKER UNSPECIFIED

TEACHERS
WHYTE & MACKAY
VAT 69
OTHER ANSWERS (WRITE IN)
NO MOST OFTEN BRAND
DON'T KNOW

If there is more than one brand in the repertoire, we now try to isolate the brand bought most often for drinking at home at Q18. One response only is allowed here.

Note we must not assume that there will be one brand that is bought more often than any other, which is conveyed in the question by the phrase 'if any'. Without that phrase, respondents may feel that they have to nominate a brand even if there is no most often brand.

The list of pre-codes includes a category for 'No most often brand'.

Q19. IF BUY IT MYSELF AT Q13 OR HAVE A SAY AT Q14
Is there one brand that you buy/ask for (AS APPROPRIATE) more often than any other?
YES
NO

For efficiency the question appears on the paper questionnaire as it is here, and the interviewer is expected to use the words 'buy' and 'ask for' as appropriate for purchasers and specifiers respectively. With electronic CAPI and Web versions of the questionnaire, purchasers and specifiers can be routed to a version of the question that is worded appropriately.

Questions 19 to 22 are designed to establish the brand repertoire and most often brand where the respondent is the usual purchaser or is the brand specifier. However, the question sequence is different to that asked in questions 17 and 18. In the previous section the interview established the repertoire first and then the most often brand. Here it establishes the most often brand first and then asks for other brands bought in order to establish the brand repertoire. Inconsistent sequencing of questions like this is to be avoided.

The different sequences are likely to result in different responses and make it difficult to combine data from the two sets of questions to provide an overall brand repertoire. Even where it is felt that the two sets of data are sufficiently comparable to be combined, the differences in the questions increase the likelihood of data-processing errors occurring. The second sequence requires four questions compared to two in the first sequence, so is less efficient. There is also more filtering of respondents through different question routes, so increasing the possibility of interviewer error on paper questionnaires or of a questionnaire programming error with electronic questionnaires.

Q20. IF YES AT Q19
Which brand is that?
BELLS
CHIVAS REGAL
CRIANLARICH
FAMOUS GROUSE
GLENFIDDICH
GLENMORANGIE
GRAND PRIX
J&B
JACK DANIELS
JOHNNIE WALKER RED LABEL
JOHNNIE WALKER BLACK LABEL
JOHNNIE WALKER UNSPECIFIED
TEACHERS
WHYTE & MACKAY
VAT 69
OTHER ANSWERS (WRITE IN)
DON'T KNOW

Q20 establishes which brand is bought most often. As it is a spontaneous question the code list is again the longer list of brands in order to minimize the number of 'other answers' written in.

Q21. IF YES AT Q19
Which other brands, if any, do you buy at all?
BELLS
CHIVAS REGAL
CRIANLARICH
FAMOUS GROUSE
GLENFIDDICH
GLENMORANGIE
GRAND PRIX
J&B

JACK DANIELS
JOHNNIE WALKER RED LABEL
JOHNNIE WALKER BLACK LABEL
JOHNNIE WALKER UNSPECIFIED
TEACHERS
WHYTE & MACKAY
VAT 69
OTHER ANSWERS (WRITE IN)
DON'T KNOW
NO OTHER BRANDS

Again, this is a spontaneous response question, so the longer brand list is used on the questionnaire.

Q22. IF NO AT Q19
Which brands have you bought in the last six months?
BELLS
CHIVAS REGAL
CRIANLARICH
FAMOUS GROUSE
GLENFIDDICH
GLENMORANGIE
GRAND PRIX
J&B
JACK DANIELS
JOHNNIE WALKER RED LABEL
JOHNNIE WALKER BLACK LABEL
JOHNNIE WALKER UNSPECIFIED
TEACHERS
WHYTE & MACKAY
VAT 69
OTHER ANSWERS (WRITE IN)
DON'T KNOW
NO PURCHASES MADE IN LAST SIX MONTHS

One of the inefficiencies of the approach adopted for questions 19 to 22 is that a separate question is needed for people with no most often brand, as the question wording has to be different from Q21. Compare this with questions 17 and 18, where the same questions suffice for people with a most often brand and those without.

Up to now, as all of the questions about buying have been asked in the present tense the time period has implicitly been 'these days' or 'nowadays'. There is a danger that respondents will assume different time periods. Lighter purchasers are likely to assume a longer time period than heavier purchasers, as otherwise they may have no purchases to report. To avoid this, the questionnaire writer could have changed the questions to ask for brands bought or drunk over the last six months or some other specified period, as has now been used at Q22. For some respondents, particularly heavy drinkers with no fixed pattern of brand purchase, this might be difficult to answer accurately, while for light drinkers too it might be difficult to answer accurately because of the low importance of the purchase to them.

Whichever approach is chosen it is important to be consistent and not to mix time periods or whether they are specified, as this would make it impossible to cumulate a full brand repertoire analysis.

Q23. ASK ALL.

I am now going to show you a number of pairs of words or phrases that describe some of the things that you might take into account when choosing a brand of Scotch whisky. For each pair I would like you to tell me which of the two is the more important to you when deciding which brand to buy by allocating 11 points between them. SHOW EXAMPLE ON SELF-COMPLETION PAGE. For example, the two phrases might be 'the depth of the colour' and 'the smoothness of the taste'. If one is much more important in your choice of whisky than the other, then you might give 11 points to the more important and none to the other. But if you think that they are about equally important then you would give five points to one of them and six to the other. You can give any combination of points providing that they add to 11. Do you follow me?

IF ANY DOUBT REPEAT EXPLANATION.

Whether or not it is drunk in Scotland
The smoothness of the taste
How traditional the brand is
How well you know the brand
The richness of the colour
The price of the brand
How different it is to other brands

Q23 is a fixed-points allocation question to determine the relative importance of the key brand-positioning dimension against other factors believed to be key drivers of brand choice.

Note that respondents are asked to compare dimensions rather than attributes. We are not interested in whether they would be more likely to buy a brand drunk by Scots than a brand with a rich colour (although we will be able to deduce that) but in how important the dimension of Scottishness is compared to the dimension of colour richness. There are many ways in which this question could be asked, some of which would involve attributes rather than dimensions. Care must be taken with this type of question to distinguish between the two and use them appropriately.

The question as written above is for face-to-face interviews. It is long and not particularly easy for the respondents to follow. The length is alleviated by showing the example halfway through the question script. This is to try to involve the respondents and maintain their interest rather than present them with a lengthy speech from the interviewer.

Avoid being condescending. The check question 'Do you follow me?' or 'Have I explained that properly?' is preferable to 'Do you understand?'

It is important to show an example for most self-completion scalar questions, particularly when the task is as complex as this is.

With seven dimensions, there are 21 possible pairs. To ask respondents to answer for all pairs is too great a task, which would lead to boredom and fatigue. We have chosen to ask each respondent to complete seven. There will be three alternative versions for the self-completion section on paper, which between them include all of the possible pairs. Each version will be asked of exactly one-third of the sample at random. A simple summation of the scores across all respondents will provide a ranking and a rating score for each dimension. Care must be taken with analysis of sub-groups to ensure that each sub-group contains an equal number of respondents with the three versions of the question. Data may have to be weighted to achieve this. With the Web-based questionnaire, the pairs will be shown at random, such that each pair is shown the same number of times across the total sample.

Q24. ASK ALL.
I am now going to read out a number of words and phrases that

have been used to describe brands of Scotch whisky. For each one I would like you to tell me which of the brands on this card it applies to. SHOW CARD E. There is no right or wrong answer. Each phrase can apply to all of the brands, some of them or none of them.

BELLS
CRIANLARICH
FAMOUS GROUSE
GRAND PRIX
TEACHERS
WHYTE & MACKAY

READ OUT:
Has a strong heritage
Is traditional
Is old-fashioned
Is different to the others
Is a cheaper brand
Is a more expensive brand
A favourite of the Scots
A brand I like

Q24 is a brand-attribute association question designed to determine the perceived brand images of Crianlarich and the five brands that are thought to be the main competitors. The question emphasizes that each phrase can apply to all, some or none of the brands.

This question is asked after Q23. This is because, if it is asked before Q23, brand perceptions elicited at this question could force respondents into saying that something was important in order to appear consistent rather than because they think it really is. For example, if a respondent has said earlier that Crianlarich is their most frequently bought brand, and here they say that Crianlarich is a traditional brand, then they may feel compelled to say that tradition is an important dimension in their brand choice. They are less likely to say that Crianlarich is a traditional brand as a result of having said that tradition is important to them, because they are likely to have a more clearly defined brand image of Crianlarich than they do of what is important.

The attributes are chosen because they are believed to be the key image dimensions on which these brands are positioned. They would probably be a different set, though, if the client was a brand other than Crianlarich because the competitive set of brands would be different.

Some attributes may be associated with most or all of the brands. While it may be important to know this, such a finding decreases the discrimination between the brands and makes it difficult to see if any brand 'owns' the particular attribute. Discrimination between brands can be increased by changing the question, for example to 'Which one brand would you choose if you were looking for one with this attribute?'

The layout of the question on the paper questionnaire is columnated by brand rather than by attribute. This layout facilitates analysis of brand image profiles for the total sample and sub-analysis by those aware of a brand, brand users, etc.

Q25. ASK ALL.
SHOW AD N7.
Here is an advertisement for a Scotch whisky. Have you seen it before?
YES
NO
DON'T KNOW

The final section of the main questionnaire is advertising recognition. This is kept until after any brand image questions in order to avoid prompting and influencing brand image with the advertisements shown.

Here we are showing a de-branded press advertisement for Crianlarich, in order to measure recognition.

Although not strictly necessary here, it is good practice not to label prompt material in alphabetical order, as in some circumstances this may suggest a hierarchy and influence the findings.

Q26. IF YES
Which brand is it for?
BELLS
CHIVAS REGAL
CRIANLARICH
FAMOUS GROUSE
GLENFIDDICH
GLENMORANGIE
GRAND PRIX
J&B
JACK DANIELS
JOHNNIE WALKER RED LABEL

JOHNNIE WALKER BLACK LABEL
JOHNNIE WALKER UNSPECIFIED
TEACHERS
WHYTE & MACKAY
VAT 69
OTHER ANSWERS (WRITE IN)
DON'T KNOW

Responses to this question are spontaneous, so again the longer brand list is used.

Q27. ASK ALL.
SHOW AD K3.
Here is another advertisement for a Scotch whisky. Have you seen it before?
YES
NO
DON'T KNOW

Q28. IF YES
Which brand is it for?
BELLS
CHIVAS REGAL
CRIANLARICH
FAMOUS GROUSE
GLENFIDDICH
GLENMORANGIE
GRAND PRIX
J&B
JACK DANIELS
JOHNNIE WALKER RED LABEL
JOHNNIE WALKER BLACK LABEL
JOHNNIE WALKER UNSPECIFIED
TEACHERS
WHYTE & MACKAY
VAT 69
OTHER ANSWERS (WRITE IN)
DON'T KNOW

Questions 27 and 28 repeat questions 25 and 26 for a competitor advertisement in order to provide a benchmark against which to assess results for the Crianlarich ad.

CLASSIFICATION
Age
18 to 24
25 to 34
35 to 44
45 to 54
55 to 64
65 plus

Gender
Male
Female

Social group
AB
C1
C2
DE

Classification questions are usually asked at the end of the interview unless they are criteria for quota controls, when they must be asked as part of the screening process at the beginning of the interview. They may be seen as intrusive, and a greater rapport may have been built up with the interviewer by this time, which reduces the apparent intrusiveness. Any refusals at this stage will not endanger the rest of the interview, while age and social class can be estimated by the interviewer (and recorded as estimates) if refused.

Note that the minimum age of respondent is 18 years. For most surveys of adults this would be 16 years but is higher here because of the subject matter of this interview. Age is collected in six bands, although it would be unlikely that the sample size of this study would allow us to analyse by each band. However, having the six bands allows us to select age groups for analysis, which we would not be able to do if only three age bands were used. It costs no more to collect the more detailed information and not having it may limit the analysis possibilities.

Social group is recorded in four categories, and not individually for each of the six groups. This reflects analysis needs and information required to determine whether quota controls have been kept.

If the online Web-based survey is carried out using an access panel, then the classification data are likely to already be known and will not need to be asked again. If respondents are recruited to the survey through other methods such as pop-ups or other types of invitation, this will not be known and must be asked. As social grade cannot be asked in a self-completion questionnaire, the nearest approximation is job type.

Note that, because the subject of the survey is alcohol, no one under 18 should be interviewed. This therefore requires that the online version asks age at the beginning of the interview in order to screen out anyone under that age.

QUESTIONNAIRE FLOW DIAGRAMS

The flow diagram helps us to ensure that all respondents are asked the questions that they should be, and is an important aid in checking electronic questionnaires, where routeing instructions are not obvious.

The overview flow diagram is relatively straightforward for this question. However, there is a complex sub-routine within the behavioural data section, for which a separate flow diagram has been prepared, as this is the area in which the final questionnaire is most likely to contain routeing errors.

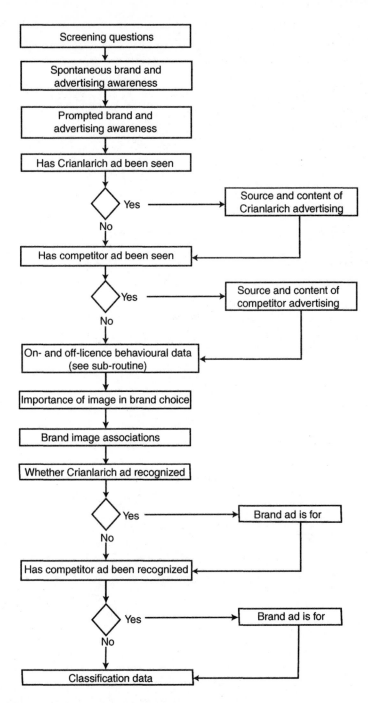

Figure A.1 *Overview flow diagram*

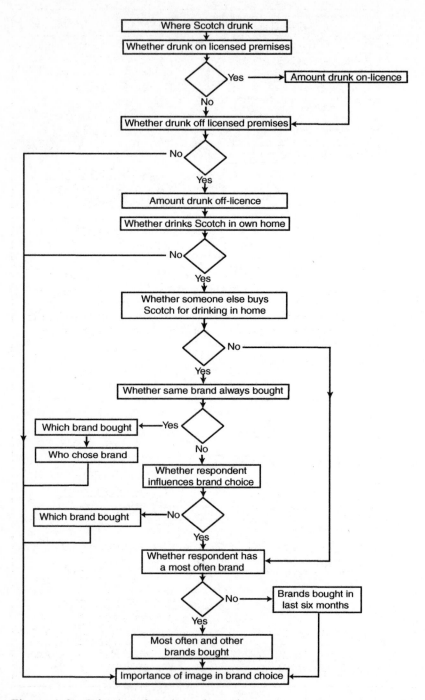

Figure A.2 *Behavioural section sub-routine*

SCREENING QUESTIONNAIRE

Good morning/afternoon/evening. I am (interviewer name) from Acme Surveys, a market research company. I am carrying out a survey about alcoholic drinks. The interview will take about 15 minutes to complete, and is carried out in accordance with the Code of Conduct of the Market Research Society.

QA SHOW CARD A.

Do you or anybody in your household work in any of the industries or professions on this card?

	(120)
ACCOUNTANCY	1
ADVERTISING*	2
COMPUTERS OR INFORMATION TECHNOLOGY	3
MARKETING/MARKET RESEARCH*	4
ALCOHOLIC DRINK PRODUCTION OR RETAILING*	5
BANKING OR INSURANCE	6
GROCERY RETAILING	7
NONE OF THESE	0

IF ANY CODED*, THANK AND CLOSE.

QB SHOW CARD B.

Which of the products on this card have you drunk in the last month either in licensed premises such as a restaurant, pub or bar, or at home or anywhere else?

	(121)
ALE	1
LAGER	2
STOUT	3
WINE	4
GIN	5
SCOTCH WHISKY	6
IRISH WHISKEY	7
NONE OF THESE	0

IF SCOTCH WHISKY (CODE 6) DRUNK, CONTINUE.

IF SCOTCH WHISKY NOT DRUNK, THANK AND CLOSE

QC SHOW CARD C.

Which of the phrases on this card best describes how often you drink Scotch whisky?

	(122)	
MOST DAYS	1	
AT LEAST ONCE A WEEK	2	
AT LEAST ONCE A MONTH	3	
AT LEAST ONCE EVERY THREE MONTHS	4	CONT
AT LEAST ONCE EVERY SIX MONTHS	5	CLOSE
LESS OFTEN THAN ONCE EVERY SIX MONTHS	6	

MAIN QUESTIONNAIRE

Q1 What brands of whisky can you think of? Please name as many as you can think of. DO NOT PROMPT.

RECORD BRAND FIRST MENTIONED SEPARATELY ON LEFT BELOW.

RECORD OTHER MENTIONS IN CENTRE BELOW.

Q2 Which brands of whisky have you seen or heard advertised anywhere recently?

DO NOT PROMPT.

RECORD ON RIGHT BELOW.

	Q1 FIRST MENTION	Q1 OTHERS	Q2 ADVERTISED
	(123)	(125)	(127)
BELLS	1	1	1
CHIVAS REGAL	2	2	2
CRIANLARICH	3	3	3
FAMOUS GROUSE	4	4	4
GLENFIDDICH	5	5	5
GLENMORANGIE	6	6	6
GRAND PRIX	7	7	7
J&B	8	8	8
JACK DANIELS	9	9	9
JOHNNIE WALKER RED LABEL	0	0	0
JOHNNIE WALKER BLACK LABEL	X	X	X
JOHNNIE WALKER UNSPECIFIED	V	V	V
	(124)	(127)	(128)
TEACHERS	1	2	3
WHYTE & MACKAY	1	2	3
VAT 69	1	2	3
OTHERS (WRITE IN AND CODE)			
Q1 FIRST _____	4		
Q1 OTHERS _____		4	
Q2 ADVERT _____			4
NONE	5	5	5 Q3

Q3 **SHOW CARD D.**

Which of the brands of whisky on this card have you heard of? Please include any that you have already mentioned.

RECORD BELOW ON LEFT

Q4 **SHOW CARD D AGAIN.**

Which of the brands of whisky on this card have you seen or heard advertised anywhere recently? Again please include any that you have already mentioned.

	Q3 **AWARE**	**Q4** **ADVERT-** **ISED**	
	(129)	(130)	
BELLS	1	1	
CHIVAS REGAL	2	2	
CRIANLARICH	3	3*	
FAMOUS GROUSE	4	4	
GLENFIDDICH	5	5	
GLENMORANGIE	6	6	
GRAND PRIX	7	7*	
JOHNNIE WALKER RED LABEL	8	8	
JOHNNIE WALKER BLACK LABEL	9	9	
TEACHERS	0	0	
WHYTE & MACKAY	X	X	INSTRU-
NONE OF THESE	V	V	CTION

IF CRIANLARICH SEEN ADVERTISED AT Q4 GO TO Q5.

IF GRAND PRIX SEEN ADVERTISED AT Q4 AND NOT CRIANLARICH GO TO Q7.

ALL OTHERS GO TO Q9.

IF CRIANLARICH MENTIONED AT Q2 OR Q4

Q5   Where did you see or hear advertising for Crianlarich?

	(131)
CINEMA	1
DIRECT MAIL SHOT	2
INTERNET	3
MAGAZINE	4
NEWSPAPER (INCLUDING MAGAZINE SUPPLEMENT)	5
RADIO	6
TELEVISION	7
OTHER	8
DON'T KNOW	9 Q6

IF CRIANLARICH MENTIONED AT Q4

Q6   Please describe to me everything that you can
       remember about the advertising for Crianlarich.
       PROBE: What was it about? What did it say or
       show? PROBE: What else?
       WRITE IN VERBATIM BELOW.

	(132)	
_____	123	
_____	456	
_____	789	
_____	0XV	
_____	(133)	SEE
_____	123	INSTR-
_____	456	UCTION
_____	789	
	0XV	

**IF GRAND PRIX SEEN ADVERTISED AT
Q4 ASK Q7.
OTHERS GO TO Q9.**

IF GRAND PRIX MENTIONED AT Q4

Q7   Where did you see or hear advertising for Grand Prix?

	(134)
CINEMA	1
DIRECT MAIL SHOT	2
INTERNET	3
MAGAZINE	4
NEWSPAPER (INCLUDING MAGAZINE SUPPLEMENT)	5
RADIO	6
TELEVISION	7
OTHER	8 Q8
DON'T KNOW	9

IF GRAND PRIX MENTIONED AT Q4

Q8   Please describe to me everything that you can
remember about the advertising for Grand Prix.
PROBE: What was it about? What did it say or show?
WRITE IN VERBATIM BELOW.

(135)
123
456
789
0XV

(136)
123
456
789
0XV   Q9

ASK ALL.

Q9   Do you drink whisky only on licensed premises such as a restaurant, pub
or bar, or only at home or someone else's home, or do you drink it both
on licensed premises and at home.

(137)

ONLY ON LICENSED PREMISES   1   Q10

ONLY AT HOME/SOMEONE ELSE'S HOME   2   Q11

BOTH ON LICENSED PREMISES AND AT HOME   3   Q10

IF DRINKS AT ALL ON LICENSED PREMISES

Q10   How many glasses of Scotch whisky would you say you drank in the last
seven days before today in pubs, bars or restaurants? By glasses I mean
single pub measures.

WRITE IN BOX BELOW. USE LEADING ZERO IF UNDER 10.

(138)	(139)

eg 05

IF REFUSES WRITE IN 98.   **SEE**
IF DON'T KNOW WRITE IN 99.   **INSTRUCTION**

IF ALSO DRINKS OFF-LICENCE AT Q9 ASK Q11.
OTHERS TO Q23.

IF DRINKS OFF LICENSED PREMISES

Q11 How many glasses of Scotch whisky would you say you drank at home, either in your own home or in anyone else's in the last seven days? By glasses I mean the equivalent of a single measure in a pub.

WRITE IN BOX BELOW. USE LEADING ZERO IF UNDER 10.

(140)	(141)

eg 05

IF REFUSES WRITE IN 98   Q12
IF DON'T KNOW WRITE IN 99

IF DRINKS OFF-LICENCE

Q12 Do you drink Scotch whisky in your own home, in someone else's home or both?

(142)

OWN HOME	1	Q13
SOMEONE ELSE'S HOME	2	Q23
BOTH OWN AND SOMEONE ELSE'S	3	Q13

IF DRINKS AT HOME

Q13 Do you yourself usually buy the Scotch to drink at home or does someone else usually buy it for you?

(143)

BUY IT MYSELF   1   Q19

SOMEONE ELSE BUYS IT   2   Q14

SOMETIMES MYSELF, SOMETIMES SOMEONE ELSE   3   Q19

GIVEN AS GIFT   4   Q23

OTHER ANSWER   5

IF SOMEONE ELSE USUALLY BUYS (Q13 CODE 2)

Q14 Do you have a say in which brand of Scotch whisky they buy or do they decide, or do they always buy the same brand?

(144)

HAVE A SAY   1   Q19

HAVE NO SAY   2   Q17

ALWAYS BUY SAME BRAND   3   Q15

IF ALWAYS BUYS THE SAME BRAND

Q15   Which brand do they buy?

		(145)	
	BELLS	1	
	CHIVAS REGAL	2	
	CRIANLARICH	3	
	FAMOUS GROUSE	4	
	GLENFIDDICH	5	
	GLENMORANGIE	6	
	GRAND PRIX	7	
	J&B	8	
	JACK DANIELS	9	
	JOHNNIE WALKER RED LABEL	0	
	JOHNNIE WALKER BLACK LABEL	X	
	JOHNNIE WALKER UNSPECIFIED	V	
		(146)	
	TEACHERS	1	
	WHYTE & MACKAY	2	
	VAT 69	3	
	OTHER (WRITE IN AND CODE)		
	———————————————	4	Q16
	DON'T KNOW	5	Q23

IF SAYS 'JOHNNIE WALKER' PROBE
FOR RED OR BLACK LABEL BEFORE
ACCEPTING 'UNSPECIFIED'.

IF KNOWS WHICH BRAND IS BOUGHT

Q16   Did you decide to always buy that brand, or was
that someone else's decision, or a decision made
by both of you?

		(147)	
	RESPONDENT'S CHOICE	1	
	SOMEONE ELSE'S CHOICE	2	
	CHOICE OF BOTH	3	
	DON'T KNOW/CAN'T REMEMBER	4	Q23

IF HAVE NO SAY AT Q14

Q17 Which brands do they buy? Which others? CODE ON LEFT BELOW.

IF MORE THAN ONE BRAND BOUGHT – OTHERS TO Q23

Q18 Which brand, if any, do they buy most often? SINGLE CODE ONLY.

Q18	Q17 BOUGHT AT ALL	MOST OFTEN	
	(148)	(150)	
BELLS	1	1	
CHIVAS REGAL	2	2	
CRIANLARICH	3	3	
FAMOUS GROUSE	4	4	
GLENFIDDICH	5	5	
GLENMORANGIE	6	6	
GRAND PRIX	7	7	
J&B	8	8	
JACK DANIELS	9	9	
JOHNNIE WALKER RED LABEL	0	0	
JOHNNIE WALKER BLACK LABEL	X	X	
JOHNNIE WALKER UNSPECIFIED*	V	V	
	(149)	(151)	
TEACHERS	1	1	
WHYTE & MACKAY	2	2	
VAT 69	3	3	
OTHER (WRITE IN AND CODE)			
_____	4	4	
NO MOST OFTEN BRAND	5	5	
DON'T KNOW	6	6	Q23

*IF SAYS 'JOHNNIE WALKER' PROBE FOR RED OR BLACK LABEL BEFORE ACCEPTING 'UNSPECIFIED'.

IF BUY IT MYSELF AT Q13 OR HAVE A SAY AT Q14

Q19 Is there one brand that you buy/ask for (AS APPROPRIATE) more often than any other?

	(152)	
YES	1	Q20
NO	2	Q22

IF YES AT Q19

Q20 Which brand is that?
RECORD BELOW ON LEFT.

Q21 Which other brands, if any, do you buy at all?

	Q20 MOST OFTEN	Q21 OTHERS BOUGHT	
	(153)	(154)	
BELLS	1	1	
CHIVAS REGAL	2	2	
CRIANLARICH	3	3	
FAMOUS GROUSE	4	4	
GLENFIDDICH	5	5	
GLENMORANGIE	6	6	
GRAND PRIX	7	7	
J&B	8	8	
JACK DANIELS	9	9	
JOHNNIE WALKER RED LABEL	0	0	
JOHNNIE WALKER BLACK LABEL	X	X	
JOHNNIE WALKER UNSPECIFIED*	V	V	
	(154)	(154)	
TEACHERS	1	1	
WHYTE & MACKAY	2	2	
VAT 69	3	3	
OTHER (WRITE IN AND CODE)			
_____	4	4	
DON'T KNOW	5	5	
NO OTHER BRANDS BOUGHT	6	6	Q23

*IF SAYS 'JOHNNIE WALKER' PROBE FOR RED OR BLACK LABEL
BEFORE ACCEPTING 'UNSPECIFIED'

IF NO AT Q19

Q22 Which brands have you bought in the last six months?

	(157)
BELLS	1
CHIVAS REGAL	2
CRIANLARICH	3
FAMOUS GROUSE	4
GLENFIDDICH	5
GLENMORANGIE	6
GRAND PRIX	7
J&B	8
JACK DANIELS	9
JOHNNIE WALKER RED LABEL	0
JOHNNIE WALKER BLACK LABEL	X
JOHNNIE WALKER UNSPECIFIED*	V
	(158)
TEACHERS	1
WHYTE & MACKAY	2
VAT 69	3
OTHER (WRITE IN AND CODE)	
_____	4
DON'T KNOW	5
NO PURCHASES MADE IN LAST SIX MONTHS	

IF SAYS 'JOHNNIE WALKER' PROBE
FOR RED OR BLACK LABEL BEFORE
ACCEPTING 'UNSPECIFIED'.   Q23

ASK ALL.

Q23 I am now going to show you a number of pairs of phrases that describe some of the things that you might take into account when choosing a brand of Scotch whisky. For each pair I would like you to tell me which of the two is the more important to you when deciding which brand to buy by allocating 11 points between them. **SHOW EXAMPLE ON SELF-COMPLETION PAGE.** For example, the two phrases might be 'the depth of the colour' and 'the smoothness of the taste'. If one is much more important in your choice of whisky than the other, then you might give 11 points to the more important and none to the other. But if you think that they are about equally important then you would give five points to one of them and six to the other. You can give any combination of points providing that they add to 11. Do you follow me?

IF ANY DOUBT REPEAT EXPLANATION.

HAND SELF-COMPLETION PAGE AND PEN TO RESPONDENT.

WHEN COMPLETED TAKE PAGE BACK AND GO TO Q24.

HOW IMPORTANT ARE THE FOLLOWING TO YOU IN DECIDING WHICH WHISKY TO BUY?

Please divide 11 points between each pair of statements depending on how important each one is to you in deciding which brand of whisky to buy.

EXAMPLE:

a) Whether or not it has a deep colour is much more important than how smooth the taste is.

THE DEPTH OF | 11 | 0 | THE SMOOTHNESS
THE COLOUR | | | OF THE TASTE

b) Whether or not it has a deep colour and whether or not it has a smooth taste are of about the same importance

THE DEPTH OF | 5 | 6 | THE SMOOTHNESS
THE COLOUR | | | OF THE TASTE

Please complete the rest of the page to show how important they are to you.

| THE SMOOTHE-NESS OF THE TASTE | | | HOW TRADITIONAL THE BRAND IS | (162 – 164) |
| THE RICHNESS OF | | | | |

THE SMOOTHE-
NESS OF THE
TASTE ☐ ☐ HOW TRADITIONAL   (162 –
THE BRAND IS   164)

HOW WELL YOU
KNOW THE
BRAND ☐ ☐ THE RICHNESS OF   (165 –
THE COLOUR   168)

HOW TRADITI-
ONAL THE
BRAND IS ☐ ☐ THE RICHNESS OF   (169 –
THE COLOUR   172)

WHETHER IT IS
DRUNK IN
SCOTLAND ☐ ☐ THE SMOOTHNESS   (173 –
OF THE TASTE   176)

THE PRICE OF
THE BRAND ☐ ☐ HOW DIFFERENT   (177 –
IT IS TO OTHER   180)

THE RICHNESS
OF THE COLOUR ☐ ☐ THE SMOOTHNESS   (181 –
OF THE TASTE   184)

HOW TRADITI-
ONAL THE
BRAND IS ☐ ☐ HOW WELL YOU   (185 –
KNOW THE BRAND   188)

THANK YOU. PLEASE HAND PAGE BACK TO INTERVIEWER.

ASK ALL.

Q24 I am now going to read out a number of words and phrases that have been used to describe brands of Scotch whisky. For each one I would like you to tell me which of the brands on this cardit applies to. **SHOW CARD E.** There is no right or wrong answer. Each phrase can apply to all of the brands, some of them or none of them.

READ OUT:	BELLS	CRIANLARICH	FAMOUS GROUSE	GRAND PRIX	TEACHERS	WHYTE & MACKAY	NONE	DON'T KNOW
	(189)	(190)	(191)	(192)	(193)	(194)	(195)	(196)
Has a strong heritage	1	1	1	1	1	1	1 1	
Is traditional	2	2	2	2	2	2	2	2
Is old-fashioned	3	3	3	3	3	3	3 3	
Is different to the others	4	4	4	4	4	4	4 4	
Is a cheaper brand	5	5	5	5	5	5	5 5	
Is a more expensive brand	6	6	6	6	6	6	6 6	
A favourite of the Scots	7	7	7	7	7	7	7 7	
A brand I like	8	8	8	8	8	8	8	8

Q25

ASK ALL.
SHOW DE-BRANDED AD N7.

Q25 Here is an advertisement for a Scotch whisky. Have you seen it before?

	(197)	
YES	1	Q26
NO	2	Q27
DON'T KNOW	3	

IF YES

Q26   Which brand is it for?

	(198)	(200)
BELLS	1	1
CHIVAS REGAL	2	2
CRIANLARICH	3	3
FAMOUS GROUSE	4	4
GLENFIDDICH	5	5
GLENMORANGIE	6	6
GRAND PRIX	7	7
J&B	8	8
JACK DANIELS	9	9
JOHNNIE WALKER RED LABEL	0	0
JOHNNIE WALKER BLACK LABEL	X	X
JOHNNIE WALKER UNSPECIFIED*	V	V

	(199)	(201)
TEACHERS	1	1
WHYTE & MACKAY	2	2
VAT 69	3	3
OTHER (WRITE IN AND CODE)		
————————————————	4	4
DON'T KNOW	5	5

*IF SAYS 'JOHNNIE WALKER' PROBE
FOR RED OR BLACK LABEL BEFORE
ACCEPTING 'UNSPECIFIED'.   Q27

ASK ALL.
SHOW AD K3.

Q27   Here is another advertisement for a Scotch
       whisky. Have you seen it before?

	(202)	
YES	1	Q28
NO	2	CLASS
DON'T KNOW	3	AND
		CLOSE

IF YES

Q28   Which brand is it for?

	(203)
BELLS	1
CHIVAS REGAL	2
CRIANLARICH	3
FAMOUS GROUSE	4
GLENFIDDICH	5
GLENMORANGIE	6
GRAND PRIX	7
J&B	8
JACK DANIELS	9
JOHNNIE WALKER RED LABEL	0
JOHNNIE WALKER BLACK LABEL	X
JOHNNIE WALKER UNSPECIFIED*	V
	(204)
TEACHERS	1
WHYTE & MACKAY	2
VAT 69	3
OTHER (WRITE IN)	4
DON'T KNOW	5

*IF SAYS 'JOHNNIE WALKER' PROBE FOR RED OR BLACK LABEL
BEFORE ACCEPTING 'UNSPECIFIED'.

**COMPLETE CLASSIFICATION QUESTIONS, THANK RESPONDENT
AND CLOSE INTERVIEW.**

Figure A.3 *Example questionnaire*

Appendix 2: The Market Research Society Code of Conduct

INTRODUCTION

The Market Research Society

With over 8,000 members in more than 50 countries, The Market Research Society (MRS) is the world's largest international membership organisation for professional researchers and others engaged in (or interested in) marketing, social or opinion research.

It has a diverse membership of individual researchers within agencies, independent consultancies, client-side organisations, and the academic community, and from all levels of seniority and job functions.

All members agree to comply with the MRS Code of Conduct, which is supported by the Codeline advisory service and a range of specialist guidelines on best practice.

MRS offers various qualifications and membership grades, as well as training and professional development resources to support these. It is the official awarding body in the UK for vocational qualifications in market research.

MRS is a major supplier of publications and information services, conferences and seminars and many other meeting and networking opportunities for researchers.

MRS is 'the voice of the profession' in its media relations and public affairs activities on behalf of professional research practitioners, and aims to achieve the most favourable climate of opinions and legislative environment for research.

The purpose of the 'Code of Conduct'

This edition of the Code of Conduct was agreed by The Market Research Society to be operative from July 1999. It is a fully revised version of a self-regulatory code which has been in existence since 1954. This Code is based upon and fully compatible with the ICC/ESOMAR International Code of Marketing and Social Research Practice. The Code of Conduct is designed to support all those engaged in marketing or social research in maintaining professional standards. It applies to all members of The Market Research Society, whether they are engaged in consumer, business to business, social, opinion or any other type of confidential survey research. It applies to all quantitative and qualitative methods for data gathering. Assurance that research is conducted in an ethical manner is needed to create confidence in, and to encourage co-operation among, the business community, the general public, regulators and others.

The Code of Conduct does not take precedence over national law. Members responsible for international research shall take its provisions as a minimum requirement and fulfil any other responsibilities set down in law or by nationally agreed standards.

The purpose of guidelines

MRS Guidelines exist or are being developed in many of these areas in order to provide a more comprehensive framework of interpretation. These guidelines have been written in recognition of the increasingly diverse activities of the Society's members, some of which are not covered in detail by the Code of Conduct. A full list of guidelines appears on the Society's Web site, and is also available from the Society's Standards Manager.

One particular guideline covers the use of databases containing personal details of respondents or potential respondents, both for purposes associated with confidential survey research and in cases where respondent details are passed to a third party for marketing or other purposes. This guideline has been formally accepted by the Society, following extensive consultation with members and with the Data Protection Registrar/Commissioner.

Relationship with data protection legislation

Adherence to the Code of Conduct and the database Guidelines will help to ensure that research is conducted in accordance with the principles of data protection legislation. In the UK this is encompassed by the Data Protection Act 1998.

Data Protection Definitions

Personal Data means data which relates to a living individual who can be identified

- from the data, or
- from the data and other information in the possession of, or likely to come into the possession of, the data controller

and includes any expression of opinion about the individual and any indication of the intentions of the data controller or any other person in respect of the individual.

Processing means obtaining, recording or holding the information or data or carrying out any operation or set of operations on the information or data, including

- organisation, adaptation or alteration
- retrieval, consultation or use
- disclosure by transmission, dissemination or otherwise making available
- alignment, combination, blocking, erasure or destruction.

It is a requirement of membership that researchers must ensure that their conduct follows the letter and spirit of the principles of Data Protection legislation from the Act. In the UK the eight data protection principles are:

▓ **The First Principle**
Personal data shall be processed fairly and lawfully.[1]

▓ **The Second Principle**
Personal data shall be obtained only for one or more specified and lawful purposes, and shall not be further processed in any manner incompatible with that purpose or those purposes.

▓ **The Third Principle**
Personal data shall be adequate, relevant and not excessive in relation to the purpose or purposes for which they are processed.

▓ **The Fourth Principle**
Personal data shall be accurate and, where necessary, kept up to date.

▓ **The Fifth Principle**
Personal data processed for any purpose or purposes shall not be kept longer than is necessary for that purpose or those purposes.

▓ **The Sixth Principle**
Personal data shall be processed in accordance with the rights of data subjects under this Act.

▓ **The Seventh Principle**
Appropriate technical and organisational measures shall be taken against unauthorised or unlawful processing of personal data and against accidental loss or destruction of, or damage to, personal data.

▓ **The Eighth Principle**
Personal data shall not be transferred to a country or territory outside the European Economic Area, unless that country or territory ensures an adequate level of protection for the rights and freedoms of data subjects in relation to the processing of personal data.

Exemption for Research Purposes

Where personal data processed for research, statistical or historical purposes are not processed to support decisions affecting particular individuals, or in such a way as likely to cause substantial damage or distress to any data subject, such processing will not breach the Second Principle and the data may be retained indefinitely despite the Fifth Principle.

As long as the results of the research are not published in a form which identifies any data subject, there is no right of subject access to the data.

Code Definitions

▓ **Research**

Research is the collection and analysis of data from a sample of individuals or organisations relating to their characteristics, behaviour, attitudes, opinions or possessions. It includes all forms of marketing and social research such as consumer and industrial surveys, psychological investigations, observational and panel studies.

▓ **Respondent**

A respondent is any individual or organisation from whom any information is sought by the researcher for the purpose of a marketing or social research project. The term covers cases where information is to be obtained by verbal interviewing techniques, postal and other self-completion questionnaires, mechanical or electonic equipment, observation and any other method where the identity of the provider of the information may be recorded or otherwise traceable. This includes those approached for research purposes whether or not substantive information is obtained from them and includes those who decline to participate or withdraw at any stage from the research.

▓ **Interview**

An interview is any form of contact intended to provide information from a respondent.

▓ **Identity**

The identity of a respondent includes, as well as his/her name and/or address, any other information which offers a reasonable chance that he/she can be identified by any of the recipients of the information.

▓ **Children**

For the Purpose of the Code, children and young people are defined as those aged under 18. The intention of the provisions regarding age is to protect potentially vulnerable members of society, whatever the source of their vulnerability, and to strengthen the principle of public trust. Consent of a parent or responsible adult should be obtained for interviews with children under 16. Consent must be obtained under the following circumstances:

▓ In home/at home (face-to-face and telephone interviewing)
▓ Group discussions/depth interviews
▓ Where interviewer and child are alone together.

Interviews being conducted in public places, such as in-street/

in-store/central locations, with 14 and 15 years olds may take place without consent if a parent or responsible adult is not accompanying the child. In these situations an explanatory thank you note must be given to the child.

Under special circumstances, a survey may waive parental consent but only with the prior approval of the Professional Standards Committee.

- **Records**

  The term records includes anything containing information relating to a research project and covers all data collection and data processing documents, audio and visual recordings. Primary records are the most comprehensive record of information on which a project is based; they include not only the original data records themselves, but also anything needed to evaluate those records, such as quality control documents. Secondary records are any other records about the Respondent.

- **Client**

  Client includes any individual, organisation, department or division, including any belonging to the same organisation as the research agency which is responsible for commissioning a research project.

- **Agency**

  Agency includes any individual, organisation, department or division, including any belonging to the same organisation as the client which is responsible for, or acts as, a supplier on all or part of a research project.

- **Professional Body**

  Professional body refers to The Market Research Society.

- **Public Place**

  A 'public place' is one to which the public has access (where admission has been gained with or without a charge) and where an individual could reasonably expect to be observed and/or overheard by other people, for example in a shop, in the street or in a place of entertainment.

PRINCIPLES

Research is founded upon the willing co-operation of the public and of business organisations. It depends upon their confidence that it is conducted honestly, objectively, without unwelcome intrusion and without harm to respondents. Its purpose is to collect and analyse information, and not directly to create sales nor to influence the opinions of anyone participating in it. It is in this spirit that the Code of Conduct has been devised.

The general public and other interested parties shall be entitled to complete assurance that every research project is carried out strictly in accordance with this Code, and that their rights of privacy are respected. In particular, they must be assured that no information which could be used to identify them will be made available without their agreement to anyone outside the agency responsible for conducting the research. They must also be assured that the information they supply will not be used for any purposes other than research and that they will not be adversely affected or embarrassed as a direct result of their participation in a research project.

Wherever possible respondents must be informed as to the purpose of the research and the likely length of time necessary for the collection of the information. Finally, the research findings themselves must always be reported accurately and never used to mislead anyone, in any way.

RULES

A. Conditions of Membership and Professional Responsibilities

A.1 Membership of the professional body is granted to individuals who are believed, on the basis of the information they have given, to have such qualifications as are specified from time to time by the professional body and who have undertaken to accept this Code of Conduct. Membership may be withdrawn if this information is found to be inaccurate.

General Responsibilities

A.2 Members shall at all times act honestly in dealings with respondents, clients (actual or potential), employers, employees, subcontractors and the general public.

A.3 Members shall at all times seek to avoid conflicts of interest with clients or employers and shall make prior voluntary and full disclosure to all parties concerned of all matters that might give rise to such conflict.

A.4 The use of letters after an individual's name to indicate membership of The Market Research Society is permitted in the case of Fellows (FMRS) and Full Members (MMRS). All members may point out, where relevant, that they belong to the appropriate category of the professional body.

A.5 Members shall not imply in any statement that they are speaking on behalf of the professional body unless they have the written authority of Council or of some duly delegated individual or committee.

Working Practices

A.6 Members shall ensure that the people (including clients, colleagues and subcontractors) with whom they work are sufficiently familiar with this Code of Conduct and that working arrangements are such that the Code is unlikely to be breached through ignorance of its provisions.

A.7 Members shall not knowingly take advantage, without permission, of the unpublished work of a fellow member which is the property of that member. Specifically, members shall not carry out or commission work based on proposals prepared by a member in another organisation unless permission has been obtained from that organisation.

A.8 All written or oral assurances made by anyone involved in commissioning of conducting projects must be factually correct and honoured.

Responsibilities to Other Members

A.9 Members shall not place other members in a position in which they might unwittingly breach any part of this Code of Conduct.

Responsibilities of Clients to Agencies

A.10 Clients should not normally invite more than four agencies to tender in writing for a project. If they do so, they should disclose how many invitations to tender they are seeking.

A.11 Unless paid for by the client, a specification for a project drawn up by one research agency is the property of that agency and may not be passed on to another agency without the permission of the originating research agency.

Confidential Survey Research and Other Activities

(apply B.15 and Notes to B.15)

A.12 Members shall only use the term *confidential survey research* to describe research projects which are based upon respondent anonymity and do not involve the divulgence of identities or personal details of respondents to others except for research purposes.

A.13 If any of the following activities are involved in, or form part of, a project then the project lies outside the scope of confidential survey research and must not be described or presented as such:

(a) enquiries whose objectives include obtaining personal information about private individuals per se, whether for legal, political, supervisory (eg job performance), private or other purposes:

(b) the acquisition of information for use by credit-rating or similar purposes;

(c) the compilation, updating or enhancement of lists, registers or databases which are not exclusively for research purposes (eg which will be used for direct or relationship marketing);

(d) industrial, commercial or any other form of espionage;

(e) sales or promotional responses to individual respondents;

(f) the collection of debts;

(g) fund raising;

(h) direct or indirect attempts, including the framing of questions, to influence a respondent's opinions or attitudes on any issue other than for experimental purposes which are identified in any report or publication of the results.

A.14 Where any such activities referred to by paragraph A.13 are carried out by a member, the member must clearly differentiate such activities by:

(a) not describing them to anyone as confidential survey research and

(b) making it clear to respondents at the start of any data collection exercise what the purposes of the activity are and that the activity is not confidential survey research.

Scope of Code

A.15 When undertaking confidential survey research based on respondent anonymity, members shall abide by the ICC/ESOMAR International Code of Conduct which constitutes Section B of this Code.

A.16 MRS Guidelines issued, other than those published as consultative drafts, are binding on members where they indicate that actions or procedures *shall* or *must* be adhered to by members. Breaches of these conditions will be treated as breaches of the Code and may be subject to disciplinary action.

A.17 Recommendations within such guidelines that members should behave in certain ways are advisory only.

A.18 It is the responsibility of members to keep themselves updated on changes or amendments to any part of this Code which are published from time to time and announced in publications and on the web pages of the Society. If in doubt about the interpretation of the Code, members may consult the Professional Standards Committee or its Codeline Service set up to deal with Code enquiries.

Disciplinary Action

A.19 Complaints regarding breaches of the Code of Conduct by those in membership of the MRS must be made to The Market Research Society.

A.20 Membership may be withdrawn, or other disciplinary action taken, if, on investigation of a complaint, it is found that in the opinion of the professional body, any part of the member's research work or behaviour breaches this Code of Conduct.

A.21 Members must make available the necessary information as and when requested by the Professional Standards Committee and Disciplinary Committee in the course of an enquiry.

A.22 Membership may be withdrawn, or other disciplinary action taken, if a member is deemed guilty of unprofessional conduct. This is defined as a member:

(a) being guilty of any act or conduct which in the opinion of a body appointed by Council might bring discredit on the profession, the professional body or its members;

(b) being guilty of any breach of the Code of Conduct set out in this document;

(c) knowingly being in breach of any other regulations laid down from time to time by the Council of the professional body;

(d) failing without good reason to assist the professional body in the investigation of a complaint;

(e) having a receiving order made against him/her or making any arrangement or composition with his/her creditors;

(f) being found to be in breach of the Data Protection Act by the Data Protection Registrar.

A.23 No member will have his/her membership withdrawn, demoted or suspended under this Code without an opportunity of a hearing before a tribunal, of which s/he will have at least one month's notice.

A.24 Normally, the MRS will publish the names of members who have their membership withdrawn, demoted or are suspended or have other disciplinary action taken with the reasons for the decision.

A.25 If a member subject to a complaint resigns his/her membership of the Society whilst the case is unresolved, then such resignation shall be published and in the event of re-admission to membership the member shall be required to co-operate in the completion of any outstanding disciplinary process.

B. ICC/ESOMAR Code of Marketing and Social Research Practice

General

B.1 Marketing research must always be carried out objectively and in accordance with established scientific principles.

B.2 Marketing research must always conform to the national and international legislation which applies in those countries involved in a given research project.

The Rights of Respondents

B.3   Respondents' co-operation in a marketing research project is entirely voluntary at all stages. They must not be misled when being asked for co-operation.

B.4   Respondents' anonymity must be strictly preserved. If the respondent on request from the Researcher has given permission for data to be passed on in a form which allows that respondent to be identified personally:

(a) the Respondent must first have been told to whom the information would be supplied and the purposes for which it will be used, and also

(b) the Respondent must ensure that the information will not be used for any non-research purpose and that the recipient of the information has agreed to conform to the requirements of the Code.

B.5   The Researcher must take all reasonable precautions to ensure that Respondents are in no way directly harmed or adversely affected as a result of their participation in a marketing research project.

B.6   The Researcher must take special care when interviewing children and young people. The informed consent of the parent or responsible adult must first be obtained for interviews with children.

B.7   Respondents must be told (normally at the beginning of the interview) if observation techniques or recording equipment are used, except where these are used in a public place. If a respondent so wishes, the record or relevant section of it must be destroyed or deleted. Respondents' anonymity must not be infringed by the use of such methods.

B.8   Respondents must be enabled to check without difficulty the identity and bona fides of the Researcher.

The Professional Responsibilities of Researchers

B.9   Researchers must not, whether knowingly or negligently, act in any way which could bring discredit on the marketing research profession or lead to a loss of public confidence in it.

B.10 Researchers must not make false claims about their skills and experience or about those of their organisation.

B.11 Researchers must not unjustifiably criticise or disparage other Researchers.

B.12 Researchers must always strive to design research which is cost-efficient and of adequate quality, and then to carry this out to the specification agreed with the Client.

B.13 Researchers must ensure the security of all research records in their possession.

B.14 Researchers must not knowingly allow the dissemination of conclusions from a marketing research project which are not adequately supported by the data. They must always be prepared to make available the technical information necessary to assess the validity of any published findings.

B.15 When acting in their capacity as Researchers the latter must not undertake any non-research activities, for example database marketing involving data about individuals which will be used for direct marketing and promotional activities. Any such non-research activities must always, in the way they are organised and carried out, be clearly differentiated from marketing research activities.

Mutual Rights and Responsibilities of Researchers and Clients

B.16 These rights and responsibilities will normally be governed by a written Contract between the Researcher and the Client. The parties may amend the provisions of rules B.19–B.23 below if they have agreed this in writing beforehand; but the other requirements of this Code may not be altered in this way. Marketing research must also always be conducted according to the principles of fair competition, as generally understood and accepted.

B.17 The Researcher must inform the Client if the work to be carried out for that Client is to be combined or syndicated in the same project with work for other Clients but must not disclose the identity of such clients without their permission.

B.18 The Researcher must inform the Client as soon as possible in advance when any part of the work for that Client is to be sub-contracted outside the Researcher's own organisation (including the use of any outside consultants). On request the Client must be told the identity of any such subcontractor.

B.19 The Client does not have the right, without prior agreement between the parties involved, to exclusive use of the Researcher's services or those of his organisation, whether in whole or in part. In carrying out work for different clients, however, the Researcher must endeavour to avoid possible clashes of interest between the services provided to those clients.

B.20 The following Records remain the property of the Client and must not be disclosed by the Researcher to any third party without the Client's permission:

(a) marketing research briefs, specifications and other information provided by the Client;

(b) the research data and findings from a marketing research project (except in the case of syndicated or multi-client projects or services where the same data are available to more than one client).

The Client has, however, no right to know the names or addresses of Respondents unless the latter's explicit permission for this has first been obtained by the Researcher (this particular requirement cannot be altered under Rule B.16).

B.21 Unless it is specifically agreed to the contrary, the following Records remain the property of the Researcher:

(a) marketing research proposals and cost quotations (unless these have been paid for by the Client). They must not be disclosed by the Client to any third party, other than to a consultant working for the Client on that project (with the exception of any consultant working also for a competitor of the Researcher). In particular, they must not be used by the Client to influence research proposals or cost quotations from other Researchers.

(b) the contents of a report in the case of syndicated research and/or multi-client projects or services when the same data are available to more than one client and where it is clearly understood that the resulting reports are available for general purchase or subscription. The Client may not disclose the findings of such research to any third party (other than his own consultants and advisors for use in connection with his business) without the permission of the Researcher.

(c) all other research Records prepared by the Researcher (with the exception in the case of non-syndicated projects of the report to the Client, and also the research design and questionnaire where the costs of developing these are covered by the charges paid by the Client).

B.22 The Researcher must conform to current agreed professional practice relating to the keeping of such records for an appropriate period of time after the end of the project. On request the Researcher must supply the Client with duplicate copies of such records provided that such duplicates do not breach anonymity and confidentiality requirements (Rule B.4); that the request is made within the agreed time limit for keeping the Records; and that the Client pays the reasonable costs of providing the duplicates.

B.23 The Researcher must not disclose the identity of the Client (provided there is no legal obligation to do so) or any confidential information about the latter's business, to any third party without the Client's permission.

B.24 The Researcher must, on request, allow the Client to arrange for checks on the quality of fieldwork and data preparation provided that the Client pays any additional costs involved in this. Any such checks must conform to the requirements of Rule B.4.

B.25 The Researcher must provide the Client with all appropriate technical details of any research project carried out for that Client.

B.26 When reporting on the results of a marketing research project the Researcher must make a clear distinction between the findings as such, the Researcher's interpretation of these and any recommendations based on them.

B.27 Where any of the findings of a research project are published by the Client, the latter has a responsibility to ensure that these are not misleading. The Researcher must be consulted and agree in advance the form and content of publication, and must take action to correct any misleading statements about the research and its findings.

B.28 Researchers must not allow their names to be used in connection with any research project as an assurance that the latter has been carried out in conformity with this Code unless they are confident that the project has in all respects met the Code's requirements.

B.29   Researchers must ensure that Clients are aware of the existence
of this Code and of the need to comply with its requirements.

NOTES

How the ICC/ESOMAR International Code of Marketing and Social Research Practice should be Applied

These general notes published by ICC/ESOMAR apply to the interpretation of Section B of this Code in the absence of any specific interpretation
which may be found in the MRS Definitions, in Part A of the MRS Code
or in Guidelines published by the MRS. MRS members who are also
members of ESOMAR will in addition be subject to requirements of the
guidelines published by ESOMAR.

These Notes are intended to help users of the Code to interpret and
apply it in practice.

The Notes, and the Guidelines referred to in them, will be reviewed
and reissued from time to time. Any query or problem about how to
apply the Code in a specific situation should be addressed to the
Secretariat of MRS.

The Rights of Respondents

All Respondents are entitled to be sure that when they agree to co-
operate in any marketing research project they are fully protected by
the provisions of this Code and that the Researcher will conform to
its requirements. This applies equally to Respondents interviewed as
private individuals and to those interviewed as representatives of
organisations of different kinds.

Note on Rule B.3

Researchers and those working on their behalf (e.g. interviewers) must
not, in order to secure Respondents' co-operation, make statements or
promises which are knowingly misleading or incorrect – for example,
about the likely length of the interview or about the possibilities of
being re-interviewed on a later occasion. Any such statements and
assurances given to Respondents must be fully honoured.

Respondents are entitled to withdraw from an interview at any stage and to refuse to co-operate further in the research project. Any or all of the information collected from or about them must be destroyed without delay if the Respondents so request.

Note on Rule B.4

All indications of the identity of Respondents should be physically separated from the records of the information they have provided as soon as possible after the completion of any necessary fieldwork quality checks. The Researcher must ensure that any information which might identify Respondents is stored securely, and separately from the other information they have provided; and that access to such material is restricted to authorised research personnel within the Researcher's own organisation for specific research purposes (e.g. field administration, data processing, panel or 'longitudinal' studies or other forms of research involving recall interviews).

To preserve Respondents' anonymity not only their names and addresses but also any other information provided by or about them which could in practice identify them (e.g. their Company and job title) must be safeguarded.

These anonymity requirements may be relaxed only under the following safeguards:

(a) Where the Respondent has given explicit permission for this under the conditions of 'informed consent' summarised in Rule 4 (a) and (b).
(b) where disclosure of names to a third party (e.g. a Subcontractor) is essential for any research purpose such as data processing or further interview (e.g. an independent fieldwork quality check) or for further follow-up research. The original Researcher is responsible for ensuring that any such third party agrees to observe the requirements of this Code, in writing, if the third party has not already formally subscribed to the Code.

It must be noted that even these limited relaxations may not be permissible in certain countries. The definition of 'non-research activity', referred to in Rule 4(b), is dealt with in connection with Rule I5.

Note on Rule B.5

The Researcher must explicitly agree with the Client arrangements regarding the responsibilities for product safety and for dealing with any complaints or damage arising from faulty products or product misuse. Such responsibilities will normally rest with the Client, but the Researcher must ensure that products are correctly stored and handled while in the Researcher's charge and that Respondents are given appropriate instructions for their use. More generally, Researchers should avoid interviewing at inappropriate or inconvenient times. They should also avoid the use of unnecessarily long interviews; and the asking of personal questions which may worry or annoy Respondents, unless the information is essential to the purposes of the study and the reasons for needing it are explained to the Respondent.

Note on Rule B.6

The definitions of 'children' and 'young people' may vary by country but if not otherwise specified locally should be taken as 'under 14 years' and '14–17 years' (under 16, and 16–17 respectively in the UK).

Note on Rule B.7

The Respondent should be told at the beginning of the interview that recording techniques are to be used unless this knowledge might bias the Respondent's subsequent behaviour: in such cases the Respondent must be told about the recording at the end of the interview and be given the opportunity to see or hear the relevant section of the record and, if they so wish, to have this destroyed. A 'public place' is defined as one to which the public has free access and where an individual could reasonably expect to be observed and/or overheard by other people present, for example in a shop or in the street.

Note on Rule B.8

The name and address/telephone number of the Researcher must normally be made available to the Respondent at the time of interview. In cases where an accommodation address or 'cover name' are used for data collection purposes arrangements must be made to enable Respondents subsequently to find without difficulty or avoidable expense the name and address of the Researcher. Wherever possible 'Freephone' or similar facilities should be provided so that Respondents can check the Researcher's bona fides without cost to themselves.

The Professional Responsibilities of Researchers

This Code is not intended to restrict the rights of Researchers to undertake any legitimate marketing research activity and to operate competitively in so doing. However, it is essential that in pursuing these objectives the general public's confidence in the integrity of marketing research is not undermined in any way. This Section sets out the responsibilities which the Researcher has towards the public at large and towards the marketing research profession and other members of this.

Note on Rule B.14

The kinds of technical information which should on request be made available include those listed in the Notes on Rule B.25. The Researcher must not however disclose information which is confidential to the Client's business, nor need he/she disclose information relating to parts of the survey which were not published.

Note on Rule B.15

The kinds of non-research activity which must not be associated in any way with the carrying out of marketing research include: enquiries whose objectives are to obtain personal information about private individuals *per se*, whether for legal, political supervisory (e.g. job performance), private or other purposes; the acquisition of information for use for credit-rating or similar purposes; the compilation, updating or enhancement of lists, registers or databases which are not exclusively for research purposes (eg which will be used for direct marketing); industrial, commercial or any other form of espionage; sales or promotional attempts to individual Respondents; the collection of debts; fund-raising; direct or indirect attempts, including by the design of the questionnaire, to influence a Respondent's opinions, attitudes or behaviour on any issue.

Certain of these activities – in particular the collection of information for databases for subsequent use in direct marketing and similar operations – are legitimate marketing activities in their own right. Researchers (especially those working within a client company) may often be involved with such activities, directly or indirectly. In such cases it is essential that a clear distinction is made between these activities and marketing research since by definition marketing research anonymity rules cannot be applied to them.

Situations may arise where a Researcher wishes, quite legitimately, to become involved with marketing database work for direct marketing (as distinct from marketing research) purposes: such work must not be carried out under the name of marketing research or of a marketing research organisation as such.

The Mutual Rights and Responsibilities of Researchers and Clients

This Code is not intended to regulate the details of business relationships between Researchers and Clients except in so far as these may involve principles of general interest and concern. Most such matters should be regulated by the individual business. It is clearly vital that such Contracts are based on an adequate understanding and consideration of the issues involved.

Note on Rule B.18

Although it is usually known in advance what subcontractors will be used, occasions do arise during the project where subcontractors need to be brought in, or changed, at very short notice. In such cases, rather than cause delays to the project in order to inform the Client it will usually be sensible and acceptable to let the Client know as quickly as possible after the decision has been taken.

Note on Rule B.22

The period of time for which research Records should be kept by the Researcher will vary with the nature of the project (eg ad hoc, panel, repetitive) and the possible requirements for follow-up research or further analysis. It will normally be longer for the stored research data resulting from a survey (tabulations, discs, tapes etc.) than for primary field records (the original completed questionnaires and similar basic records). The period must be disclosed to, and agreed by, the Client in advance. In default of any agreement to the contrary, in the case of ad hoc surveys the normal period for which the primary field records should be retained is one year after completion of the fieldwork while the research data should be stored for possible further analysis for at least two years. The Researcher should take suitable precautions to guard against any accidental loss of the information, whether stored physically or electronically, during the agreed storage period.

Note on Rule B.24

On request the Client, or his mutually acceptable representative, may observe a limited number of interviews for this purpose. In certain cases, such as panels or in situations where a Respondent might be known to (or be in subsequent contact with) the Client, this may require the previous agreement of the Respondent. Any such observer must agree to be bound by the provisions of this Code, especially Rule B.4.

The Researcher is entitled to be recompensed for any delays and increased fieldwork costs which may result from such a request. The Client must be informed if the observation of interviews may mean that the results of such interviews will need to be excluded from the overall survey analysis because they are no longer methodologically comparable.

In the case of multi-client studies the Researcher may require that any such observer is independent of any of the Clients.

Where an independent check on the quality of the fieldwork is to be carried out by a different research agency the latter must conform in all respects to the requirements of this Code. In particular, the anonymity of the original Respondents must be fully safeguarded and their names and addresses used exclusively for the purposes of back-checks, not being disclosed to the Client. Similar considerations apply where the Client wishes to carry out checks on the quality of data preparation work.

Notes on Rule B.25

The Client is entitled to the following information about any marketing research project to which he has subscribed:

(1) Background

- for whom the study was conducted
- the purpose of the study
- names of subcontractors and consultants performing any substantial part of the work

(2) Sample

- a description of the intended and actual universe covered
- the size, nature and geographical distribution of the sample (both planned and achieved); and where relevant, the extent to which any of the data collected were obtained from only part of the sample
- details of the sampling method and any weighting methods used
- where technically relevant, a statement of response rates and a discussion of any possible bias due to non-response

(3) Data Collection

- a description of the method by which the information was collected
- a description of the field staff, briefing and field quality control methods used

- the method of recruiting Respondents; and the general nature of any incentives offered to secure their co-operation
- when the fieldwork was carried out
- (in the case of 'desk research') a clear statement of the sources of the information and their likely reliability

(4) Presentation of Results

- the relevant factual findings obtained
- bases of percentages (both weighted and unweighted)
- general indications of the probable statistical margins of error to be attached to the main findings, and the levels of statistical significance of differences between key figures
- the questionnaire and other relevant documents and materials used (or, in the case of a shared project, that portion relating to the matter reported on).

The Report on a project should normally cover the above points or provide a reference to a readily available document which contains the information.

Note on Rule B.27

If the Client does not consult and agree in advance the form of publication with the Researcher the latter is entitled to:

(a) refuse permission for his name to be used in connection with the published findings and
(b) publish the appropriate technical details of the project (as listed in the Notes on Rule B.25).

Note on Rule B.29

It is recommended that Researchers specify in their research proposals that they follow the requirements of this Code and that they make a copy available to the Client if the latter does not already have one.

CODELINE

Codeline is a free, confidential answer service to Market Research Society Code of Conduct related queries raised by market researchers, clients, respondents and other interested parties. The aim of Codeline is to provide an immediate, personal and practical interpretation and advice service.

Codeline is directly responsible to the MRS Professional Standards Committee (PSC) to which each query and its response is reported at PSC's next meeting. Queries from enquirers are handled by an individual member of the Codeline panel, drawn from past members of the PSC. As long as contact can be made with the enquirer, queries will be dealt with by Codeline generally within 24 hours. Where necessary, the responding Codeline member can seek further specialist advice.

Codeline's response to enquirers is not intended to be definitive but is the personal interpretation of the individual Codeline member, based on personal Code-related experience. PSC and Codeline panellists may highlight some of the queries and responses for examination and ratification by the PSC, the ultimate arbiter of the Code, at its next meeting. In the event that an individual Codeline response is not accepted by the PSC the enquirer will be notified immediately.

Enquirer details are treated as totally confidential outside the PSC but should 'Research' or any other MRS journal wish to refer to a particularly interesting or relevant query in 'Problem Page' or similar, permission is sought and obtained from the enquirer before anonymous publication and after that query's examination by PSC.

Codeline operates in the firm belief that a wide discussion of the issues arising from queries or anomalies in applying the Code and its associated guidelines within the profession will lead both to better understanding, awareness and application of the Code among members and to a better public appreciation of the ethical standards the market research industry professes and to which it aspires.

How to Use Codeline

Codeline deals with any market research ethical issues. To contact Codeline please phone or fax the MRS Secretariat who will then allocate your query to a Codeline panellist.

If you choose to contact MRS by phone, the MRS Secretariat will ask you to confirm by fax the nature of your query, whether or not the caller is an MRS member or works for an organisation which employs an MRS member and a phone number at which you can be contacted. This fax will then be sent to the allocated panellist who will discuss your query directly with you by phone as soon as possible after receipt of your enquiry.

Please forward any queries about the MRS Code of Conduct and Guidelines, in writing to the:

MRS Secretariat, 15 Northburgh Street, London EC1V OJR
Tel: 020 7490 4911 Fax: 020 7490 0608

NOTES

[1] In particular shall not be processed unless at least one of the conditions in Schedule 2 is met, and in the case of sensitive data, at least one of the conditions of Schedule 3 is also met. (These schedules provide that in determining whether personal data has been processed fairly, consideration must be given to the basis on which it was obtained.)

References

Albaum, G (1997) The Likert scale revisited, *Journal of the Market Research Society*, **39** (2), pp 331–48

Artingstall, R (1978) Some random thoughts on non sampling error, *European Research*, **6** (6)

Basi, R K (1999) WWW response rates to socio-demographic items, *Journal of the Market Research Society*, **41** (4), pp 397–401

Bearden, W O and Netemeyer, R G (1999) *Handbook of Marketing Scales*, Sage Publications, Thousand Oaks, CA

Booth-Kewley, S, Edwards, J E and Rosenfeld, P (1992) Impression management, social desirability and computer administration of attitude questionnaires: does the computer make a difference?, *Journal of Applied Psychology*, **77** (4), pp 562–66

Brace, I, Nancarrow, C and McCloskey, J (1999) MR Confidential: a help or a hindrance in the new marketing era?, *Journal of Database Marketing*, **7** (2), pp 173–85

Bradley, N (1999) Sampling for Internet surveys: an examination of respondent selection for Internet research, *Journal of the Market Research Society*, **41** (4), pp 387–95

Brown, G, Copeland, T and Millward, M (1973) Monadic testing of new products: an old problem and some partial solutions, *Journal of the Market Research Society*, **15** (2)

Cobanoglu, C, Warde, B and Moreo, P J (2001) A comparison of mail, fax and web-based survey methods, *International Journal of Market Research*, **43** (4), pp 441–52

Crowne, D P and Marlowe, D (1960) A new scale of social desirability independent of psychopathology, *Journal of Consulting Psychology*, **24**, pp 349–54

References

Diamantopolous, A, Schlegelmilch, B and Reynolds, N (1994) Pre-testing in questionnaire design: the impact of respondent characteristics on error detection, *Journal of the Market Research Society*, **36** (4), pp 295–311

Dillman, D A *et al* (1996) Effects of benefits appeals and variations in statements of confidentiality on completion rate for census questionnaires, *Public Opinion Quarterly*, **60** (3)

Duffy, B (2003) Response order effects – how do people read?, *International Journal of Market Research*, **45** (4), pp 457–66

Edwards, A L (1957) *The Social Desirability Variable in Personality Assessment*, Dryden Press, New York

Greenwald, H J and Satow, Y (1970) A short social desirability scale, *Psychology Rep*, **27**, pp 131–35

Hogg, A and Masztal, J J (2001) A practical learning about online research, Advertising Research Foundation Workshop, October

Holtgraves, T, Eck, J and Lasky, B (1997) Face management, question wording and social desirability, *Journal of Applied Psychology*, **27**, pp 1650–69

Ilieva, J, Baron, S and Healey, N M (2002) Online surveys in marketing research: pros and cons, *International Journal of Market Research*, **44** (3), pp 361–76

Kalton, G and Schuman, H (1982) The effect of the question on survey responses: a review, *Journal of the Royal Statistical Society*, Series A, **145** (1), pp 42–73

Kellner, P (2004) Can online polls produce accurate findings?, *International Journal of Marketing Research*, **46** (1), pp 3–21

Lautenschlager, G J and Flaherty, V L (1990) Computer administration of questions: more desirable or more socially desirable, *Journal of Applied Psychology*, **75**, pp 310–14

McDaniel, C, Jr and Gates, R (1993) *Contemporary Marketing Research*, 2nd edn, Chapter 11/12, West Publishing Company, St Paul, MN

McFarland, S G (1981) Effects of question order on survey responses, *Public Opinion Quarterly*, **45**, pp 208–15

Nancarrow, C, Brace, I and Wright, L T (2000) Tell me lie, tell me sweet little lies: dealing with socially desirable responses in market research, *Marketing Review*, **2** (1), pp 55–69

Nancarrow, C, Pallister, J and Brace, I (2001) A new research medium, new research populations and seven deadly sins for Internet researchers, *Qualitative Market Research: An international journal*, **4** (3), pp 136–49

Oppenheim, A N (1992) *Questionnaire Design, Interviewing and Attitude Measurement*, 2nd edn, Continuum, London

Osgood, C E, Suci, G J and Tannenbaum, P (1957) *The Measurement of Meaning*, University of Illinois Press, Urbana, IL

Paulhus, D L and Reid, D B (1991) Enhancement and denial in socially desirable responding, *Journal of Personality and Social Psychology*, **60** (2), pp 307–17

Peterson, R A (2000) *Constructing Effective Questionnaires*, Sage Publications, Thousand Oaks, CA

Phillips, D L and Clancy, K J (1972) Some effects of 'social desirability' in survey studies, *American Journal of Sociology*, **77** (5), pp 921–38

Ring, E (1975) Asymmetrical rotation, *European Research*, **3** (3), pp 111–19

Schober, M F (1999) Making sense of questions: an interactional approach, in *Cognition and Survey Research*, ed M G Sirken *et al*, John Wiley & Sons, New York

Schwarz, N, Hippler, H and Noelle-Neumann, E (1991) A cognitive model of response-order effects in survey measurement, in *Context Effects in Social and Psychological Research*, ed N Schwarz and S Sudman, pp 187–201, Springer-Verlag, New York

Singer, E, Hippler, H-J and Schwarz, N (1992) Confidentiality assurances in surveys: reassurance or threat, *International Journal of Public Opinion Research*, **4** (34), pp 256–68

Singer, E, Von Thurn, D R and Miller, E R (1995) Confidentiality assurances and response: a quantitative review of the experimental literature, *Public Opinion Quarterly*, **59** (1), pp 67–77

Sparrow, N and Curtice, J (2004) Internet polls: an evaluation, *International Journal of Marketing Research*, **46** (1), pp 23–44

Strahan, R and Gerbasi, K C (1972) Short homogeneous versions of the Marlowe–Crowne social desirability scale, *Journal of Clinical Psychology*, **28**, pp 191–93

Sudman, S and Bradburn, N (1973) Effects of time and memory factors on response in surveys, *Journal of the American Statistical Association*, **68**, pp 805–15

Sudman, S and Bradburn, N (1982) *Asking Questions: A practical guide to questionnaire design*, Jossey-Bass, San Francisco

Taylor, H (2000) Does internet research work?, *International Journal of Market Research*, **42** (1), pp 51–63

Tourangeau, R, Rips, L J and Rasinski, K (2000) *The Psychology of Survey Response*, Cambridge University Press, Cambridge

Wable, N and Pall, S (1998) You just do not understand! More and more respondents are saying this to market researchers today, ESO-MAR Congress

Warner, S L (1965) Randomised response: a survey technique for eliminating evasive answer bias, *Journal of the American Statistical Association*, **60**, pp 63–69

Worcester, R and Downham, J (1978) *Consumer Market Research Handbook*, 2nd edn, Van Nostrand Reinhold, Wokingham

Wright, L T and Crimp, M (2000) *The Marketing Research Process*, 5th edn, Pearson Education, Harlow

Zaichkowsky, J L (1999) Personal involvement inventory for advertising, in *Handbook of Marketing Scales*, ed W O Bearden and R G Netemeyer, Sage Publications, Thousand Oaks, CA

Further reading

Bethlehem, Jelke (2000) The routing structure of questionnaires, *International Journal of Market Research*, **42** (1), pp 95–110

Brennan, M, Esslemont, D and Hini, D (1995) Obtaining purchase predictions via telephone interviews, *Journal of the Market Research Society*, **37** (3), pp 241–50

Caffyn, J M and Wells, C (1982) Picture scaling: a new quantitative technique for measuring aspects of personality and perceptions, *Proceedings of the Conference of the Market Research Society*, pp 237–52

Childers, T L and Skinner, S J (1985) Theoretical and empirical issues in the identification of survey respondents, *Journal of the Market Research Society*, **27** (1), pp 39–53

Crask, M R and Fox, R J (1987) An exploration of the interval properties of three commonly used marketing research scales: a magnitude estimation approach, *Journal of the Market Research Society*, **29** (3), pp 317–39

Crowne, D P and Marlowe, D (1964) *The Approval Motive*, Wiley, New York

Dommeyer, C J (1985) Does response to an offer of mail survey results interact with questionnaire interest?, *Journal of the Market Research Society*, **27** (1), pp 27–38

Douglas, S and Shoemaker, R (1981) Item non-response in cross-national attitude surveys, *European Research*, **9** (3), pp 124–32

Downs, P E (1978) Testing the upgraded semantic differential, *Journal of the Market Research Society*, **20** (2), pp 99–103

Durant, H and Simmons, M (1986) The paradox of memory in market research, *Journal of the Market Research Society*, **10** (4)

Elder, A and Incalcatera, T (2000) Pushing the envelope: moving a major syndicated study to the web, ESOMAR Congress

Garg, R K (1996) The influence of positive and negative wording and issue involvement on responses to Likert scales in marketing research, *Journal of the Market Research Society*, **38** (3), pp 235–46

Holmes, C (1974) A statistical evaluation of rating scales, *Journal of the Market Research Society*, **16** (2)

Jenkins, S and Solomonides, T (2000) Automating questionnaire design and construction, *International Journal of Market Research*, **42** (1), pp 79–94

Kalton, G, Roberts, J and Holt, D (1980) The effects of offering a middle response option with opinion questions, *Statistician*, **29**, pp 65–78

Kirk-Smith, M (1995) Handedness bias in preference rating scales, *Journal of the Market Research Society*, **37** (2), pp 195–202

Lickert, R (1932) A technique for the measurement of attitudes, *Archives of Psychology*, **140**, pp 5–55

O'Brien, J (1984) How do market researchers ask questions?, *Journal of the Market Research Society*, **26** (2), pp 93–107

Powers, E A *et al* (1977) Serial order preference in survey research, *Public Opinion Quarterly*, **36** (1), pp 80–85

Presser, S and Schuman, H (1980) The measurement of a middle position in attitude studies, *Public Opinion Quarterly*, **44**, pp 70–85

Reynolds, N, Diamantopolous, A and Schlegelmilch, B (1993) Pre-testing in questionnaire design: a review of the literature and suggestions for further research, *Journal of the Market Research Society*, **35** (2), pp 171–82

Sampson, P (1986) Importance revisited: the importance of attributes issue – a contemporary viewpoint, Proceedings of the Conference of the Market Research Society, pp 73–92

Sampson, P and Harris, P (1970) A user's guide to Fishbein, *Journal of the Market Research Society*, **12** (3)

Wildman, R C (1977) Effects of anonymity and social setting on survey responses, *Public Opinion Quarterly*, **36** (1), pp 74–79

Wilson, N and McClean, S (1994) *Questionnaire Design: A practical introduction*, University of Ulster, Coleraine

Yu, J H, Albaum, G and Swenson, M (2003) Is a central tendency inherent in the use of semantic differential scales in different cultures?, *International Journal of Market Research*, **45** (2)

Index

absolute performance scale   98
accompanied interviewing
    167–68
accuracy of findings   118
    of recording responses   94,
        119, 121, 123
    of responses   2, 3, 14–22, 27,
        33, 34, 43, 66, 67, 181
acquiescence   87, 88
adaptive conjoint   27
administrative information
    150–51
advertising awareness,
    spontaneous   57, 59
advertising content recall   57, 59
advertising testing   28, 52, 90–91
ambiguity in question   13, 16,
    24, 113, 114, 118, 119, 129, 164
    in response   113, 120, 144, 145
    in routeing instructions   156
analysis of data   8, 9, 10, 41,
    43, 44, 53, 54, 61, 62, 70, 79,
    84, 94, 111, 124, 151, 176,
    179, 206
anchor points   96, 159
anchor strength   96

appearance of questionnaire   40,
    151, 154, 157, 158
asymmetric rotation   131–32
attitude batteries, fatigue in
    128–29
    rotating of   129
    statement clarification   129
attitude dimensions   79–81,
    86–96, 99–101, 148, 203
attitudinal questions   21, 37, 45,
    48, 50, 60, 78, 133, 194, 203
    in international surveys   203
attitudinal segments   99
attributes, determining of
    99–100
    number of   100–01
audience design   116, 117

back translating   205
banner ads, recruitment by   38
behavioural questions   18, 49,
    50, 78, 133, 201
bipolar scales   89, 96, 107, 158
bogus pipeline   192–93
bold, use of   142
booklet presentation   154

boredom, of interviewer   14, 18
    of respondent   14, 17, 18, 72,
        88, 100–01, 108, 114,
        128–29, 164, 173, 179
brand awareness, prompted   51,
    125
    spontaneous   51, 52, 57, 58–59
brand image measurement,
    attribute association   108–11
    itemized rating scales
        107–08
brand image, effect of brand set
    111
    in international surveys
        201–02, 203
    indirect measurement of
        111–12
    measurement of   107–12
    quality   110
    strength   110
brand lists, in international
    surveys   199, 201
brand logos as prompts   94,
    124–25
bridging phrase   139
brief, interrogation of   11, 12, 114
business objectives   10, 11
business to business interviews
    27, 34, 176

CAPI   26–28, 41, 58, 63, 69, 72,
    84, 93, 124, 127, 158, 160
card sorting   104, 106
case, upper and lower   143
CASRO   173, 185
CATI   34, 41, 58, 63, 69, 72, 84,
    93, 124, 127, 158, 160
CAWI (see web-based surveys)
central tendency   88

children, interviewing   95
classification questions   44, 53,
    150
client, international survey input
    197, 205
    requirements of   9, 19, 11
    responsibilities to 180
closed questions   2, 55–56, 66, 67
closed web   37
codes of conduct   173
coding, open ended questions
    63, 150
colour, use of   154
column numbering   208
comparative scaling   102–07
confidentiality   176, 185
conjoint analysis   82
consistency effect   134, 136–37
constant sum   102–04, 105
continuous rating scale   93, 94,
    95–96
conversation, interview as   4, 5,
    15, 114, 115–17
conversational tone of interview
    114
correlation analysis   82, 97, 107,
    111
correspondence analysis   111,
    203
cost to respondent   178
covering letter   157
Crowne-Marlowe scale   195
cultural differences, in
    international surveys   95,
    198, 203
cultural response differences
    206–07
customer databases   36, 174, 176,
    177

customer satisfaction research
75, 82, 96–99, 138

data controller   175
data entry   41, 151, 157, 208
data processing   9, 10, 109
Data Protection Act 1998   174,
175, 176
database marketing   172
demographic data   44, 150
international classification   206
depth interview   2
dichotomous questions   66–67
dimension, rating of   79
direct marketing   172
directive questions   62
discrimination, maximisation
of   72, 82, 84, 92, 96,
110, 206
disguising interest   48, 49
don't know codes   39, 68–69,
121, 145–46, 160–61
don't know responses, pre-coded
questions   68–69
rating scales   84
drop down boxes   159–60, 169
dynamic pilot survey   170–71

Edwards scale   195
ego defence   184, 186
eligibility criteria   47, 48
e-mail surveys   37,38
ESOMAR   173, 185
ethnic differences, in international surveys   198
examples, provision of   101
exclusion question   44, 45–46
expectations scale   98
extended prompts   191

face management   185
face saving questions   189–90
face to face interviewing   2, 18,
24, 25–33, 47, 58, 86, 104, 106,
107, 186
compared to web-based
interviewing   38, 39, 40,
42
laying out for   142
order bias in   127
using prompts in   124
factor analysis   86, 87, 100, 107
factor score   87
fatigue see boredom
flow of questionnaire   44, 50,
142, 143, 164
focus groups   13
font size   142–43
funnelling   133–35, 134

graphic scales   93–95
grids   148
grounding   116–17
group discussions see focus
groups

hidden web 37
hotel surveys 97–98

image dimensions, international
surveys   199, 201, 202–03
impression management   184,
185
indirect questioning   190
informal pilot survey   165–67
instrumentation   184, 186
interaction lack of   5
interest, maintaining
respondent's   18

internet surveys see web surveys
interval data 70, 74–75, 79, 94, 96, 107
interviewer identification 151
interviewer instructions 142, 143, 147
interviewer, failure to record responses accurately 16
  removal of 185–86
  errors made by 13, 14, 33, 47, 62, 68, 117, 143, 167
  needs of 9, 10
italics, use of 142
itemised rating scales 79–85, 104, 107
  balanced scales 81–82
  number of points 82–84, 85, 93
  position of mid-point 79

job identification number 150

language, everyday 8, 61, 113, 114–16
language, in international surveys 198
languages, minority 117–18
laptop computers 26
layout conventions in international surveys 207
length of interview 40, 142, 165, 166, 174, 176–77
Likert scale 75, 86–89, 91, 107
literacy levels, in international surveys 95, 198

manipulation of survey outcome 46
market research society 138, 173, 176, 185

market segments, variation between countries 199–200
mean scores 74, 77, 86, 97, 106, 107
measuring sdb, checking known facts 194–95
  matched cell experiment 193–94
  matching known facts 194
  question rating 195
memory, failure of 14, 19, 20, 125
multi-chotomous questions 67–68
multinational surveys 196, 197
multiple choice questions 66, 67–68
multiple response questions 144, 145–47

native speakers, for translation 204–05
needs scale 98
nominal data 70–71
non-directive questions 62
non-sampling error 1
not answered code 146–47, 160–61, 169, 179
not answering, right to 178–79
numeric scale 95, 206
numerical data 27

objectives of survey 7, 8, 13
omnibus surveys 139–40
open questions 34
open web 37
open-ended questions 16, 42, 55–56, 57, 61–64, 150, 156

order bias, attitudinal
    dimensions   127, 128–30
  prompt lists   127–33
  prompts   113
  question order   133–37, 138
  questions   113
  response lists   127, 130–33
  scales   127–28
order effect, between questions
    13
  in Likert scale   87, 88
  within questions   13
ordinal data   70, 71–74
other answers   65, 144

pack tests   40
paired comparisons   102
paraphrasing of questions
    14–15, 164
paraphrasing of response   16
pattern responding   18, 88–89,
    90, 91
Paulhus scale   195
personal digital assistants   26
pictorial prompts, advertising
    recognition   126–27
  brand awareness   124–25
  brand image   125–26
  likelihood to purchase   125
pictorial representation   28, 113
pictorial scales   95–96
pilot survey, de-briefing   169–70
pilot survey, large scale   168–70
pop-ups   37, 38
postal surveys   39, 40, 157, 176,
    177, 178
pre-coded questions   55, 56, 60,
    65–69
pre-codes, common lists of   145

determining of   65, 113,
    119–24, 164
exclusivity of   120
exhaustiveness   17, 120, 144
order of   143–44
orientation of   155
precision of   120, 121, 123
provision of   16
primacy effect   128, 131
priming effects, question order
    135
probing   24, 64
product tests   26
product usage, variation between
    countries   199
prompt cards   25, 27, 34, 113
prompt material   124–27
prompted attitudes   52
prompted questions   46, 51, 55,
    56, 58, 60–61
prompting   64
proprietary techniques   12, 112,
    197

Q sort   106–07
qualitative research   2, 6, 13, 60,
    66, 99, 190, 202, 207
question enhancements   190–92
question numbering in
    international surveys
    207–08
questionnaire design guidelines
    (MRS)   173
questionnaire errors, repairing of
    24, 41

radio buttons   158–59
random response technique
    186–88

randomising question order 27,
41
randomising response order 27,
41
ranges, construction of 121–24
ranking 71–74, 102, 106
rating scales *see* itemized rating
scales
ratio data 70, 75–77
read outs 147–48
reassurance, about behaviour
190
recency effect 128, 131
recording interview 174
recruitment interview 2, 9
recruitment questionnaires 13
regression analysis 97, 107, 111
religious differences, in
international surveys
198, 203
research objectives 10, 11, 12
research organization, name
of 175
respondents, competency to
answer question 69, 164
difficulty in articulating 62,
78
failure to answer accurately
19, 20, 21, 62
failure to understand
question 13, 15, 101,
164, 167
needs of 9, 10, 114, 164
thanking of 150
verbosity of 63
response categories 77
length of 77
response codes 13
failures of 13, 14

responses, disguised by codes
191
rotated start points 129
rotating question order 41, 107,
157
response prompts 41, 158
scale points 128
routeing 13, 26, 27, 41, 50, 134,
148–49, 156, 157, 161, 162,
164, 166, 167, 169, 179, 208

sampling error 1
satisficing 132–33
scanning 151, 157
screening questions 44, 47–49
security question 44, 45–46
selection bias 25
self deception 184, 186
self-completion questionnaire,
use of space 154–56
self-completion questions 23,
26, 27, 88, 89, 101, 106, 107,
108, 110, 120, 128, 129, 187
self-completion surveys, 16, 18,
19, 23, 36–42, 96, 124, 135,
141, 147, 174, 185, 186, 198
electronic 37–42, 157–62, 168,
179
paper 36, 37, 151–58, 164, 167,
168
self-presentation bias 25
semantic differential scale 75,
86, 89–91, 92, 107
semi-structured interviews 2
sensitive questions 34, 39, 47,
52–52, 179, 186–88
sensitive subjects 175
sensitizing 52
serial numbers 150

show cards   25, 124, 127
  identification of   147
sight lines   148
signing off the questionnaire
  180
single response questions
  144–45, 147
smiley scales   95–96
social desirability bias   14, 39,
  181–95
  in commercial markets
    183–84
source of name   177–78
spontaneous questions   37, 41,
  51, 55, 57–60
stakeholders in questionnaire   7,
  9, 10
standard deviations   86, 107
standardised questionnaires   5,
  137–38
Stapel scale   86, 92–93
stimulus material   25, 34, 35, 36,
  40, 42
structured interview   2
subject of survey   174, 175

technical terms, avoiding use of
  15, 114–15

telephone interviewing,
  advantages of   33, 34
  disadvantages of   35–56
telescoping   14, 20, 21
thermometer scale   95–96
third-party bias   25
threatening questions   186–88
tick start   129
touch screen computers   26
tracking studies   138–39
trade off analysis   82
translating questions   93, 203
unease, physical manifestations
  of   195

values, recording of   120–21
vocabulary of respondents   8

warm-up statement   207
web-based surveys   19, 35,
  37–42, 58, 63, 69, 72, 84, 93,
  106, 124, 127, 157, 158, 161,
  178
  advantages of   38–41
  disadvantages of   41–42
write-in box   159, 160

yea saying   88

THE *MARKET RESEARCH IN PRACTICE* SERIES

£18.99 0 7494 4200 X
Paperback 240 pages

£18.99 0 7494 4201 8
Paperback 232 pages

£18.99 0 7494 4181 X
Paperback + CD ROM 224 pages

£18.99 0 7494 4180 1
Paperback 256 pages

Forthcoming titles include:

- BUSINESS-TO-BUSINESS MARKET RESEARCH
- CONSUMER INSIGHT
- CUSTOMER SATISFACTION RESEARCH
- EMPLOYEE RESEARCH
- ON-LINE RESEACH
- POLICY-MAKING RESEARCH
- RESEARCHING BRANDS

For further information on how to order, please visit

www.kogan-page.co.uk